PHENOMENOLOGIC.

14,90

EDMUND HUSSERL

PHENOMENOLOGICAL PSYCHOLOGY

LECTURES, SUMMER SEMESTER, 1925

translated by

JOHN SCANLON

1977

MARTINUS NIJHOFF

THE HAGUE

Translated from Edmund Husserl, Phänomenologische Psychologie. Vorlesungen Sommersemester 1925. Herausgegeben von W. Biemel. (Husserliana ix), pages 3–234. The Hague. Martinus Nijhoff, 1962.

ISBN 90 247 1978 X

Printed in The Netherlands by Intercontinental Graphics

CONTENTS

TRANSLATOR'S INTRODUCTION

THE TEXT

In the summer semester of 1925 in Freiburg, Edmund Husserl delivered a lecture course on phenomenological psychology, in 1926/27 a course on the possibility of an intentional psychology, and in 1928 a course entitled "Intentional Psychology." In preparing the critical edition of *Phänomenologische Psychologie* (*Husserliana* IX),[1] Walter Biemel presented the entire 1925 course as the main text and included as supplements significant excerpts from the two subsequent courses along with pertinent selections from various research manuscripts of Husserl. He also included as larger supplementary texts the final version and two of the three earlier drafts of Husserl's *Encyclopedia Britannica* article, "Phenomenology"[2] (with critical comments and a proposed formulation of the Introduction and Part I of the second draft by Martin Heidegger[3]), and the text of Husserl's Amsterdam lecture, "Phenomenological Psychology," which was a further revision of the Britannica article. Only the main text of the 1925 lecture course (*Husserliana* IX, 1–234) is translated here.

In preparing the German text for publication, Walter Biemel took as his basis Husserl's original lecture notes (handwritten in shorthand and

---

[1] Hague: Nijhoff, 1962, 1968. The second impression, 1968, corrects a number of printing mistakes which occur in the 1962 impression.

[2] English translation by Richard E. Palmer in *Journal of the British Society for Phenomenology*, II (1971), 77–90.

[3] Heidegger's part of the second draft is available in English as Martin Heidegger, "The Idea of Phenomenology," tr. John N. Deely and Joseph A. Novak in *The New Scholasticism* XLIV (1970), 324–344. For a discussion of Heidegger's comments as leading beyond transcendental idealism into thinking about the problem of being, see Walter Biemel, "Husserls encyclopaedia Britannica Artikel und Heideggers Ammerkungen dazu," *Tijdschrift voor Filosophie* XII (1950), 246–280. For a discussion of Husserl's reasons, based upon his understanding of the phenomenological approach to anthropology, for not following Heidegger's suggestions, see John Scanlon, "The Epoché and Phenomenological Anthropology," *Research in Phenomenology* (II), 1972, 95–109.

containing numerous insertions, corrections, bracketings and underlinings). Those notes have been catalogued by the Husserl Archives of Louvain as Ms FI 36, with the exception of the introductory part which Husserl had inserted into his notes for the 1928 course, catalogued as Ms FI 44 (the notes for the 1926–27 course are Ms FI 33). Two additional sources were taken into account in preparing the critical German edition of the main text: for the section corresponding to *Husserliana* IX, page 20, line 30 to page 45, line 22 ("Task and Significance of the *Logical Investigations*"), Ms MI 4 I, a typed copy prepared by Ludwig Landgrebe, then Husserl's assistant; and for the section corresponding to *Husserliana* IX, page 72, line 14 to page 86, line 39 ("Seeing Essences as Genuine Method for Grasping the A Priori"), Mss MI 4/F 136 II–V, four typed copies prepared and edited by Landgrebe (Landgrebe also used Mss MI 4 II, III, IV as basis for pages 411–427 of his edition for publication of Edmund Husserl, *Erfahrung und Urteil*[4]).[5]

The division into sections is the work of the editor, Walter Biemel, and usually does not correspond to the beginnings and endings of the individual lectures of the original course. Husserl's original chronological sequence is followed except in the case of the final two lectures which the editor has presented in reverse order. The section headings, with few exceptions, are also the editor's contribution. Husserl's own original titles are only the following: "Task and Significance of the *Logical Investigations*" (§3), "Reduction to Pure Realities as Substrates of Exclusively Real Properties. Exclusion of Irreal Cultural Senses" (§17), "Spatial Primal Presence" (§30), "Hyle – Hyletic Data as Matter for Intentional Functions" (§31), "Objective Temporality and Temporality of the Stream" (§33).

In the translation, the pages of *Husserliana* IX are indicated in the margin, and the beginning of each of Husserl's lectures is signaled by an asterisk in the margin. The divisions and section headings of *Husserliana* IX are maintained. Unless otherwise specified, footnotes are Husserl's.

SCOPE OF THE WORK

Because Husserl avoids asking any transcendental questions here and consequently refrains from executing the transcendental reduction, he does not consider this course one in philosophy, strictly speaking. However,

---

[4] 2. Auflage (Hamburg: Claassen und Goverts, 1948). English translation by James S. Churchill and Karl Ameriks (Evanston: Northwestern University Press, 1973).
[5] For fuller text-critical discussion, see *Husserliana* IX, 543–546. For a correlation of the pagination of the manuscripts, of *Husserliana* IX, and of *Erfahrung und Urteil*, see *ibid.*, 647–649.

neither does he ask any questions concerning empirical psychological regularities, not even such as might involve a phenomenological orientation toward actually observable psychic or mental life in its factuality. While recognising that level of work as pertaining to psychology, Husserl neither enters into it nor discusses the method which would be appropriate to it. Instead, he discusses throughout the task of a phenomenological clarification of the basic concepts of psychology, concepts which would faithfully express the essential features and structures of any possible psychic and mental life. To distinguish two senses of "phenomenological psychology," this course discusses not what would comprise a phenomenologically based psychology but what is required for a phenomenological clarification of the conceptual foundations of psychology. Thus, this work can be considered a distinctively phenomenological contribution to philosophical psychology or philosophy of mind. The point is that it is neither transcendental philosophy nor empirical psychology, nor even a discussion of the program for empirical psychology.

Within that scope, the work is still further limited. In 1925 phenomenological psychology was not an ongoing enterprise to which Husserl could simply contribute new findings; it did not exist yet.[6] Accordingly, the bulk of Husserl's work consists not in detailed phenomenological clarifications but in a penetrating and orderly discussion of the need for and possibility of a phenomenological approach to the conceptual foundations of psychology.[7] Only by recognizing this limited but pioneering purpose can the reader begin to appreciate and evaluate the character of Husserl's contribution to phenomenological psychology.[8]

---

[6] See Herbert Spiegelberg, *Phenomenology in Psychology and Psychiatry* (Evanston: Northwestern University Press, 1972), p. 11. There Spiegelberg cites the following passage of a letter of Martin Heidegger to Husserl, October 22, 1927, "You remark repeatedly during the past days: actually there is not yet any pure psychology." (*Husserliana* IX, 601).

[7] Spiegelberg, e.g., suggests that the work might accurately be called "Guiding Ideas Toward . . . " [Phenomenological Psychology], *ibid.*

[8] For a fairly thorough summary of some of the chief themes raised by Husserl in this context, see Aron Gurwitsch, "Edmund Husserl's Conception of Phenomenological Psychology," *The Review of Metaphysics*, XIX (1966), 689–727. Reprinted in L. Embree, ed., Aron Gurwitsch, *Phenomenology and the Theory of Science* (Evanston: Northwestern University Press, 1974), 77–112. For an appreciation of the basic contribution of direction and orientation provided by Husserl, see Herbert Spiegelberg, "The Relevance of Phenomenological Philosophy for Psychology" in Edward N. Lee and Maurice Mandelbaum, eds., *Phenomenology and Existentialism* (Baltimore: Johns Hopkins University Press, 1967), 219–241, and F.J.J. Buytendijk, "Die Bedeutung der Phänomenologie Husserls für die Psychologie der Gegenwart," in *Husserl und das Denken der Neuzeit* (Hague: Nijhoff, 1959), 78–114. For a comprehensive attempt to show the internal coherence of Husserl's published and unpublished statements about phenomenological psychology, see Hermann Drüe, *Edmund Husserls System der phänomenologischen Psychologie* (Berlin: De Gruyter, 1963). See also Joseph Kockelmans, *Edmund Husserl's Phenomenological Psychology* (Pittsburgh: Duquesne University Press, 1967).

STRUCTURE OF THE WORK

While it is certainly true that Husserl's lecture notes do not display the unity of a closely structured book, that there is no strict system of phenomenological psychology to dictate the course of his lectures, and that he avails himself of a lecturer's freedom to follow for a while particularly interesting tangential questions, nevertheless the lectures are not simply a string of disjointed or random thoughts on the subject of phenomenological psychology. The lectures do not meander: they follow a unitary direction, a main route from which Husserl wanders afield now and then but to which he always returns. That route is the gradual unfolding of all that is required for a thoroughgoing critique of physicalism in psychology.

That central, unifying theme is introduced by Husserl's reflections upon the historical situation in psychology at the turn of the century, the time when his own phenomenology emerged. The prevailing model of scientific research was then that of experimental physics and chemistry. Experimental concepts and procedures taken from those natural sciences were applied to the subject matter of psychology, especially of physiological psychology. The very success in accumulating solidly acceptable results by that approach and even of instituting new practically useful branches of study, such as industrial psychology, prompted psychologists to accept it without question as *the* way of finally making psychology scientific.

Husserl centers attention upon two parallel and mutually independent critiques of the sense and appropriateness of this approach to psychology, that of Dilthey and that of his own phenomenology. By proposing reasons for Dilthey's inability to find broad acceptance for his critical remarks, Husserl in effect suggests what has to be done in order for such a critique to be made scientifically sound. Thus, the subsequent lectures can be read as a reopening of the entire issue of physicalism in psychology, as pursuing that question more thoroughly and more methodically than Dilthey had done, and as offering phenomenology as a suitably scientific alternative approach to the conceptual foundations of psychology.

Dilthey's objection was that because mental life is intrinsically unified in an intuitively intelligible fashion, it made no sense to isolate single psychic or mental events from their inherent nexus of significance and subject them as thus abstractly isolated to the sort of extrinsic hypothetically postulated causal connections required by the sciences of nature. Husserl maintains that part of the reason for Dilthey's failure to convince psychologists and philosophers of his views stems from the dazzling technical success of physicalism. But he sees also a limitation in Dilthey's own reform proposals: Dilthey offered brilliant examples of the interpretation of broad historical events and movements, and individual and typical historical figures, but he never established a rational foundation for such studies by scientifically disclosing the universal concepts proper to mental life. Thus, though his negative critique is cogent and his positive studies are highly suggestive, he does not offer a positive alternative to the conceptual foundation provided by physicalism. Satisfied that phenomenology provides just such a fundamental approach to consciousness, Husserl painstakingly unravels the many strands of the complex issue of the undeniable success yet fundamental inadequacy of physicalism in psychology. At stake throughout is the sense of scientific objectivity and universality.

Husserl's distinctive first move is to turn our attention to the world as it presents itself to pre-scientific experience in order to clarify first its all-pervasive structures and then its less general determinate areas which can provide differentiated subject matters for distinct sciences. Thus, by implication at least, one sense of scientific objectivity is accuracy to features and structures discernible within the world as given to experience.

However, if each step of Husserl's discussion is to be scientifically acceptable, before proceeding further, he has to step back and present a scientific method for discovering and testing essential concepts and necessary laws, a method of investigation which, to be materially significant, applicable to everything experienceable, and yet intrinsically diversifiable, cannot be the materially indeterminate method of formal analysis. The method of ideation via imaginative variation, once it is developed rigorously, allows Husserl to point to the possibility of a fundamental science of the world given to experience, on the basis of which specific regional sciences can in turn be scientifically differentiated. At the same time, it is a method which can subsequently be called upon, within the specific domain of the psychic, to provide a basic conceptualizing procedure which is not hypothetically deductive in character and thus can supply an appropriate dimension of universality in psychology, not provided by Dilthey.

The next step along the way is to discover by the application of the method of ideation to the world of experience the essential contrasts between the psychic, mental, and subjective in various forms and the non-psychic, non-mental, non-subjective, as well as their intertwinings, and consequently to retrace the various stages of elimination of the psychic, mental and subjective involved in that isolating and purifying abstraction which produces the purely physical as the exclusive subject matter of the physical sciences. This step is crucial to Husserl's central purpose. Insofar as the psychic is essentially involved with the organic and insofar as the organic can, as material, be subjected to the physicalistic abstraction, the method of physics can legitimately establish inductive regularities which govern all material entities as such and consequently govern also organisms considered merely as material entities, and finally indirectly govern also the psychic in its essential involvement with the organic. Hence, this step renders intelligible the limited sense and success of physiology for psychology. At the same time, this step displays the absurdity of physicalism as a fundamental position in psychology, since the physicalistic abstraction achieves its orientation toward the purely physical by deliberately disregarding all that is psychic, mental, or subjective and thus disregards all that is of direct interest to psychology.

The fourth major stage of Husserl's route is to propose and clarify a purifying reflective method which can provide access to the purely psychic, purely mental, purely subjective, in its own appropriate mode of self-givenness, and thus meet the demand for scientific objectivity concerning the subjective: the method of phenomenological reduction.

Finally, once such access to the subjective as such has been secured, Husserl's last step is to present a few exemplary analyses of selected phenomenological themes, such as the phenomenology of perception, of spatial primal presence, of the body, of the I, to illustrate how scientific results can be worked out at a fundamental level of phenomenological psychology.

At that point, Husserl has reached the end of his route. He has clarified and illustrated a positive scientific alternative to physicalism as the conceptual foundation for psychology and has displayed the absurdity of physicalism in psychology.

ACKNOWLEDGMENTS

All who are familiar with Dorion Cairn's *Guide for Translating Husserl*[9] will recognize the debt which this translation owes to his suggestions. I am grateful to the Husserl Archives of Louvain, under the direction first of Professor van Breda and then of Professor IJsseling for making that work available to me prior to publication, to Professor José Juertas-Jourda for being instrumental in transmitting it to me in photocopy. This translation grew out of the needs of teaching a graduate course in Husserl's phenomenological psychology; thanks are due to the Philosophy Department of Duquesne University, and Professor André Schuwer, Chairman, for making it possible for me to schedule that course on three occasions, and to all the students who participated in that course. I am especially grateful to Dr. Eduard Marbach and Dr. Reto Parpan, both of the Husserl Archives at Louvain, for their valuable suggestions and constant encouragement;

[9] Hague: Nijhoff, 1972.

thanks are due also to Mr. Thomas Nemeth who noted many ambiguities and typographical errors in a manuscript version, to Miss Anita Ruppen for her expert typing of the final version and to Mr. Peter Madsen for his invaluable assistance in the tedious work of proofreading.

Above all, thanks to my wife Mary, besides all else, long-suffering and diligent typist and re-typist of several versions.

JOHN SCANLON
Duquesne University, 1976

INTRODUCTION

1. THE DEVELOPMENT OF MODERN PSYCHOLOGY, DILTHEY'S DECISIVE ⟨3⟩
CRITIQUE AND HIS PROPOSALS FOR A REFORM (EXPLANATORY AND
DESCRIPTIVE PSYCHOLOGY).

Psychology is one of the oldest of all sciences. Like logic, ethics, political theory, and metaphysics, it was already founded by Plato and given a systematic completion and presentation by Aristotle. It has never subsequently lacked diligent cultivation, especially since the beginning of scientific modernity. The first attempts at a new establishment of natural science are already matched by similar attempts for psychology. When an exact science of nature, novel in its method and prospering with unheard of successes, had arisen in the beginning of the seventeenth century as a result of the life work of such men as Kepler, Galileo, and Descartes, it reacted as a model upon psychology and the concrete socio-cultural sciences. A passionate endeavor to carry out just such a methodical reform in psychology, to reshape it also as a science which explains its subject matter exactly, on the basis of elementary laws, arose immediately.

However, neither the psychology of Cartesian dualism, nor that of Hobbesian materialism, nor of the metaphysical monism of Spinoza, nor even the great Lockean impulse to an empirical psychology on the basis of internal experience, led to the desired success. They did not lead to a psychology which had the shape and power of a continually progressing development, to the unity of firmly established and constantly expanding theories and methods.

When we think of the theoretical gain of the seventeenth and eighteenth centuries in the mathematical and physical sciences, we are overcome ⟨4⟩ with admiration. At every step in its development, it was compelling in the evidence of its method, which was becoming ever more polished, and in the quantity of its useful applications. Of psychology one can report nothing similar, especially if we consider the time from the seventeenth to the nineteenth century, although the researchers in this field were certainly not inferior in mental power to the great natural scientists.

Profound difficulties, deeply concealed until our own time, hindered a similar prosperity here. From the beginning, psychology was unable to resist the temptation of naturalism, of an extrinsic imitation of the model of natural science. Whereas the new natural science, once set on the right methodic course, could never come to a standstill, and continued to grow in an almost miraculously mounting progression – we find that psychology, in spite of all great intentions was unable, for sheer promising beginnings, to arrive at a definitive beginning, which could be followed by a definitive continuation.

In the nineteenth century, psychology received a new, great, even splendid, impetus. The impulse came from leading German physiologists and physicists, such as J. v. Müller, E.H. Weber, Volkmann, Helmholtz, Hering, G.T. Fechner, and was especially expedited by the organising power of Wundt. There sprang up a psychology intimately connected with natural science and especially with physiology, to which it was faithfully adapted as to the nature of its method. The naturalistic psychology already intended in the times of Descartes and Hobbes was actualized in an essentially new shape by first approaching psychophysical problems of the psychology of the senses, or rather the psychophysics of the senses, with the highly developed experimental skill of physiology. As a matter of fact, this psychophysical, physiological, experimental psychology did achieve international recognition, internationally homogeneous institutes and methods of work, and an accord of convictions which for a time seemed hardly inferior to that of the less exact biological disciplines of natural science. ‹5› This psychology undoubtedly brought to light a profusion of very noteworthy facts which had previously been hidden. And they were really psychological facts, even though physiologists include many large groups of them in their own science. Although unanimity in the theoretical interpretation of these facts is far inferior to that of the exact natural-scientific disciplines, still it is complete in a certain respect, namely with regard to the methodic style of the theories sought. In any case, in the international scientific circles of the new psychology, one is of the firm conviction – a conviction unbroken until recently – that finally the only true and genuine psychology has been set in motion, as a rigorous science upon whose paths the totality of all psychological problems, all those pertaining to individual and cultural mentality, must lie. As in every experiential science which is directed toward explanation on the basis of elementary laws, there would be need only of patient restraint and a quite cautious advance; one ought not too hastily grasp at problems which were not yet ripe for scientific treatment, for which the substratum of facts was not yet prepared nor the necessary experiential concepts created. The new psychology acquired no slight increase in its inner certainty through the successful creation of an industrial psychology. Indeed, psychology seemed actually to be on a par with exact physics. It had even advanced so far as to make its psychological knowledge practically useful, just like physical and chemical knowledge.

And yet it could come to pass that a very radical scepticism could be directed against this psychology – surely successful in a certain manner – such as could never be directed against the exact science of nature. This scepticism has gained ground from year to year and has taken on various forms. The most radical sceptical reaction which originates with Dilthey and on the other hand with the new phenomenology, shall interest us here. This sceptical critique turns toward nothing less than the entire methodology of this psychology insofar as it ever raised the claim actually to explain the facts of the life of mind mentally and that is, psychologically. ‹6› Indeed, this scepticism, in its later, matured form, even turns toward the nature of the method of establishing psychic facts as psychological, which means: not simply making experimental facts apparent as facts, but analyzing them in explicit internal experience, further subsuming them under concepts which express the structural essential species of these facts as psychic. Here also the most radical rebuke springs up. The new psychology was reproached for being actually blind to the unique essential species of psychic life, blind to all essential forms specific to mentality as an intentionally active subjectivity, constituting mental formations and also cultural community. Therefore it was said to be quite incapable of accomplishing what so-called exact and explanatory science had to do everywhere; for, all explanation is knowledge derived from essential concepts and guided by essential necessities based on them.

In the year 1894, in the midst of a time which was filled with exaggerated hopes in the new psychology, a time which expected of it simultaneously an exact grounding of the socio-cultural sciences and a reform of logic, theory of knowledge, and all specifically philosophical sciences, W. Dilthey's "Ideen über eine beschreibende und zergliedernde Psychologie" appeared (in the *Sitzungsberichten der Berliner Akadamie*) – as the first assault against this naturalistic psychology. This work, characterized by genius though also incompletely matured, will surely never be forgotten in the history of psychology. Dilthey, whose studies were rooted entirely in the socio-cultural sciences and who was without doubt one of the very great socio-cultural scientists of the nineteenth century, was much more a man of brilliant intuitions of the whole than of analyses and abstract theorizings. The capacity for elementary experiential analysis, but also for logical precision and thinking in precise concepts, as it is learned and practiced in mathematical natural science, was not his particular strength.

Instead, he had incomparable capacity for surveying everywhere the con-
‹7› crete life of the mind, individual and socio-historical, in its living concretions, for grasping intuitively its typical shapes, its forms of change, its
motivational connections, and for carrying out with respect to them great
surveying explications which make intelligible to us the characteristic being
and genesis of historical mentality in its concrete necessity.

He was the first to sense how little modern philosophy satisfied the socio-
cultural sciences and that all reform movements of modern logic and critique of reason, whether they reached back to Kant or to British empiricism,
were all too onesidedly determined by natural science. He began early to be
concerned about a "critique" of that reason which operates in the socio-
cultural sciences, about an epistemological clarification of the essence and
the possibility of those imposing performances which were there as the
new socio-cultural sciences. And here he immediately confronted the question, to what extent the new physiological and experimental psychology
could ever satisfy these sciences of the mind, to what extent its pretention
to be the theoretical foundation-science for the explanation of concrete
mentality was justified. The result at which he arrives is one of decisive
rejection.

He seeks to show in comprehensive presentations that over against this
"explanatory" or "constructive" psychology, as he expresses himself,
there is need of a "descriptive and analytic" psychology, the idea of which
he attempts to sketch extensively in a continuing critique of experimental
psychology, which has become dominant. This experimental psychology
follows, he states, the ideal of the exact science of nature, especially that
of modern *atomistic* physics. As *the latter* does with physical appearances,
so *it* wants to subordinate the appearances of psychic life to a causal nexus
by means of a limited number of univocally determined elements. In doing
so, it proceeds, like physics, hypothetically and constructively by means
of inferences which transcend experiencing intuition. Therefore, on the
basis of experience it projects hypothetical substructions of causal nexus
which are not experienced and of hypothetical laws referring to them. *But*
‹8› *this entire procedure is completely inappropriate to the essence of the psychic.*
It has arisen from an unjustified extension of natural-scientific concepts
to the region of psychic life and of history.[1] This procedure has a sense and
a necessity in natural science; for it rests upon external experience which
gives us nature as merely spatial mutual externality, while the objective
nexus of universal causality which provide regulative unity for this mere
mutual externality are not also given in immediate intuitiveness. But psychology and consequently all socio-cultural sciences refer to the one *men-*

---

[1] Cf. Dilthey, *Werke.* V, 195.

tal nexus universally given by internal experience [*innere Erfahrung*]. Internal experience gives no mere mutual externality; it knows no separation of parts consisting of self-sufficient elements. It knows only *internally* interwoven states, interwoven in the unity of one all-inclusive nexus, which is itself necessarily given along with them as nexus in internal intuition. Whether or not we look at it and its moments becoming singly prominent – the single perceptions, recollections, feelings, willings – whether or not we direct our noticing special regard toward their intertwinings, their passing over into one another and proceeding forth from one another: all that and as *one* nexus, is *lived experience* [*Erlebnis*]. The living life streams on continually and it not only *is*, it is *lived* [*erlebt*] and at every time a notice, a pondering, a valuing, etc., can be directed toward it. But they themselves are merely new pulses of this life, not external to it, but taking place in it as moments, as lived experience making its appearance in life and directed toward life becoming singly prominent in the unbroken unity of one life and lived experience.

The fact that psychic life is not merely given externally and as mutual 〈*〉 externality, but is given in its nexus, given by self-knowledge, by internal experience, constitutes the basic difference between psychological knowledge and the knowledge of nature. And that is also the basis for the fundamental peculiarity of the socio-cultural sciences as opposed to the sciences of nature. While the latter can only "explain" in hypothetical substructions 〈9〉 and constructions, it is the essence of the socio-cultural sciences to understand, or to make intelligible.

Speaking more precisely, their distinctive task is to make intelligible the unity of mental living, of mental doing, performing, creating, by establishing a unitary intuition which goes back to the internally experienceable mental nexus (to one's own and others', the singly subjective and communally subjective nexus). In a brief formulation: natural-scientific explanation is contrasted to socio-cultural-scientific understanding. But this understanding is not achieved simply by the establishment of the mere unitary intuition, in which the concrete nexus are re-lived. Indeed, every poetic presentation does that sort of thing. But the much discussed psychology of the great poets and authors is in truth no psychology; it is no science. Rather, there is required a scientific analysis, formation of concepts and systematic description, carried out on a purely intuitive basis. As will be explained fully, this task concerns not only the descriptive exhibiting of the types of single psychic data, but also of the types of nexus. For the single datum is a mere abstraction in the psychic. A feeling, a mood, an emerging thought, a hope which makes itself felt, etc. – nothing of the sort is ever an

---

* Beginning of new lecture [indicated thus throughout]. *Tr.*

isolated lived experience; it is what it is in the psychic milieu, in its intertwinings, its motivations, indications, etc.; and these are moments of the
nexus, of the psychic function, which are lived together inseparably. Thus
the great task is to analyze systematically and describe in their typology
the many-sided intertwinings which unite in the respective unity of a structural nexus. "Structure" designates the complex intertwining which belongs to every concrete phase of the streaming psychic life. Even the series
of phases which successively give unity to the life-stream has its typology.
The psychic nexus is a nexus of efficacy, a nexus of development, and is
governed throughout by an immanent teleology which can be exhibited
analytically. A directedness toward values runs through life, a unitary
striving toward happiness, toward contentment, an instinctive or con-
‹10› sciously purposeful directedness. Thus, at times instinctively, at times with
conscious purposefulness, new mental forms arise from previous ones. The
subjective psychic activities and the *performances* of the single subjects
combine in common activities and performances. Therefore all levels of
creative mentality including the high forms of art, science, and religion
also become thematic; they must be clarified in an understanding manner,
must be brought to descriptive understanding by means of elementary and
systematically progressing analysis.

The great significance of Dilthey's expositions lay above all in what he
said positively about the unity of psychic life as a unity of lived experience,
and in the demand derived therefrom for a descriptive psychology drawing
purely upon intuition: a psychology which, in spite of being "mere" description, should accomplish its own species of the highest performance of
clarification, i.e., that which Dilthey expressed with the word *understanding*.
For, can one not say in a very good sense, as historians say: to understand a
historical nexus is its only meaningful explanation?

Dilthey had penetrated to the recognition that scientific description on
the basis of external experience designates a performance which differs
essentially and fundamentally from scientific description on the basis
of internal experience, the experience of the purely mental. He saw that
scientific description in the region of mentality already includes as its result
a complete clarification, precisely because of the capacity of all mental
intertwinings to be relived, including the intertwining of motivation. Pure
analysis and description pursued far enough explains and even explains
with full satisfaction what concrete, historical socio-cultural science in-
quires about, because here explaining can have no other sense than that of
making apparent on mental grounds the internal necessities of mental
genesis, of mental origination. Mentality includes, purely in itself, a species
of causality, the causality of motivation. And it itself belongs to the content
of lived experience, and is therefore directly accessible to simple intuition

and description. To understand the origin of a work of art in the way of
socio-cultural sciences is not to do psychophysics; it does not mean inquir- ‹11›
ing into the psychophysical causalities which occur between the psychic
life of the artists and physical nature. It means, rather, to project oneself
into the living and striving of the artist, to bring it to an appropriate and
fully living intuition and to make intelligible on the basis of his motives the
system of goal-positings and realizing activities. If that is done completely,
then no meaningful question is left for history of art.

2. THE REASONS FOR THE LIMITED INFLUENCE OF DILTHEY UPON HIS
CONTEMPORARIES: THE INADEQUACY OF THEIR UNDERSTANDING AND THE
LIMITS OF HIS BEGINNING.

At first, the time was not ripe for the acceptance of such thoughts. Those
who stood under the spell of the naturalistic attitude of the prevailing
psychology were incapable of entering deeply into the problems raised by
Dilthey. In one respect Dilthey's influence was very strong, not only
through the Academy Treatise which occupies us, but already through
his earlier works, viz., in his ever new endeavors to demonstrate and to
characterize in principle the irreconcilable difference between natural
sciences and socio-cultural sciences. In any case, the naiveté of the naturalistic interpretation of the socio-cultural sciences, prevalent until then, was
broken. One can say that the entire great literature of the last decades concerning the nature and method of history and the historical socio-cultural
sciences in contrast to that of the natural sciences originates with Dilthey.[1]
He had already struck up all motivating thoughts of any value. But just the
most significant thoughts to which he sees himself led back by these problems, those of a purely intuitive, descriptive-analytic psychology in opposition to the dominant natural-scientific psychology, at first meet with no
approval at all. Of course it must be confessed that Dilthey's critique lacks a
sufficiently fundamental sharpness. No matter how suggestively he man-
ages to speak against the socio-cultural scientific pretensions of naturalistic
psychology, he does not penetrate to a clarity of principles concerning its
own peculiar sense and the limits of its possible results. Indeed such results ‹12›
already existed in the large groups of psychological facts and regularities of
facts which it had been the first to expose and which could be established
only by its inductive experimental method. On the other hand the persua-
sive power of the most valuable positive expositions concerning the method
and problem area of a purely descriptive internal psychology was also inadequate and unsuccessful for various reasons. Above all the exemplary

[1] Perhaps, that is saying too much.

illustrations fell short, insofar as they were unable to awaken conviction as
to how a psychology, a clarifying, elementary and fundamental science,
should result from intuitive singularities and from a description attached to
them. In the historical socio-cultural sciences[1] which have to do with historically given individual mentality, with nations and laws in their respective individual typology, with the conditions and historical origins of
peoples, with artistic movements, artists, and works of art, scientific formations, etc., given as historical facts, it is always a question of something
individual and of producing that clarification of the individual by intuitive
and descriptive analysis of which we have spoken. The creative origin of
a work of art becomes individually intelligible, finds a purely individual
"explanation", if we succeed in projecting ourselves into the artist, into
his mental life, into the surrounding world which motivates him mentally –
of course, on the basis of interpretation of the historical data. Following the
motives which have determined the artist, we reach from within an understanding of what he has striven for, willed, realized, and what original
sense the work itself received creatively from him. Therefore, the art of
historical description and explanation is restricted purely to the individual.
The same with every socio-cultural science. But psychology does not want
to be the science which makes the individual and historical facticities in
‹13› their individual motivational nexus individually intelligible. Rather, it is
to be a science which recognizes the laws of psychic life and the laws
according to which common mentality and culture, taken universally,
develops. We want to be enabled by it to explain on the basis of laws, thus
to bring about the result of explanation by law also for the socio-cultural
sciences, beyond their individual explanation.

But Dilthey offers no satisfying information in this regard. How is a
description on the basis of mere inner experience or of mere bringing to
intuition of another's mental life and of a community life, to be able to
produce more than individual understanding? How is it to be able to lead
to universally psychological laws; how is it ever to get beyond vague empirical generalizations? Must it be satisfied with an inductive morphological
typology, with a mere natural history of historical forms of mind? This
may have its value. But is that all? Doesn't every morphology and every
natural history demand a rational explanation according to laws? Later
you will learn to understand the radical deficiency of Dilthey's idea of a
descriptive psychology. Here I merely mention briefly in anticipation:
he has not yet seen that there is such a thing as a generic essential description on the basis of intuition, but now of an intuition of essence, as he has

---

[1] Dilthey distinguishes between history and systematic socio-cultural sciences which like
the natural sciences aim at universal concepts and laws. (*Werke*, V, 258.)

also not yet seen that the relationship to objects of consciousness, which comprises the radical essence of psychic life, is the proper and infinitely fruitful theme of systematic analyses of the psyche, and indeed as analyses of essence.

Since the continuity of thought with our first two lectures may perhaps ⟨*⟩ have been broken by the unfortunate intermission, the first thing to do is to re-awaken what has already been said. I wish not merely to recapitulate, but also to add some thoughts which are apt to elucidate further the character of Dilthey's psychological intentions and to make more intelligible the critical words with which I closed.

As opposed to the "explanatory" psychology led by the natural-scientific ⟨14⟩ model, he demands a "descriptive-analytic" psychology.[1] The former seeks in a hypothetico-constructive procedure to construct from assumed psychic elements, for instance, sense data and feeling data, a causal nexus which is itself inexperienceable and to produce, like the physical science of nature (and interwoven with it in psychophysics), "explanation" through causal laws. Dilthey behaves skeptically in a certain respect toward this psychology, the modern naturalistically experimental psychology. It is incapable of serving the socio-cultural sciences as foundation. Rather, a psychology proceeding purely intuitively (and not hypothetico-constructively), a descriptive and analytic psychology, is needed. This is (I cite almost literally) the presentation of the component parts and nexus which appear uniformly in every developed human psychic life. The naturalistic psychology overlooks the fact that psychic nexus are lived and that they are all combined in one single nexus, namely, the total nexus of the onflowing psychic life. Nexus is therefore not something hypothetically added on by thought, something inferred, but, as lived in purely internal experience, accessible to a direct articulating analysis and description. Psychology is nothing else but description and analysis of this one nexus given internally as life itself and indeed, according to Dilthey, the question concerns always the life-nexus of the developed "typical human." Nature we explain; psychic and mental life we understand; to produce understanding is the task of all historical and systematic socio-cultural sciences, which for that very reason are referred back to descriptive and analytic psychology as the fundamental science of understanding. The hypothetical substructions of experimental, natural-scientific psychology can only confuse them and burden them with useless hypotheses. A psychology which foregoes

[1] In the lectures further details were given and in them the Aristotelian expression "apodictic" was used for "explanatory" knowledge. – Explanation on the basis of laws; a) pure a priori, b) in relation to it, the apodictic form of the empirical regularity of mathematical physics. Afterwards, in the subsequent lectures use was always made thereof (orally).

‹15› grounding what happens in the mind upon the intelligible nexus of mental life is necessarily unfruitful. E.g., religion is a realm of mental culture. Whenever we speak of it, we come necessarily to universal concepts such as feeling, will, dependency, freedom, motive, etc. But it is clear that such concepts can be clarified only in the universally regular psychic nexus, as it is given purely intuitively to internal experiences. Starting from there we must produce an understanding of how, e.g., the consciousness of God arises and gains strength. The procedure is the same if in jurisprudence the all-inclusive mental fact, *Right*, becomes our theme. Then we are led back to fundamental concepts such as norm, law, accountability, etc. How could we clarify these concepts otherwise, how make intelligible what purposes are effective in Right, and how the single wills are subordinate to the law – except by reverting to regular connections in the interiority of human psychic life? Likewise in the political sciences, where concepts of community, sovereignity, dependency, etc., again lead us back to inner psychic facts; likewise, of course, in those socio-cultural sciences which seek to give a theory of literature and art. It is clear that this holds of all socio-cultural sciences, no matter which cultural systems or which external organizations of human society they refer to, such as family and local community, church and state. Having originated in the living nexus of the human psyche, they can be understood only on this same basis. Only because there is uniformity and regularity in psychic life can they arise as forces overreaching the individual and making the same order possible for all individuals. Another significant point is their combination with the theory of knowledge.

No matter how much the theory of knowledge claims a special position vis-a-vis the socio-cultural sciences, the same thing holds for it, as Dilthey sets forth in detail. For, the title "knowledge" with all its particular forms traces back finally to the unity of the psychic nexus as the substratum of all cognitive processes. Theory of knowledge, then, if it does not want to operate with the unclarified concepts of a contingently arisen psychological ‹16› tradition, is also traced back to a descriptive, analytic psychology as its basis.

Last time I already indicated critically that as significant as were the impulses attempted in Dilthey's expositions and as brilliant as were the intuitions contained in them, still great lacks became perceptible. His contrasting of naturalistically externally directed and descriptively internally directed psychology was not yet traced back to an ultimate clarity, to the ultimate fundamental sources. I call your attention to a main point, which played no express role in his contemporaries' response to his criticism, but operated unnoticed. In any case it is the decisive reason why we, in spite of all our admiration for Dilthey's intuition, can not abide by his ideas and can by no means recommend the imitation of the methodology which he had in mind.

The return to internal experience and to the descriptive analysis to be carried out in pure internal seeing makes possible an individual understanding, an understanding of the appearance of an individual mental act and product in the nexus of lived experience: an understanding on the basis of the individually motivating reasons. The reconstruction of the concrete motivation makes necessity apparent, e.g., the necessity as to why just this decision of a political figure had to arise or why a scientist had to come precisely to this theoretical train of thought. This is a species of producing an explanation of something individual. But psychology is supposed to explain in terms of general insights; it is supposed to be a science of laws; it is supposed to acquire a universally theoretical base of laws, which does the same for the socio-cultural sciences (and if Dilthey is right, also for theory of knowledge) as mathematical theory and theoretical physics do for the sciences of nature. But, in a psychology which relies solely upon internal experience and description of psychic life, how do we arrive at universalities of law? Or, are they not possible here, and is a psychology which explains by means of laws possible only as psychophysical psychology? It almost seems that, according to Dilthey, a descriptive, analytic psychology could and should be nothing else and nothing more than a descriptive natural history of human psychic life, of the "developed typical human" –as Dilthey says expressly. But is the typology of psychic life which ⟨17⟩ we trace back through elementary analyses to impressions, sense feelings, perceptions, memories, expectations, multiple types of judicative knowing, valuing, desiring, willing behavior – is this typology, I ask, any such thing as a merely natural-historical typology? And if we then pursue the typical personal forms, do we not arrive at a merely comparative empirical psychology of the oldest style, which supplies us with a multiplicity of typical forms of personalities, of characters, temperaments, of associations, but never anything like a universal necessity, an explanation capable of knowledge in terms of laws? All performance of natural-scientific explanation which takes place under the title of physics and which, normally understood, holds as an unconditioned task of knowledge of nature, rests upon the fact that nature, the realm of so-called external experience, has a so-called "a priori" structure. To speak more accurately, beyond all empirical typology of given nature as it is systematically pursued in the natural-historical disciplines and exhibited in descriptive typical concepts, is a realm of necessary and exact universalities. Every question concerning particular empirical forms of a physical thing is preceded by the fact that it is a thing at all, that in this respect it maintains, amid all its transformations, an ideal norm, a form, which we call its mathematical essence. Insofar as it can be identified harmoniously and also intersubjectively in all empirical procedure, and is to hold up as the same thing, it is a temporally enduring, spatially extended material entity. But what is so taken in the factually subjective experience is in principle nothing stable; however, amid the alteration of "intuitions" it supports a mathematical ideal, an ideal in relation to which the empirical is an approximation.

Whenever one says, "spatially-temporally extended entity," one has already indicated a powerful title for transempirical necessities which the mathematics of space-time seeks to develop according to axioms and theorems: an infinite realm of ideal laws by which every natural object as such and every intuitive empirical procedure as an approximation, is ab-
‹18› solutely restricted.[1] What is essential is not that nature is subject to quantitative concepts, as if they alone conveyed necessities, but that nature has an all-inclusive form, an all-inclusive frame of law, by which everything natural is restricted in unconditioned necessity. This is not the place to show how the reference back to this a priori makes possible a theoretically explanatory science of experience à la physics – as long as you see, what is anyhow quite manifest, that if we leave out of consideration this a priori frame, this reference of what is in each case actually emprically given back to the infinite idea, then only a universal natural history is possible, but no longer explanation by law, explanation by necessities.

Now, should not the realm of "internal" experiences, should not the nexus of lived experience which comprises our internally streaming life, or the nexus of the person taken concretely, a nexus which is accessible to direct seeing, also support a formal frame of law, a universal form of absolutely inviolable necessities or laws, to which an explanatory result of socio-cultural scientific work could be referred back methodically? And should not the same hold also with regard to the most all-inclusive structural forms for the uniting of single personal mentalities in common mentalities? If the critical thought just suggested had no footing, then we would stand before a marvelous paradox which Dilthey had not noticed. To make individual mental acts and products intelligible means nothing other than making their individual necessity apparent. By intuitive reconstruction of the concrete persons, of their individual nexus of lived experience and of capability, in which these acts are embedded, but in which also they have arisen from the motivation proper to such an intersubjective nexus of lived experience in such a motivated manner, we see their individual necessity;

---

[1] It is not easy to describe briefly the true relation of the intuitive thing as appearance, vis-a-vis the ideally mathematical which appears in this appearance, since it can be understood as approximation to the idea. In the attitude of exact science the thing and its properties are themselves meant as mathematical. Exactness = mathematical ideality.

and understanding means nothing else. It may be that we are mistaken ⟨19⟩ in the reconstruction, e.g., in the historical reconstruction of the personality of a Bismarck and of the motives which guided him in a certain decision. But, if the reconstruction is historically correct and has arrived at an actually unitary and complete intuition, then it becomes evident to us, why Bismarck as the one he was and who was so motivated, necessarily decided in such a way. And even if the reconstruction was false, if it is completely intuitive, it contains individual necessity: if Bismarck had been such and if he had been so motivated, then he would have had to act in such a way. Understanding extends exactly so far as the analysis and reconstruction of the motivation extends. If it is incomplete, then the necessity is also incompletely clarified. Now, the paradox lies in this, that there should be necessity in the individual case and yet no pure laws of necessity, which like all pure laws present hypothetical connections, connections of pure universalities, which refer to pure possibilities. Already in the individual instance, Dilthey seems not to have made clear to himself the difference between strict necessity, or *explanatory* understanding, and empirical induction; otherwise, this paradox would have struck him and guided him.

Here also, the paralleling by Dilthey of the grounding of the socio-cultural sciences and of the grounding of the critique of knowledge by a descriptive psychology is illuminating. The parallel paradox appears indeed and has even greater weight. Briefly stated, the theory of knowledge wants to make intelligible, generically and in principle, how cognitive activity in its psychic interiority can succeed in producing objective validity. But, how could it ever solve such a problem if it depended upon a psychological empirical procedure which would supply it with only natural-historical universalities instead of inviolable and intuitively evident necessities? Principles of knowledge can not possibly be clarified by vague biological universalities of types. Thus in every respect, a psychology which provides necessities is a desideratum.

The incomplete maturation of Dilthey's ideas explains the at first victo- ⟨20⟩ rious reaction on the part of experimental psychology. The October 1895 issue of the *Zeitschift für Psychologie und Physiologie der Sinnesorgane* brought a brilliantly written response on the part of Hermann Ebbinghaus, the founder of the experimental psychology of memory. The tenor of his reply to the criticism is best expressed in some sentences of a private letter which Ebbinghaus had already addressed to Dilthey the previous year (Misch, Dilthey's *Gesammelte Schriften*, V, 423). Ebbinghaus explains that he considers the entire idea completely mistaken and misleading, and says further, "I was really not prepared for so much injustice toward contemporary psychology and for so little clarity concerning the fact that what you are recommending to people is just what people have been doing for the longest time." Now, the latter remark is certainly not correct, concerning the most essential points, although it is correct that many of Dilthey's expositions admitted of such an interpretation. The lack of a pure fundamental clarity makes it also intelligible that Dilthey's many attempts to compose a response did not succeed, and that accordingly a detailed published reply never appeared. In any case, success was at first on the side of experimental psychology – even in the eyes of non-participant philosophers, to the very great vexation of Dilthey, who nearly despaired of being able to make convincingly clear to his contemporaries what extremely significant insights he had grasped in his brilliant intuition.

3. Task and significance of the *LOGICAL INVESTIGATIONS*.

At the turn of the century a complete change of Dilthey's internal situation took place, and soon also a change of his external situation. In 1900–01 my *Logical Investigations* appeared as the result of ten-year long efforts for a clarification of the pure idea of logic by a return to the bestowing of sense or the performance of cognition which occurs in the nexus of lived experiences of logical thinking. More accurately speaking, the single investigations of the second volume involved a turning of intuition back toward the logical lived experiences which take place in us whenever we think but which we do not see just then, which we do not have in our noticing view whenever we carry out thought activity in a naturally original manner. The thinker knows nothing of his lived experiences of thinking but only of the thoughts which his thinking engenders continuously. The point was to bring this obscurely occurring life of thinking into one's grip by subsequent reflection and to fix it in faithful descriptive concepts; further, to solve the newly arising problem, namely, to make intelligible how the forming of all those mentally produced formations takes place in the performance of this internal logical lived experiencing, formations which appear in assertively judicative thinking as multiply formed concepts, judgments, inferences, etc., and which find their generic expression, their universally objective mental stamp in the fundamental concepts and axioms of logic..

〈21〉

a) *Critique of psychologism; the essence of irreal (ideal) objects and of irreal (ideal) truths.*

In the *Logical Investigations*, an important preliminary work preceded the single investigations. It involved a pure grasping of these stamped sense-forms themselves and the combatting of all empiricistic or psychologistic mixing of psychological ingredients of thinking activity into the logical concepts and propositions themselves. E.g., the expressed proposition which is won as a result in logical thinking contains as formation of sense nothing of thinking in its own sense itself, no more than the number counted in the lived experience of counting contains in the content of its sense anything of the psychic activity of counting. Numbers, propositions, truths, proofs, theories, form in their ideal objectivity a self-contained realm of objects – not things, not realities such as stones or horses, but objects nonetheless. The formal logic systematically grounded by Aristotle is, as to its principal core, a theory of propositions, a discipline which establishes the pure forms of possible judgment-propositions and the formal *laws* which ⟨22⟩ propositions as such – if they are to be able to be true – must satisfy. The entire "syllogistic" belongs to it. Let us now consider the chief basic concept of this logical theory, that of the proposition, and let us stick with a clarifying example.

The Pythagorean theorem in the realm of propositions is one single proposition whenever I or anyone thinks it and proves it; just as the number four is one single number, whenever and by whomsoever it is thought or becomes consciously given by counting. A proposition or a number is not a real event in the universe, thus not something which occurs here and there, in individual irrepeatability, moving or resting, and exercising real causality. That holds only of the written number and of the spoken proposition, spoken now or some other time. But the written or spoken expression of a number or of a proposition is not the Pythagorean proposition itself or the number 4 itself, as Leibniz already saw, in fact even earlier, the scholastics, and as Bolzano developed most consistently. Such irreal or as one also says, ideal objects are, in their numerically identical singularity, substrates of true and false judgments just as real objects are; conversely, "object" in the most universal logical sense means nothing else than anything at all concerning which statements can be made sensefully and in truth.

For our purposes it is useful if I now emphasize that properly speaking two points had to be maintained in the systematic-critical preliminary considerations of the first volume of the *Logical Investigations*: 1) against logical psychologism, the just mentioned irreality and yet objectivity, the ideal identical existence of such objects as concepts, propositions, arguments, truths, true proofs, etc. That meant that these objects are unities of significance in such a manner that nothing of the psychic acts and other subjective lived experiences which comprise the varying consciousness of the objects occurs in the content of their sense itself, that they are also in no way restricted to real men or other subjects. Psychic acts themselves, like their subjects, belong to the real world; and in close connection with what was just said: 2) pertaining to the ideal objectivities ⟨23⟩

there are purely ideal truths which assert nothing about the world, nothing about what is real. Thus in syllogistic, pure logic asserts true laws and theories about pure concepts and pure propositions the sense of which includes not the least assertion about the spatio-temporal factual world; the same holds for what pure arithmetic asserts about pure numbers of the number series. The truth that $2 + 3 = 5$ stands all by itself as a pure truth whether there is a world, and this world with these actual things, or not. It includes not the least bit of real factualities in its sense. The same holds for the logical principle of contradiction and so forth. Purely ideal truths are "a priori" and are discerned as truths in the unconditioned necessity of their universality. But this universality does need to be characterised. Though ideal objects do not refer to actual facts, in their sense they refer implicitly to *possible* facts – ideally possible, ideally conceivable. In pure arithmetic no counted things or events of the factual world are pre-supposed; but every number does have a universal extension. All conceivable groups, all that can be in any way imagined, are included in the idea "3," to the extent that they are denumerable as 3. Accordingly every arithmetical proposition and all arithmetic is a priori applicable to every conceivable group and consequently, for instance, to every group which in fact actually exists. Likewise, the logic of propositions (the Aristotelian syllogistic) is applicable to all conceivable cases in which conceivable men or other rational beings might judge and in their judging express the corresponding propositions as asserted sense. Therefore, to every ideal object there belongs inseparably an ideal extension, the idea of a totality of conceivable single instances, and together with it a validity without exception, a universal validity which is not restricted by the presupposition of factual singularities, factual data. This is just what unconditioned universal validity means. "Before" the givenness of a fact and a world of facts (a priori) we can be unconditionally certain of this, that whatever we assert as logicians, arithmeticians and so forth, must be able to find application to anything and everything which is to be able to confront us as corresponding actuality of fact.

⟨24⟩   The universality extends even further insofar as ideal objects with their extension of corresponding singularities can refer again to ideal objects. Thus, numbers count not only possible realities; one can also again count pure numbers themselves, just as the logical ideal truths speak about propositions as such. But propositions are not only propositions about the earth, about the Black Forest, about the factual nature in which we live, but also propositions about ideal objects; at any time there can also be statements made about statements, as the logical laws are themselves propositions about propositions.

If pure logic asserts that every contradictory proposition is false, every non-contradictory proposition possible, this holds also for the propositions which are asserted in logic itself, in which nothing is said about the factual world. In summary: there are thus without a doubt *irreal* objectivities and *irreal* truths pertaining to them, with an ideal extension, by which they are referable perhaps to something ideal, but always also referable to some possibly real thing, but note well, to that which is ideally a real possibility, the factual existence of which is not presupposed. Accordingly, there are sciences of irrealities, "a priori sciences," the idea of which theoretically governs a self-contained realm of ideal objects.

b) Researching the correlation: ideal object – psychic lived experiencing (forming of sense) by means of essential description in the reflective attitude

But the greatest theme of the *Logical Investigations* was not such establishments in the "Prolegomena," which were always limited to pure logic, but descriptive investigations of psychic lived experiences to which all sorts of ideal objects of logic and mathematics are inseparably related in a certain way. For, apart from the necessary relation of extension which is implied in the sense of ideal objects, by which for instance every "number" has a relation to possible groups of single objects and specifically of possible single real entities, ideal objects also have necessarily another relation to ‹ 25 › possible reality, namely to psychic subjects and activities. It is this very relation which played the chief role in the struggle against psychologism in logic. What had to be eliminated in this struggle as a pernicious contamination of ideality in order to secure a purely formal logic as a parallel to pure mathematics, namely the subject matter of the psychology of cognition, was to become the chief theme, and it had to.

Let us consider the issue more closely: a proposition can say something about stones, heavenly bodies, and so forth, thus about something real. This it does then by its sense. But, whatever an assertion may be about, it has infinitely many possibilities of being asserted factually by us or by any conceivable someone in possible acts of judgment on the basis of possible subjective lived experiences of perceiving, remembering, representing. Nevertheless, nothing of a counting individual and his counting lived experiences pertains to the sense or content of a pure number. But ideally we can conceive any psychic subject whatever, a human being of given actuality or a fictitious centaur, who counts and by counting becomes conscious of the respective number. Indeed, we even see ourselves compelled to say: the numbers are produced in counting, the judicative propositions are produced in the judging activity.

In this way a marvelous state of affairs confronts us with regard to the ideal objectivities with which the logician deals. On the one hand, as objectivities, they have a proper species of existing all by themselves, of existing in themselves; and in this regard then we have the a priori truths related purely to their existence by themselves and in themselves, the truths of arithmetic and pure logic. This "in themselves" means: they are what they are whether or not they are counted, thought, judged, known – every mathematical proposition and every number. On the other hand, it is inconceivable that ideal objects of this sort should not be able to become objects of consciousness and become knowable in subjective psychic lived experiences and activities corresponding to them; and even in such a way that we see ourselves compelled to say that if the occasion arises, the number is produced in counting, the respective proposition, the respective truth is subjectively formed in the judging activity.

⟨26⟩ Precisely this circumstance that if the occasion arises, ideal objects confront us as subjectively produced formations in the lived experiencing and doing of the forming, had been the source for the then almost universal psychologising of ideal objects. If now it was also made evident that ideal objects, in spite of the fact that they become formed in consciousness, have their own existence, their existence in themselves, then there existed here a great task never seriously seen and begun: namely this task, to make of this unique *correlation* between *ideal objects* of the purely logical sphere and *subjectively psychic lived experiencing as forming activity* a theme for research. If a psychic subject, for instance, I, this thinking human being, carry out in my psychic life certain psychic activities (and of course, not just any arbitrary ones, but of a very particular character), then there occurs in them a gradual forming of sense and a producing, in conformity with which the respective number-formation, the respective truth, the respective conclusion and proof, and so forth, appears as the gradually generated product. If I "repeat" a like producing, if I exercise once again like counting, predicating, inferring actions, then they are psychically a new fact, but I can recognize evidently that what has come to be here is identically the same pure number, identically the same truth, etc. But to speak about this in vague and empty generality does not yet yield any scientific knowledge. How do the hidden psychic lived experiences look, which are correlated to the respective idealities and which must occur as quite determinately appropriate producings, in order that the subject can have consciousness and evidently knowing consciousness of these idealities as objects?

This designates the proper theme of the *Logical Investigations* and, in corresponding amplification, of all phenomenology. You see that in this way the primary interest does not lie with the idealities and will not be content and satisfied with their proper sphere. Arithmetic, the a priori science of numbers and of other purely mathematical formations, is the business of the mathematician. With regard to traditional logic the case is no different; only, here a purification had to be carried out first, and it had to be shown that with regard to the subject matter of formal logic there is an exactly parallel, purely logical and ideal objectivity. Indeed in this ‹27› way it was shown that this discipline of pure propositions and truths as such is inseparable from arithmetic and from the whole of formal mathematical analysis, so that under the heading of *mathesis universalis* a single science had to be bordered off, as, only now become intelligible, Leibniz had already recognized. Thus, speaking now universally: one can pursue mathematics precisely as a mathematician, and then the theme is mathematical idealities purely by themselves and in their ideal relations among one another. As a mathematician one lives through the correlative mathematical activities continually, but one knows nothing at all about them; one can do the latter only by reflection. In any case, they are not a scientific theme for the mathematician. But if one turns one's theoretical interest precisely toward the multiplicity of subjective activity, the entire nexus of subjective life, in which the mathematical is born forth in the mathematician, then a correlative direction of research is opened up. Manifestly it is one in which the mathematical also occurs, namely as the respective ideal formation as it "appears" in the lived experiencing which forms it or makes it an object of consciousness in some other way, and it has a species of participation in temporality and reality without itself being a really, and thus temporally, individuated object.

What was taken up here in single investigations to be pursued concretely was, as can also be said now, a theory of logical-mathematical knowledge, a thorough scientific investigation of mathematical knowing together with the mathematically known, but quite concretely, showing step by step in psychological reflection the correlative internal events which so to speak bring it about in logical-mathematical knowledge that the mathematical can appear as object, appear as concept, as proposition, as propositional connection, as theory and entire science, but also as number, group, multiplicity, as the substrate of a theory of multiplicities, etc.

You can understand now why the *Logical Investigations*, this work directed toward the psychic, could also be designated as descriptive psychology. In fact, the sole purpose which they intended and had to intend was the establishing of an inner viewing which discloses the lived exper- ‹28› iences of thinking hidden from the thinker, and an essential description pertaining to these pure data of lived experience and moving within a pure inner viewing. But on the other hand, in order to characterize the novel peculiarity of method, the name *phenomenology* was chosen. In fact, a novel method of dealing with the psychic emerged here. On the one hand, the task was new, the attempt to go back radically and consistently from the respective categories of objectivities and ask about the modes of consciousness determinately belonging to them, about the subjective acts, act-structures, foundations of lived experience, in which objectivities of such a character become objects of consciousness, and above all become evidently self-given.

A new world opened up right away. It was astonishing to observe what immeasurable multiplicities of differences in internal life appear purely intuitively and become accessible to rigorously scientific work if one only has the courage quite exclusively to interrogate consciousness itself in a consistently carried out inner viewing and to witness as it were how it brings to pass within itself the becoming conscious of such objectivities, how it appears in itself as consciousness producing objectivity.

I must however add that a broadening of the problem area had to thrust itself to the fore at once. Plainly, the same problems which had arisen here starting with the logical and mathematical idealities had to be posed for all objectivities, even for real objects of knowledge. And these problems could also have been posed immediately in their regard, and were already partially so taken up in the *Logical Investigations*.

c) More precise characterization of the reflection decisive for phenomenology (step by step accomplishment of the reflection).

The following should be noted here to characterize further the specific peculiarity of the posing of the problem and the method of logical clarifications. The inquiry back from the respective objectivities to the subjective ‹29› lived experiencing and active forming of a subject which is conscious of such objectivities was from the very beginning determined by certain guiding intentions which admittedly (I was not yet that far along in reflective clarity) were not yet expressed in the form of clarified thoughts and demands.

For, the highest level of reflective clarity concerning the sense of the methodic procedure was gained only much later, precisely by reflection about what had been the deepest need in the *Investigations* and had made its fulfillment possible.

In the first place, the aim was a pure intuition and not a theoretical and hypothetical construction according to the manner of natural-scientific psychology. Logical thinking itself and the thoughts which are thought in it, the conceptual contents, the objects as their underlying objects just as they come to consciousness in thinking, purely according to the subjective and changing modes in which they "appear" in it, were to be brought into view and described in faithful descriptions. Description meant not merely the pure expression of the seen in concepts which were drawn originally from it, but rather also the most far-reaching possible analysis of the seen into its moments to be unfolded intuitively. E.g., to illustrate all that: if I make a judgment, for instance, establish that a straight line is determined by two points, I live the lived experiencing or doing of this establishing; I am conscious of it in a certain manner, but am not directed toward it in my judging. But quite obviously I can pay special attention to it by looking back and precisely by doing so make the reflective assertion also. Thus, instead of "a straight line is determined by two points," I assert then: "I judge, I am convinced, I am just now thinking by way of judgment that . . . . ;" obviously, I can now ask how does this judicative lived experiencing, the act of judgment, already passively given in its "how," look in more details? Does it admit of being further unfolded? What can I establish therein purely by intuition? And so in every case. The universal typology of thinking life had to be pursued here, and pursued in universal and yet purely intuitive descriptions. That belonged plainly to a psychology on the ground of "internal experience," which had already ⟨30⟩ been in demand and in attempted execution since the beginning of the eighteenth century, already since Locke's *Essay Concerning Human Understanding* (a psychological theory of knowledge). But at the same time for more profound reasons, it had never arrived at systematic and pure descriptions, neither for the lived experiences of experiencing and thinking, nor for those of valuing, willing, and acting, nor for their imaginative, neutral counterparts of fantasy. The reason probably lay partially in the fact that one strove all too hastily to produce explanation in psychology, and to do so after the model of explanation in the natural sciences and thus slid quickly past the region of sheer intuition, sheer givenness on the basis of internal experience.

Of particular importance, but noticed only very late, is the fact that reflective, so-called "internal," experience has very many levels and depth-dimensions and is exceedingly difficult to put into practice whenever one strives to go beyond the most superficial level. Indeed, at first one had no inkling at all of the depths and mediacies. One did not see that internal experience is not a simple reflection which would lead without further ado to the concreteness of the respective interiorities, but that the concrete admitted of being grasped as a theme only in many levels of reflection, that internal experience is a process of disclosure to be effected in ever new reflection. The demand for pure and systematically progressing description and the conviction that it designates a great field of difficult work, philosophically and psychologically fundamental, awakened soon after the blossoming of an experimental psychology. The motives lay in logic, ethics, esthetics, thus in the normative philosophical sciences, and in the critique

of reason which was interwoven with them. One must first become acquainted with cognitive life itself, valuing and willing life itself in internal
experience, and derive clear concepts from it in order to be able to gain a
theory of knowledge, a theory of value and a theory of will. In other words,
the task is to gain a clear understanding from within, of how "truth" arises
as a product of "rational" knowing, how true value arises as a product of
"rational" valuing, how ethical goodness arises as subjective product in
ethically right willing.

‹31›   *d) Brentano as pioneer for research in internal experience – discovery of
intentionality as the fundamental character of the psychic.*

Attempts at reform, especially of logic and theory of knowledge, but also of
ethics and esthetics, were the order of the day. Brentano participated in
them in his own way and, especially in his Vienna lectures, energetically
argued the point that all healthy reform here would trace back to a purely
descriptive analysis of the data of logical consciousness and of all other
consciousness, given in internal experience, especially internal perception.
And starting from there, he required for psychology taken universally, to
which all such analyses were to belong, a purely descriptive psychology
which was to be the basis for all explanatory theories, and which he later
called "psychognosy."

As vigorously as Brentano was resisted in his own time, he has provided
extraordinarily strong impulses in this respect, and that not only for
Germany but also for England and universally on an international scale.
Especially significant was a universal point of view for all psychological
descriptions, itself drawn already from the inner viewing: today we designate it with the word "intentionality." For the first time the fundamental
essence of all psychic life, consciousness as being conscious of something,
was put into the focal point, and was established descriptively as the most
universal essential character of psychic life, to be drawn directly from
the evidence of internal experience.

One could not evade the recognition that intentionality is a fundamental
characteristic of psychic life which is given quite immediately and evidently
prior to all theories. If I perceive a house, then, perhaps I might say to
myself at first, what is present is the house outside and in me a psychic
lived experience of perceiving, for instance a perceptual image, as a remote
effect of the house itself upon my psychophysical subjectivity. But, however
things may stand with this causal relation and whether or not there is
something to be said against it, it can in any case be made evident that a
relationship of consciousness is contained in the lived experience of
‹32› perceiving itself, and indeed a relation to the house perceived in it itself.

It can happen that later on I become correctly convinced that I have fallen victim to an illusion. But previously I did have purely the consciousness "house-existing-there;" descriptively it is no different from any other perceiving. Of course there can be no talk of external-internal psychophysical causality if the house is a mere hallucination. But it is clear that the momentary lived experiencing is in itself not only a subjective lived experiencing but precisely a perceiving *of* this house. Therefore, descriptively, the object-relation belongs to the lived experiencing, whether the object actually exists or not. Likewise, if I imagine a centaur, the lived experiencing of the fiction is itself a fantasy of this or that centaur; the lived experiencing which we call remembering includes the relation to the past; loving itself, the relation to the loved; hating, to the hated; willing, to what is willed, etc.

Intentionality had been seen already in scholasticism; the distinction had been made between truly actual objects, as existing in and of themselves, and merely intentional objects, as what is meant within the meaning, what is experienced within the experiencing, what is judged within the judging. This implied that psychic life as consciousness contains the property of relating to objects. But it is fundamentally mistaken to say that Brentano has simply rediscovered an old scholastic doctrine; his great discovery and his true originality consist in this, that he – guided by the idea of a descriptive psychology which he still, naturalistically oriented, thought of as the foundation for psychology which would be explanatory à la natural science – sought for a descriptive principle for the distinction between the physical and psychic and thereby was the first to establish that intentionality is the essential descriptively graspable characteristic of what is specifically psychic. Ostensibly, that is a minor change in the scholastic doctrine of intentionality. But such ostensibly slight changes make history and decide the fate of science. The consequence, obvious yet rich in implications, of this descriptive fundamental establishment was that psychology had at first to begin as a purely ‹33› descriptive science of psychic life and that, within that limit, it was nothing else but the descriptive science of intentionality, of the multiple forms of consciousness as consciousness of something, with all its constituents which can be distinguished in internal intuition.

This doctrine was admittedly laden with the greatest difficulties and obscurities, in spite of its evident descriptive rootedness in psychic life: how that of which one is conscious as such is to be treated in concrete internal experiential research, how intentional "analysis" is to be carried out, what sort of universality is possible and should be striven after in this sphere, and how from this point of departure psychology is to be grounded as a factual science of the psychophysically real psychic life – all that was in the dark. Thus, the prevailing psychology reacted on the whole by rejecting it. Nevertheless, one could not entirely escape Brentano's impulses. There were unprejudiced scientists who, after Brentano had shown it, could no longer overlook the fact that intentionality is the fundamental characteristic of psychic life, as that which is given quite immediately to the evidence of internal experience before all theories.

‹ * ›   Once clearly seen, intentionality had to be a psychological theme, indeed the central theme of psychology. Thus we find already since the 1870's in Germany, and later outside Germany, important psychologists who wanted to take account of intentionality descriptively. Simultaneously, the more universal demand for a descriptive psychology as the fundamental discipline of psychology found various spokesmen. Dilthey appears not to have been influenced by Brentano in this respect. Rather, he seems to have arrived at the demand for a pure description entirely on his own and guided by his own sphere of interests in the socio-cultural sciences. Characteristically, the central significance of intentionality plays no role in his work.

The *Logical Investigations* on the contrary, are a full development of Brentano's suggestions, as is a matter of course, since I was an immediate
‹ 34 ›   student of Brentano. And yet a new turn and an essential transformation of the idea of descriptive psychology was accomplished in these investigations by an essentially new method; so much so, that Brentano was never willing to recognize them as the mature execution of his idea; he then, secluding himself in his own intellectual circle, refused to go along in the new direction, quite differently from Dilthey who received the *Logical Investigations* with great joy and saw in them a first concrete execution of his "Ideen zu einer beschreibenden und zergliedernden Psychologie," even though they had arisen without any relation to his writings. Dilthey himself established this relationship; for, unfortunately, under the influence of Ebbinghaus' brilliant rebuttal, I had considered it unnecessary to read Dilthey's great work, all the more so since I had little receptivity at all for the significance of Dilthey's writings in those years. In my internal struggle for a fundamental overcoming of positivism, I had to repulse the strong tendency toward positivism which had appeared in Dilthey's previous work, the "Einleitung in die Geisteswissenschaften." I was at first not a little surprised to hear personally from Dilthey that phenomenology, and indeed the descriptive analyses of the second, specifically phenomenological, part of the *Logical Investigations*, were in essential harmony with his "Ideen" and could be regarded as a first fundamental piece of an actual methodologically matured execution of the psychology which he had in mind as an ideal. Dilthey always laid the greatest weight upon this coincidence of our investigations, in spite of essentially different

points of departure, and in his old age he took up once again with sheer youthful enthusiasm his investigations in the theory of the socio-cultural sciences, which he had dropped. The result was the last and most beautiful of his writings on this subject – from which he was unfortunately taken by death – "Der Aufbau der geschichtlichen Welt," (1910) in the *Abhandlungen der Berliner Akademie.* The further I myself progressed in the elaboration of the phenomenological method and in the phenomenological analysis of mental life, the more I had to recognize that Dilthey was in fact right with ‹35› his judgment which had so greatly astonished me, concerning the inner unity of phenomenology and descriptive-analytic psychology. His writings contain a gifted preview and preliminary level of phenomenology. They are in no way antiquated but even today quite rich in the most valuable sugges- tions for work in phenomenology, though phenomenology is methodologi- cally advanced and forms its entire problem area differently. Therefore, I would like to recommend to you most warmly the study of all the writings of this extraordinary mind. They bring true treasures of intuitive exhibi- tions and descriptions into the historical context, and wherever actually pure description in the most faithful accommodation to the givenness of actual intuition prevails, there phenomenology has a prepared and fruit- ful ground for work. But one can not gain from them instruction in that purely inner-directed psychology which Dilthey actually had in mind and which he himself had not yet formed into a rigorous science with a conceptually rigorous method and decisively carried out establishments. As gratifying as the belated great influence of Dilthey is, it can also work unfavorably, by an extrinsic imitation of his method – that should be very carefully noted.

Thus, the psychology to which I want to introduce you, in several impor- tant parts, will not be directly of a Diltheyan character, but will be precisely phenomenological psychology, as I have announced.

e) The further development of the thought of intentionality in the Logical Investigations. *The productive character of consciousness.*
Transition from a purely descriptive psychology to an a priori (eidetic-intuitive)
psychology and its significance for the theory of knowledge.

It is not possible here in this introduction to characterize in every regard ‹36› what presents itself as methodologically new in the *Logical Investigations.* Here I can clarify just a little, and first of all the following. Brentano had not gone beyond an externally classificatory-descriptive consideration of intentional lived experiences or, what amounts to the same, of species of consciousness. He never saw and took up the great task of going back from the basic categories of objects as possible objects of consciousness, espe- cially of cognitive consciousness, and inquiring about the entire multi-

plicity of possible modes of consciousness by which such objectivities come
to consciousness for us and in principle can come to consciousness, in order
to clarify, in further research beginning there, the teleological function of
these modes of consciousness for the synthetic producing of truth by reason.
Only by this posing of the problem (however incomplete a form it still had
even in the *Logical Investigations*) did a deeply penetrating insight into
consciousness and the performance of consciousness become at all possible. Indeed only then did it appear that consciousness is not merely an
empty, though also variegated, awareness, but a performance accomplished in multiple demonstrable forms and pertinent syntheses, everywhere intentional, directed toward goals, directed toward ideas of truth.
I can also say, only thus did a transcendental doctrine of consciousness
become possible and together with it a most intimate understanding of the
apperceiving of objects of every category, which occurs in psychological
interiority, and further a most intimate understanding of all verifying performances, as logical, axiological, and practical.

Consciousness, intentionality, revealed its true essential species only
in work with this orientation. Previously there prevailed in psychology,
and still now in all natural-scientifically oriented psychology, an interpretation of psychic life which regarded it as obviously an analogue of a
physical natural event, as a constantly self-transforming complex of
elements. Accordingly one held that the task was to reduce the complexes
to the elements and to the elementary forms of combinations and to
corresponding causal laws. On the contrary, it was now established that
this entire interpretation was senseless, that the synthesis of consciousness
‹37› is completely different from the external combination of natural elements,
that instead of spatial mutual externality, spatial intermingling and inter-
penetration, and spatial totality, it pertains to the essence of conscious
life to contain an intentional intertwining, motivation, mutual implication
by meaning, and this in a way which in its form and principle has no analogue at all in the physical. In the sense thus indicated, Brentano was still
a naturalist; he still did not see anything like intentional implication and
intentional analysis as analysis of a bestowal of perhaps continually in-
voluted sense. This designates also what comprises the radically strange
character of every intentional inner psychology, every descriptive-analytic
psychology in the genuine sense – strange vis-a-vis all experimental and
psycho-physical and otherwise external psychology, which encompasses
only the inductive exterior sphere of objectified psychic existence.

There is still one aspect of the psychological-phenomenological
method, perhaps the most important and essentially novel of all, which I
have not yet designated, and which also appeared for the first time in the
Logical Investigations and thoroughly influenced their working method.

For, it became apparent at once that a descriptive investigation with the novel aim of the *Logical Investigations* in no way has the character of a merely empirically psychological investigation, neither psycho-physical nor descriptive in the natural sense. The exclusive theme of the *Logical Investigations* was the psychic as correlative to the objectivities intended in each case (and especially the logically ideal objectivities), thus, the multiplicity of psychic modes in which, purely in the immanence of psychic life, concepts, judgments, theories, are formed as ideally identical unities of sense, with the respective modes of supposed or evidently true being.

Psychology of the millenia wanted to be and was in all its historically changing forms, an experiential science of human and animal psychic life. However, if one goes back from ideal objectivities to the consciousness which forms them subjectively, then one can soon become convinced that ⟨38⟩ the internal passivities and activities in which they are subjectively formed and become evidently given, and which can become intuitively disclosed by methodic reflection and phenomenological analysis, are not empirical contingencies of human act-living, not contingent facticities, which could also be thought differently. Rather, it is evident that whenever something like numbers, mathematical multiplicities, propositions, theories, etc., are to become subjectively given, become objects of consciousness in subjective lived experiences, the lived experiences which are needed for that to happen must have their essentially necessary and everywhere identical structure. In other words, whether we take us men as thinking subjects, or whether we imagine angels or devils or gods, etc., any sort of beings which count, compute, do mathematics – the counting, mathematising internal doing and living is, if the logical-mathematical is to result from it, in a priori necessity everywhere essentially the same. To the a priori of pure logic and pure mathematics itself, this realm of unconditionally necessary and universal truths, there corresponds *correlatively* an a priori of psychic species, namely, a realm of unconditionally necessary and universal truths referring to the mathematical *lived experiencing*, e.g., the mathematical presenting, thinking, connecting, etc., i.e., as a multiple psychic life of any subject at all insofar as it is to be thought, purely ideally, as a subject which knows in itself the mathematical. If we take logical-mathematical objectivity as having to be able to become evident intersubjectively, then we would have to add to the single subject communicative subjectivity and its communalized life.

The same holds for all investigations of psychic correlations referring to objects of every region and category, and it holds not merely in empty universality, in opinion and affirmation distant from the subject matter, but in a determinate particularity corresponding to the determinate objects, and in relation to the disclosing intuitions which pertain to them. But,

precisely thereby a novel idea of psychology is presented, novel not only by its concretely and all-inclusively understood theme, object-consciousness, but also in the fact that it is to be not an empirical but an a priori psychology. It is to be a priori in the same sober sense, in which mathe-
‹39› matics is called an a priori or non-empirical science or, as we also say, a science of essence, and thereby it displays a peculiarity which has its evidence prior to all "theory" of a priori knowledge, that is, prior to all epistemological interpretation. Instead of the fact of human subjects of this earth and world, this psychology deals, therefore, with ideal essences of any mathematising and, more universally, of any knowing subjectivity at all, one which is to be phenomenologically disclosed by way of example, but one which is ideally possible, conceivable in unconditioned universality. That Lotze had already noticed the a priori within the scope of the immanent sense-qualities and that logic passed as an a priori discipline in the unclarity of its noetic-noematic interpretation, means nothing in this respect. There had not been a single actual beginning of a phenomenological a priori psychology and no notion even of its possibility. That holds also for Brentano.

In previous times admittedly, a priori psychology was much discussed, namely, in the Leibnitzian-Wolffean school of the eighteenth century. Kant's critique put an end to that. But this psychology was ontological-metaphysical. It was not a psychology which like this new one was purely intuitive and descriptive and yet at the same time a priori, which therefore, beginning with intuitive concrete instances ascended to intuitive necessities and universalities. This new peculiarity will still find an accurate clarification to the point of obviousness in the systematic and concrete expositions to which we shall soon pass over. This a priori (eidetic-intuitive) psychology was possible only after the peculiarity of intentional analysis, of intentional implications, was concretely established and realized in some segments; but that was done at first in naïve intuitiveness and before all question concerning its empirical or a priori significance. But you will notice already that it is just this point which gave the descriptively psychological analysis of the *Logical Investigations* an essentially different character from that of the descriptive and analytic psychology, which Dilthey had demanded in the interest of the historical and systematic socio-cultural sciences, and
‹40› also one different from that of Brentano's psychognosy. The *Logical Investigations* do give also a descriptive-analytic psychology in the interest of psychology itself and also, as was the case likewise with Dilthey for his part, as the foundation of a theory of reason. But this psychology had an essentially different countenance, in accordance with the novel points of departure and objectives which led to it. From the beginning, the aim was not toward a new grounding of psychology. The aim was a purely epistemo-

logical one. Over against formal logic as an a priori science of the essential forms and essential laws of certain ideal objectivities, a science was required which had as its duty the systematic clarification of the subjective activities of thinking in which these thoughts become formed subjectively, and in particular, of the particular activities of reason in which such thoughts appropriate the normative form of evident truth as transsubjective validity.

But it is only another way of putting it if I say that it was a first concretely executed attempt at a theory of knowledge, which was however still limited by its theme, limited to the sphere of formal-logical reason and naturally extended to formal-mathematical reason. It became evident here for the first time that a theory of reason, as of a system of rational performances occurring in thinking subjectivity, can never be brought to pass by vague, distant discussions of the a priori and the empirical, as was previously customary, nor by a psychology on the basis of internal experience which was descriptive in a merely empirical sense. It became evident, rather, that in place of empirical psychology there had to appear a novel, purely a priori and yet at the same time descriptive, science of the psychic, namely, a science which makes intelligible in unconditioned and intuited (directly seen) necessity, how psychic life and especially knowing life accomplishes intentional productions in itself and in accordance with its a priori essential species, and in particular the production of that type of ideal validity which is called true being and truth.

Therefore, although at first there was no thought of a reform of the existing psychology, it became apparent to me afterwards of itself, that the beginning of a novel psychology lay here, and even a new form of the old ‹41› idea of an a priori psychology – in a similar manner to the way in which, in the "Prolegomena" and in the third and fourth investigations, the old idea of an a priori ontology had experienced a reawakening in a new, non-metaphysical shape.

Thereby a marvelous change of the historical relationship between psychology and theory of knowledge was announced. On the one side there was for centuries an empirical psychology in very variable forms (finally in the so successful form of an experimental psychology), a psychology which always raised the claim to include the theory of knowledge or at least to provide it with its foundations. On the other side, since Kant a transcendental theory of knowledge had achieved powerful influence and acceptance, a theory which sharply rejected all empirically-psychological founding and combatted it as psychologism, but which on the other hand, recognized no other psychology over against the psycho-physical psychology, and especially no a priori psychology which could be accepted as a necessary foundation. At the same time psychology, and all objective science, was to maintain the right of its own independent existence.

But it was something historically new that an epistemological investigation of logical-mathematical knowledge commenced and executed in complete independence of traditional empirical psychology, pressed toward a methodical reform of psychology and gave a new shape to the problem of the relation of epistemology and psychology. These concretely carried out epistemological-logical investigations had, without fail, to make use of a psychological analysis, but a novel one, proceeding in a priori fashion. An a priori science of the psychic, drawing upon purely inner directed intuition, as it appeared here in actual beginning segments, could not possibly be without significance for a rigorously scientific empirical psychology, just as an a priori science of space and of the formal idea of any nature at all could not be without significance for an experiential knowledge of nature.

Already Brentano and also Dilthey had seen that traditional empiricism and epistemological psychologism include a kernel of inviolable right, ⟨42⟩ namely, the demand that a theory of knowledge must by all means be grounded in an intuitive analysis of knowing and a theory of ethical reason likewise in an intuitive analysis of the life of ethical consciousness, thus in a descriptive psychology. But as long as this analysis was thought of as empirical, the objection of the anti-psychologists could not be met, as to how a theory of knowledge, a science of the a priori principles which are supposed to make intelligible the possibility of objective productions of reason could be grounded in psychology, in an empirical science. Added to this is the fact that the founding descriptive or psycho-genetic investigations remained necessarily without results, that is, they were unable to lead to an understanding of the logical and the ethical because they were incapable of penetrating to any genuine intentional analyses. If they had been capable of that, the genuine psychological a priori, to which precisely the then obvious reference back to the constitutive provided a suggestion, would also easily have had to come to the fore.

f) The consistent expansion and deepening of the question raised by the Logical Investigations. *Showing the necessity of an epistemological grounding of a priori sciences by transcendental phenomenology – the science of transcendental subjectivity.*

Of course, the horizons opened up for a new theory of knowledge and theory of all other species of reason, and on the other hand for an a priori psychology, needed to be first further traversed before complete clarity was possible for the future tasks of investigation in the theory of reason and in psychology. The highest level of clarity concerning principles was by no means already reached in the *Logical Investigations.* Only in the progress of the researches beyond the limited problem sphere of the *Logical Investigations,* only in its consistent expansion to a set of problems which embraced

the totality of all possible objects as such and the totality of possible con- ‹43›
sciousness as such, or of possible subjectivity as such, could the final
clarifications of principles arise. In the urgent need for a more inclusive
expansion beyond the *Logical Investigations*, already awakened by the
formal universality of the *mathesis universalis*, what had to be presented was
the expansion from a priori and formal logic and mathematics to the idea of
a total system of a priori sciences for every conceivable category of objective
entities, thus, at the highest level, the demand for an all-inclusive a priori of
possible worlds as such besides that of formal mathematics, but on the other
hand and correlatively, the expansion from the purely a priori consideration
of cognitive consciousness with reference to the merely formal universalities, to cognitive consciousness as more determinate with regard to its
content, related to every particular category of objectivities as such; and
finally from there an a priori pure doctrine of consciousness in full all-
inclusiveness had to arise, one which embraced every type of valuing,
striving, willing consciousness and so any type of consciousness at all, one
which therefore grasped the entire concrete subjective life in all forms of its
intentionality and opened up the totality problems of the constitution of the
world and of the unity of conscious subjectivity, individually personal and
communalized subjectivity.

As a further consequence, reflection on the sense of a radical and ultimately essential science of reason, as the transcendental philosophy developed in modernity properly wanted to be and as philosophy had to be,
necessitated an essential differentiation of the new idea of an a priori and
descriptive psychology into two parallel sciences distinguished only by
their fundamental attitude. The one was the exact analogue of pure
geometry and more concretely of the a priori science of nature, an a priori
psychology in the natural sense of the word.

In a priori science of nature we include disciplines such as pure geometry, pure mechanics, etc. Abstracting from all that is factual in nature
as given, they want to establish in concepts and laws nothing else but that
without which any nature at all would be inconceivable. As a parallel,
therefore, a priori psychology would seek to establish whatever is essentially necessary to the psychic as such, without which psyche and psychic ‹44›
life is utterly inconceivable, contrary to sense.

But all such a priori sciences need a theory of knowledge, a clarification
and subjective grounding from the point of view of the critique of reason,
just as formal logic and mathematics which are more comprehensive in
universality than they, require it. In this way it becomes apparent that no
psychology, not even an a priori psychology, is so self-sufficient that it is
capable on its own simultaneously to pose and to solve epistemological
problems. Rather, a specifically transcendental psychology (for which

however the historical word "psychology" is no longer fitting) must be distinguished from it, as that a priori science of the subjective to which all research in the theory of reason ultimately traces back. In other words, the distinction had to be made between a so-called transcendental subjectivity and a psychological subjectivity and correspondingly between a psychology which is classed with the objective sciences and a transcendental phenomenology which remains completely outside that class. According to its entire attitude of research, therefore for the most radical reason, it is distinguished from all the sciences which have come to their development in our European culture since Aristotle. All these sciences are called dogmatic (positive) or naturally-naïve vis-a-vis it; the novel problems which are traditionally called problems of the theory of reason refer to all truths established in them, no matter how exactly; and they are, as will be seen, transcendental-phenomenological problems.

⟨*⟩   The methodical grounding of an all-inclusive science of transcendental subjectivity in the phenomenological method, thus in pure description on the basis of pure intuition of essence and intentional analysis, was projected and already executed in some chief parts in the *Ideen zu einer reinen Phänomenologie und phänomenologischen Philosophie* of 1913. Since the discussion there concerned philosophy, a radical grounding of philosophy as a rigor-
⟨45⟩ ous science, it was sharply emphasized that this phenomenology was in no way identical with a naturally understood a priori psychology. This was frequently so understood, especially by those who found it more comfortable to remain in the well traveled tracks of dogmatic thinking and who shunned the toilsome practice of the strange phenomenological reflection and intuition of essence, as if the psychologist as a scientist referring to the world did not need to bother with this sort of philosophical inquiry into principles. All the more so, since I myself had said that dogmatic sciences would be hereafter as heretofore quite possible without recourse to the posing of transcendental questions. Nevertheless, transcendental phenomenology has this characteristic, that every one of its propositions admits of being transformed into an a priori psychological proposition in the natural sense. What was also not seen was the fact that a phenomenological method essentially similar can also ground a naturally objective a priori psychology from the start, if one only omits the radical change of attitude by which alone the transcendental can become thematic and if one does not permit the co-functioning of methodic intentions relating to the transcendental, nor of philosophically ultimate questions, which lead quite beyond the normal natural science.

Only quite slowly and at first among a few did the recognition force its way through, that the core theoretical content in scientific psychology (individual psychology and social psychology and as a further consequence every explanatory socio-cultural science) consists in a phenomenological and a priori essential science of the psychic. One learns to see that the psychophysical, experimental and esthetic external psychology, however much it pretends to rest upon internal experience, can never lead to an actual and proper psychology, to a psychology which provides insight, and therefore understanding, of psychic life and mental life itself. But such an internal insight is impossible as long as the founding internal experience is not the inner viewing disclosed by the phenomenological method and as long as the analysis of internal experience has not taken on the form of the unfolding of intentional implications. Once that is seen, however, it follows that the mighty abundance of systematically connected expositions of those ‹46› analyses of consciousness which are won from a transcendental interest and transcendental attitude, must be taken over into psychology by a corresponding change of attitude. But it then becomes evident that a strictly self-enclosed and infinite science of the a priori of phenomenological interiorities is bordered off, which is the central science for all socio-cultural sciences, but also the fundamental science for psychophysical, experimental psychology.

4. SUMMARIZING CHARACTERIZATION OF THE NEW PSYCHOLOGY.

We have now stated in essence what was to be said in an introduction. ‹*› Thus, you know in a most universal way, though merely by way of historically oriented predelineations (therefore, as from a far distance), what the new psychology wants to be and must be, in response to a necessary demand.

(Only a few almost obvious supplementary remarks need to be added, in order to avoid misleading anticipations.)

Let us survey the basic characteristics of the new psychology, under the mottoes: Apriority, Eidetic, Intuition or Pure Description, Intentionality; and let us mention also the characteristic of abiding by the natural dogmatic attitude instead of the specifically philosophical, that is, transcendental, attitude.

1) The title Apriority means: this psychology aims first of all at all those essential universalities and necessities, without which psychological being and living are simply inconceivable. Only subsequently does it proceed to the explanation of psychological facts, to theory, precisely their eidetic explanation, which is naturally *for us* the first interest.

2) The title of intuition or description designates for us then the source of this a priori.

The established results, as substantiations concerning essences, can be won only by inner seeing and analysis of the seen, and by an intuitive ascent

to generic necessities. These are not conjectured, assumed essential neces-
‹47› sities; rather, the necessity and unconditioned universality of their validity
become themselves something seen.

3) Further, by such a procedure, the most universal essential characteristic of psychic being and living is exposed: intentionality. Psychic life is
the life of consciousness; consciousness is consciousness of something. This
generic heading, consciousness, with the headings which belong inseparably
to it – I, personality as such, and objectivity as objectivity of consciousness – this heading under which all that is psychic stands, consciousness
taken just as it presents itself according to its own essence on the basis of
inner seeing, this twofold centering of conscious life, furnishes every inner
psychology a characteristic teleological centering in its progress: the task
necessarily arises of descriptively pursuing systematically coherent multiplicities of consciousness which pertain essentially to the cognitive becoming aware, or being able to become aware, of objectivities of every category.
Every category of possible objectivities designates an index for a methodic
regularity of possible psychic life; every possible real world, a regularity
of possible intersubjective psychic life.

4) In the transcendental attitude, all such inquiries take on the character
of fundamental philosophical investigations and lead to a radically grounded, and finally an all-inclusive philosophy.

But as psychologists we do not want to be philosophers, that is, at least we
do not want at first to be philosophers, any more than mathematicians,
physicists, philologists, etc., would want to be philosophers – as has already
been said. I merely suggest here further that, for essential reasons, no one
can be born a philosopher. Each can begin only as a natural, unphilosophi-
cal human being. Accordingly, a radical, systematic grounding of philosophy demands a priori a subjective and also a historical ascent from the
natural standpoint to the philosophical.

Perhaps our psychology provides an a priori possible and natural point
of departure for the ascent to a transcendental phenomenology and philos-
‹48› ophy. To that extent, such an inner psychology would be of special philosophical interest as a pedagogical, motivating stage preliminary to philosophy (but in no way as a founding discipline). But, although this interest
may well be effective and though the spirit of philosophy may be prepared
by this lecture course, nevertheless philosophy will neither be presupposed
nor systematically pursued here. We want to remain in the natural attitude;
we want actually to be nothing else but psychologists, directed in a natural,
human manner toward the objective world as actuality, and endeavoring
to investigate it insofar as it is a world of mind. But above all, we need to add
here a few words concerning the sense in which we speak of the natural
attitude and of dogmatic sciences as sciences of this attitude.

The world, posited and continually presupposed in the obviousness of its existence (an obviousness which it derives from the harmony of our constant experience), is the all-inclusive theme of all the sciences which we call "sciences of the natural attitude" in contrast to philosophy.

This very presupposition of the experienced actuality of the world, and the reference of all scientific striving for knowledge and of all other human practice back to the world presupposed as an experiential actuality, characterizes the natural attitude.

This suggests that another attitude is possible by exclusion of this presupposition; but we need not go into that. Properly speaking, even the a priori sciences, as they have developed historically, e.g., geometry and other purely mathematical sciences, do not lose this natural attitude, even though in their own special subject matters and in their foundations they neither contain nor presuppose anything about a factual world. They deal with their ideal objects, with ideally possible space-structures and time-structures, ideally possible groups, ideally possible things as such, etc.; equally, ideally possible forms of the psychic and the mental – thus our a priori psychology.

These a priori sciences are related to the world insofar as they are formed with a view to knowledge of the world and as means thereto. A priori investigation is at the same time mediately investigation of the world. For example, the multiple spatial facts in factual nature correspond to the spatial, or, equivalently, geomterical, a priori. Given nature as spatial must obviously satisfy the essential forms and essential laws of every conceivable space, all conceivable spatial figures. Accordingly, geometry, in the infinity of its a priori laws, is simultaneously and *eo ipso* a knowledge of nature, a knowledge of the world of experience, though a one-sided, incomplete knowledge, relating only to the form of space. ⟨49⟩

5) In the same sense, the pure essential theory of the mental, of the individually psychic as well as of the socially psychic, and of the productions of society, is *eo ipso* simultaneously a knowledge of the world, with regard to the mentality which factually permeates it.

And it is even a knowledge of the highest cognitive dignity, just like the mathematics of nature, insofar as it establishes everywhere in factual space the apodictically necessary structure of laws. Empirically inductive natural science mounted an incomparably higher level of knowledge at that moment when it appropriated the mathematics of nature and recognized that the systematic formation of that a priori which belongs inseparably to nature provides *ipso facto* an infinity of absolutely necessary laws for factual nature.

The same must hold for every experiential science. It must rise above the level of vague inductive empirical procedure. If it is to become rigorous science, its first concern must be to establish those essential laws which govern its province a priori, therefore, before any additional consideration of the contingently factual. The situation is no different for psychology. The knowledge that an infinity of essential laws, to be investigated systematically, here precedes all that is contingently factual, is the most important knowledge for shaping psychology into a rigorous science.

Of course, for a psychology which wants as it always has, to know mentality as it appears experientially in the given world, there remain also those cognitions which define and rule the factual as such, above and beyond the a priori. Everywhere, in psychology as well as in natural science, the a priori is merely an irrefrangible, formal border, within which the empirically ⟨50⟩ factual must remain if it is to be at all conceivable, a priori possible.[1]

How the method of empirical procedure is to be fashioned, and especially that of the search for empirical "laws", after knowledge of the a priori and in reference back to it, is then another question.

In any case, we want to see our task, not in constructing the idea of an empirical psychology itself, but in preparing, by merely constructing the idea of a purely a priori inner psychology as a self-enclosed science, that generic and fundamental essential understanding of mentality (in order actually to win it in future explicit execution) – an understanding which is in and of itself one of the highest goals of scientific striving.

6) In conclusion, just one more point, in order to exclude misunderstandings.

Since we have all formed the concept of a priori science in mathematics, the oldest and until recently the only developed a priori science, we tend understandably to regard any a priori science at all as something like a mathematics; *a priori* psychology, therefore, as a mathematics of the mind. But here we must be on our guard. The province or provinces of mathematics require a method and a type of science which fit them; but, by no means does this type pertain to every kind of a priori.

What I mean here is exemplified by geometry which, as its province demands, constructs a deductive theory, a theory which traces the infinity of deductive cognitions back to, or deduces them from, a small number of immediately evident truisms, its "Axioms". The psychic province, how- ⟨51⟩ ever, is of a completely different essential type; it has a multiplicity of im-

---

[1] To the a priori of every nature pertains universal causality of nature, in the sense that all facts of any possible natural universe stand under laws of facts, the determinate content of which is not knowable a priori, but is itself a fact of that particular natural universe. The question still needs to be explored how, further, in the a priori of an all-inclusive mentality, in any real world at all, or in the possibility of a real world at all, something like an exact or typical system of rules for factual mentality (lawfulness of the mental) is predelineated, if it is to be intuited a priori that as for nature so also for mind an empirical regularity must exist.

mediate essential insights which continually grows with analysis and is never to be limited. Here, mere immediate intuition delivers already a quite endless science, an intuitive and descriptive a priori – above all there is no question about that for us. The mediate, concluding and deducing procedure is not lacking at higher stages, and it leads to a higher level a priori; but by no means is the entire science of the type of a mathematics.

5. DELIMITING PHENOMENOLOGICAL PSYCHOLOGY: DISTINGUISHING IT
FROM THE OTHER SOCIO-CULTURAL SCIENCES AND FROM THE NATURAL
SCIENCES. QUESTIONING THE CONCEPTS, NATURE AND MIND.

‹ * › Now that we have concluded the historical introduction to phenomenological psychology, we begin today to develop it systematically. Our first
task must be to give to the scientific title "psychology" a sense which is clear
with regard to its origin; and that is a very necessary concern here.

Science universally and as such represents the ideal of systematic knowledge in the form of conclusiveness or in the form of a method which justifies in absolute evidence once and for all and for everyone.

Though the historically arisen sciences may not satisfy this ideal perfect-
ly, some of them do realize it in the form of an evident approximation. Thus,
the "exact" sciences. No one will consider a complete revolution possible
here, by which physics, for example, might completely alter the entire form
of its method, its theoretical countenance, so to speak. But the case is different, as we already know, with psychology. The psychology of the an-
cients, for example of Aristotle, has a completely different countenance
from that of the moderns, but not as if modern psychology had succeeded
even in approximating a methodic form of rigorous science. How great are
the differences of the empiricist psychology of the Lockean school, the
materialistic psychology of Hobbes, the metaphysical psychology of Her-
bart, etc., right down to modern experimental psychology. But, as we
heard, despite its international recognition, the conclusiveness of the
‹53› latter's goals and methods is not acknowledged by Dilthey or the phenomenological school.

When sciences are in such a condition, then there is need of a radical
sense-investigation; clearly only that can help. There is need of a return to
the concrete total context out of which its province is exposed and singled
out for thought as a theme for knowledge. Clarity must be provided con-

cerning what gives the respective scientific province its essential unity, and how it branches off essentially, both internally and externally, on the basis of its first originary sources of sense. Therefore, for psychology we have as our starting point the question: what does it deal with, what is its thematic sphere? Of course, one will answer: not material nature; that is the province of the natural sciences. Psychology has to do with mental facts, with men and animals, insofar as they are mental beings and abodes of mental, psychic happening; as universal psychology, with what holds in common everywhere, as psychological anthropology and animal psychology, with the human realm and the animal realm in their respective limits.

The multiple sciences of the socio-historical world also are concerned with mental facts, the sciences which deal with nations, states, systems of law, religions, etc., each within the historical unity of a cultural division of humanity, and also with various formed products of objectified mentality, such as languages, literature, art, with the multiple forms of products of work, as they appear amid constant change in the unity of a history. The concept of a psychological anthropology can include all these disciplines related to man. But when one speaks of psychology, one means clearly that it is to be a *science of the most universal forms and laws of mental facts* in contrast to the sciences of the individual concretions in historical actuality: similarly to the way in which, with regard to the sphere of nature, physics as an abstract science of law is contrasted to the concrete sciences of nature which have to do with the individual forms of things, with the earth, the sun, the stars, and with the concretely typical forms exhibitable within this individual nature. The science of law is then called upon to ‹54› accomplish explanatory results within the changing concretion.

On the other hand, we know that there are keenly felt unclarities concerning the execution of these intentions, ultimately unclarities concerning the mutual relation of nature and mind and of all the sciences which belong to these two titles. The natural and the mental do not confront us clearly and separately so that mere pointing would suffice: *here* is nature, and *here*, as something completely different, is mind. Rather, what seems at first obviously separated, upon closer consideration turns out to be obscurely intertwined, permeating each other in a manner very difficult to understand.

Modern science of nature arose from a one-sided orientation of interest and method, which under the heading "nature", did not simply single out of original experience a sphere of directly exhibitable experiential givens, but rather had in view what was already an artificial product of method. Thus, it was a nature which it did not have beforehand as experienced, but was an idea which it undertook to realize by theory.

A consistent elimination of all "merely subjective" properties belonging to the things of immediate experience, of all features stemming from subjectivity, belonged essentially to its method. This extraction of the subjective, and therefore mental, was however not at all interested in the mental itself, but precisely in that which remained over as residuum in such a method, as purely physical or material. The purely physical was the theme and not the mental, which here was merely to be disposed of as a contamination. And thus the subjective itself was not scientifically grasped and delimited.

On the other side, socio-cultural science and above all psychology, directed toward the radically and universally mental, was not able to reach the necessary correlative result. For, where the mental had to be the universal theme, it was not able to provide clarity concerning the unitary connection of the mental in the concrete world, concerning its various originary forms and those derived forms in which the experienced concrete ‹55› world is subjected to culture and has been subjected to it in ever new forms. Its *disjecta membra* of mentality, which the natural scientific method had cut off and thrown away in order to acquire its idea of nature, had to be brought back again into their original context. In other words, the abstractive procedure of natural science had to be considered anew and the abstraction again cancelled. But, educated in the habitualities of abstractly symbolic natural-scientific thinking, one no longer bore in mind the original sense of the natural-scientific concept of nature and treated this nature as if it were simply that which is given in concrete intuition.

Thus, both – cultural world and nature – remained equally unintelligible, although within the practice of the natural-scientific method, what one wanted to explore was readily intelligible.

6. NECESSITY OF THE RETURN TO THE PRE-SCIENTIFIC EXPERIENTIAL
WORLD AND TO THE EXPERIENCE IN WHICH IT IS GIVEN
(HARMONY OF EXPERIENCE).

As scientific themes, nature and mind do not exist beforehand; rather, they are formed only within a theoretical interest and in the theoretical work directed by it, upon the underlying stratum of a natural, pre-scientific experience [*Erfahrung*]. Here they appear in an originally intuitable intermingling and togetherness; it is necessary to begin with this concretely intuitive unity of the pre-scientific experiential world and then to elucidate what theoretical interests and directions of thought it predelineates, as well as how nature and mind can become unitary universal themes, always inseparably related to each other, in it.

If one had always returned to the complete original concretion of the world, as it is always experienced in naïve originality, and if in carrying out methodic abstractions, one had never forgotten this concretely intuitive world as their field of origin, the absurdities of naturalistic psychology and socio-cultural science would not have been possible; one would never have been able to think of interpreting mind as a merely causal supplement to material bodies, or as a causal sequence paralleling that of physical ‹56› matter. One would never have been able to regard human beings and animals as psycho-physical machines or even as parallelistic double machines.

The next project necessary for our purpose is thus already indicated. We go from the concepts in question for us, nature and mind, as concepts defining provinces of science, back to the world which precedes all sciences and their theoretical intentions, as a world of pre-scientific intuition, indeed as a world of actual living which includes world-experiencing and world-theorizing life. Universally speaking, all factual sciences are sciences of the world. If the world were not already originally given by experience, none of the sciences of the world could begin; they would have no sub-stratum for their activities of thought. But it is perpetually there for all of us – there thanks to continually progressing and concordant experience. It [experience] runs off with its sensed content, the experienced things; whether we pay heed to these things or not, they appear nonetheless and appear as existing things.

It is taken for granted that we are remaining in the natural attitude, and that means nothing else but that we accept experiential "being" just as it gives itself, that is, as concretely existing. All of natural life relates to this world which obviously passes for us as existing actuality. We act and pro-duce effects upon this existing world, our "surrounding world"; we address to it all our practical and theoretical questions, and relate to it our scienti-fic work. Admittedly, this world has quite a changing countenance. Not only do we experience it as variable and as forever transforming itself, but even our "apprehensions" change; and our opinions which stem from our theoretical or practical activities clothe our experience over, or clothe its sense with new layers of sense; whatever gives itself to our simple regard as seen, heard, or in any way experienced, upon closer consideration, includes such sediments of previous mental activities; and thus, it is ques-tionable whether an actually pre-theoretical world can ever be found in pure experience, free from sense-sediments of previous thinking.

In natural parlance we say: "there we see tables and benches, books for ‹57› lecture notes," etc.; it is clear that such words express the things seen in a reference of sense which, when clarified, leads us back to our own activi-ties and those of others. And if we designate as heavenly bodies the stars which we see, or if we take as our example experiential statements concerning degrees on the thermometer, then it is manifest that, for the most part, sediments of knowledge stemming from previous thought-activity adhere to what is in each case actually experienced. That is without doubt. But we want at first to take what is experienced just as it gives itself in any instance, and thus begin where we must begin, with this contrast which can always be shown between what gives itself to us in each case as immediately perceived, as passively experienced, as existing bodily, which we grasp by merely looking at it itself, and as its opposite, the thinking which we exercise upon it and the thoughts which are formed concerning these things, thoughts which may very well cling to them afterwards and present themselves in subsequent experience as belonging to the experienced thing itself.

Therefore, what is now guiding us is a first conception of experience and of experienced world, or in particular of experienced single realities – that is to say, a conception which it is necessary to form for a first sense-investigation. Taking a first look back and around us, we must then say: a world is at all times experienced, and in spite of all change of apprehensions and prior to any thinking which might afterwards come into play, one and the same world, concerning which assertions may be made and knowledge of truth obtained by endeavor, is continually experienced. Therefore, all questions concerning true being presuppose this experiential world, which is admittedly quite changeable with regard to its apprehensions: "the true world" designates therefore a higher product of knowledge which has its original raw material in the flowing universe of what is given to each respective experience. Or, this first actuality for experience is the primal field, from which the true world must be worked out by scientific research, as its fruit.

Amid all its subjective forms, changing in subjective living and working, this first sense of experiential world has evidently a certain universal structure and, as will soon be shown, not a contingently factual but an a priori necessary structure.

⟨58⟩⟨*⟩   In the last lecture, we began with a radical sense-investigation; its purpose was to lead us back to the place of origin of all our presentations, hence also of our scientific concepts of the mental and in particular of the psychic. The place of origin of all objective factual sciences or, equivalently, of all sciences of the world, is one and the same. The one world to which they all refer is originally given as the simple experiential world, thus as directly and immediately perceived in its present and as having been perceived and recalled to memory with regard to its past. We possess or we acquire multiple knowledge and sciences concerning the world; but, as we have said, a world, things, events, and the like, must first be simply experienced so that thought-activity may come into play and shape knowledge concerning those things to highly scientific theories concerning them (the ideality of truth). The final substrata of all thoughts and of all other ideal formations which grow out of mental activity are found in the experiential world. If we say something about it or about objects drawn from it, if we establish these assertions through arguments or theories, then we create thereby predicative determinations of a certain methodic form for that which is at first simply experienced (or experienceable) pre-theoretically; these determinations are thus theoretical formations, existing in the realm of the irreal. Truth is nothing other than a distinguishing predicate of such irreal formations and therefore, like them, presupposes what is relatively pre-theoretical, the perceptual and experiential world. But it is of great importance to hold sharply in our view how we understand this idea of the experiential world and of the experience of this world. Therefore, in continuing what was just said above, we will need determinations to make it more precise. What should matter to us is above all the following. In perception, the perceived gives itself as quite immediate and as itself presently existing; in memory, as itself having been present. Without any contribution from us, objects can enter into our sphere of affairs, and they are there for us as they themselves, or they can be there, without our paying attention to them. Nevertheless, we do allow certain activities to be included in our ‹59› conception of experience, namely those – but also only those – whereby perception is changed into attentive perception and attentive perception into more closely observing perception: in a word, into actively accomplished perception.

This means that we direct our attention to such and such objects of our perceptual field, grasp them and progressively take cognizance of them. We look more closely at the things already visible, and lay hold of what is *next to* them or *in* them, included with them in their concrete present. On the other hand, all naming, predicating, theorizing activity, as well as any other activity which would burden the experiential object with any novel sense, remains out of play. But – and this is to be emphasized – we do not ask whether or not what is given to us as perceived, or universally as experienced, owes its experiential content in part to previous sensuous activities; in these regards we ask no questions of origin. Thus, whatever gives itself in each case as perceived, as itself present existence, we let pass as perceived and universally as experienced.

But now there is need of greater precision.

The one experiential world pervades our waking life as a continuous unity. Certainly, we have always new perceptions from moment to moment, and considered singly, always something new perceived in particular. But, speaking universally, everything joins together without our assistance to one surveyable unity of experience, and indeed in such a way that on surveying it we must always say that the one world appears in one experience, one single experience which combines all perceptions and memories into one stream, the one world of which continually new domains become actually perceived, then to remain our own in memory.

But now we must take into consideration the exceptions to this rule, exceptions which themselves belong to the style of all-inclusive experience. I said, universally speaking, everything joins together into the unity of one perception and experience, and the unity of one experiential world. In single cases it happens that within the otherwise concordant unity, so-called ‹60› illusions, semblances make their appearance. It happens that what previously was actually given perceptually, thus what confronted us in original acceptance as existing actuality, is afterwards contested. Thus, what was previously perceived in normal fashion loses the character of doubtlessly existing actuality; the "actually existing" is crossed out, so to speak. While previously everything harmonized and fit together into the unity of one total actuality, what was previously experienced in it as actuality, subsequently stands out as not fitting, not agreeing.

The harmony is restored only by a modification of the experience at this place. One says then: it is not and was not the way it first appeared at this spot; upon closer examination, upon continuation of experience, it turns out that it is instead different at this spot.

By the title "experiential world" we mean clearly what makes up the unity of concordant total actuality which is continually reestablished in the course of our experiences. Our experience is of such a disposition that, in spite of all occasional discordances in single cases, everything is resolved finally into the harmony of one accord, in other words, that, to every illusion there corresponds in its place an actual existence, which fits in harmoniously there, and which is to be found by experience.

Every surveyable stretch of waking experiential life, for instance, that which we survey as ours up till now by taking it in at a glance, includes as a unitarily experienced total objectivity or total world, everything that appears as harmoniously uniting in the acceptance-character "existing actuality," and, within this stretch of experience, it is preserved from every subsequent devaluation. Since this total experience is always in motion, experiential actuality is always something relative, insofar as in the course of new experiences which are continually fitting in, existence can, no doubt, be transformed into illusion, and thus the content of the experiential world changes accordingly in later total experience.

But still another point requires more precise mention. Perhaps you will object: at every moment we experience only determinate single things and thing-complexes; we always have merely a limited field of perception, therefore only a trifling segment of the world, which however, always holds for us as stretching on endlessly. Therefore, it is not right, you will say, to ⟨61⟩ speak of a merely experienced world; the world is not given merely by simple experience, but by a thinking which is combined with it. Even every continually unitary stream of experience, such as our entire experience of our experiential life thus far, has merely a limited experiential field; and so must it always remain.

I respond immediately with a counter-question. Is even a single thing actually to be designated as perceived, since it is always more than we actually perceive of it? And can continuing experience ever have definitively taken possession of it? Do we not think that every experienced thing is more than we could ever perceive of it, since it always remains possible for something new to be experienced concerning it?

In truth, with such questions and counter-questions we have left the entire ground for exhibiting the matching concepts, world-experience and experienced world. Perception, memory, surveying total experience, designate for us that species of immediate prior givenness of things, thing-nexus, indeed of a world, in which this thing "given beforehand" gives itself to us as an actuality existing immediately in the present, as *originaliter* bodily existing or having existed.[1]

That is all given prior to our active dealings with it, in particular prior to the actions of thinking specifically, of conceiving, predicating, theorizing. And therefore, we should accept it *as* in each case it gives or gave itself. But, what gives itself to us as bodily present in perceptions is a thing, a house, a horse, etc. If we then distinguish that of it which enters into perception as its particular moment – in a closer single consideration, thus in a particular perception – from that of it which does not yet enter into the perception, that is a distinction which pertains to the proper content of perception, or which pertains to the manner in which perceived things always give themselves, and perhaps in strict necessity. The house stands there in bodily actuality and yet at the same time in such a way that it, this house, enters into particular perceptions only according to a part of its determin- ⟨62⟩ ations. But I can expand the circle of experience; I can step closer, go around, enter the house, and thereby exercise continually new particular views.

Thus, to the perceived object which gives itself in all these processes as *the* house, as one and the same, directly experienced, there belongs a subjective *how* of givenness to experience, an open horizon of possible and ever continuable experiences in which whatever emerges is experienced, or would be experienced, as a moment pertaining to the house itself.

---

[1] For all of us, for everyone, mere experience does not suffice, but agreement –therefore we must enter into intersubjective synthesis.

However, precisely in this sense, we must say that not only single world-realities are experienced, but from the start, the world is experienced. Though an especially attending and grasping perception may hold simply for this house here, still, we have the house in a broader perceptual field; the surrounding street, the gardens are also partially in this field, and even are actually seen. But, in that respect the world has no end; every field of seeing and looking has an open outer horizon, which can not be separated from that experience. To it belong, with regard to consciousness, the possible continuations of experience in which visual field lines up with visual field, actual field of experience with field of experience; and they combine in unities of experience in such a way that it is proper to say that one and the same world is continually experienced, but only this or that single province of it is experienced in particular and "actually". But we can go further, always look about us anew, and so on *in infinitum*. And even if we do not actively continue, experience expands and accepts something new into its unity.

In this way we have described the only original, genuine concept of the *natural world-experience* or of the *experienced world*, as we find it by looking back from now or from any prior now or by looking ahead in any future now. This is the pre-theoretical world, which precedes all theoretical questions, the world perpetually perceived and experienced in its relativity as existing in undoubting certainty. Here, lack of doubt does not mean truth, but means only literally that sort of unbroken certainty, belonging to every perception itself, certainty of directly intuitive existence and certainty of something's being grasped or of being able to be grasped, purely as it gives itself in perception, or as it can be ascertained from ‹63› the experience itself by questioning, through a clarifying disclosure of its own proper sense. Our experiencing in itself grasps the world itself around it, looks around at the world itself, touches the world itself around it, etc., and has it itself, *originaliter* in certainty. Doubt, as a breach in certainty, appears merely in single instances as a transition to new, again unbroken, certainty in the all-inclusive framework of a unitary certainty of existence. Truth is true judgment, a deciding of questions which arise. At the level of mere experience, doubt connotes a different level of questioning and with it the intention aimed at decisions. But the world itself, the universe of "the" existent is never in question, as long as we live naturally, with experiencing directed toward it. In the flowing on of all-inclusive experience, the world is perpetually the stable universal ground of being, upon which all our particular questions find their decisions. Truth in the strict sense of conceiving, predicating thinking, questioning, judging, theoretical deciding, has no place at all here in our realm of pure and simple experience. On the other hand, it is this experiential world to which all natural questions, that is, all world-related questions, are put, to which all judgments as natural truths, all natural factual sciences are related.

We are all of the opinion that this experiential world, always changeable as to its constituent contents, allows a world-truth to be sought and to be found, in other words, that an all-inclusive, theoretical thinking aiming at objective, decisive truth, can be established on the ground of our all-inclusive experience, and that such a goal has a rational, practical sense. This is the presupposition of all objective sciences. But this conviction, as well as every performance which originates in it, does not itself belong to all-inclusive experience. Only the constant horizon-presumption, that experience can be put into play again and again, that all horizons can be opened, that everything will finally match in accord, and that everything must lead to the disclosure of one and the same harmonious world, belongs to it. One might say that the idea of a conclusive world of experience – for which the world actually experienced at any time, which always admits of single corrections, is a variable installment payment, containing some ‹64› counterfeit coins, only not recognized as such – is included in the universal style of experience. This is, as I have said, an idea and not a mere experience.

7. CLASSIFYING THE SCIENCES BY A RETURN TO THE EXPERIENTIAL WORLD. THE SYSTEMATIC CONNECTION OF THE SCIENCES, BASED UPON THE STRUCTURAL CONNECTION OF THE EXPERIENTIAL WORLD; IDEA OF AN ALL-INCLUSIVE SCIENCE AS SCIENCE OF THE ALL-INCLUSIVE WORLD-STRUCTURE AND OF THE CONCRETE SCIENCES WHICH HAVE AS THEIR THEME THE INDIVIDUAL FORMS OF EXPERIENTIAL OBJECTS. SIGNIFICANCE OF THE EMPTY HORIZONS.

World-experience and experienced world form an important theme for ‹*› ever expanding descriptions. If this is the original source of all science related to the world, then, as we now understand in more profound clarity, every differentiation of the sciences which is clear about its origin must be carried out by a return to the experiential world (understood as we have defined it); every particular scientific province must lead us back to a province in the original experiental world. Here we see the place of origin of a radically grounded distribution or division of possible world-sciences. First, a universal consideration.

Supposing it should become apparent that the pretheoretical experiential world has a generic systematic structure, as a generic formal system which permeates all varying concretions and therefore belongs everywhere to the experienced world, in whatever stretches of experience we consider it, and whatever particular experiential objects we consider, then this structure would prescribe in advance the corresponding systematic form, a context as system, for all possible sciences: then an all-inclusive science which refers to this all-inclusive world-structure and seeks theoretical truth in its regard, would have to grow up.

In contrast to it, there would have to be concrete sciences which take as their theme the concrete and individual forms of the experiential objects and which want to determine them in their theoretical truth.

These sciences, according to the nature of things, would follow the generic sciences of what is structural, of what is all-inclusive, and would ‹65› make use of their cognitions. For, every individual object participates in whatever belongs universally to any object at all as object of this world, whatever belongs to it precisely as an all-inclusive world-structure.

If this world-structure is composed of particular structures which, taken abstractly on their own, have universal significance, then the abstract generic science of the world would be composed of particular sciences systematically related to one another. If something like a universally ordering form belongs to the generic nature of the world, then this would at the same time give order to the concrete singularities of the world and co-determine the order and connection of methodic work for the eventual sciences which, as concrete sciences, extend to these singularities.

Now, all that is in fact the case; and during this talk about forms, you have certainly all thought of space and time and whatever else belongs here as all-inclusive structural forms belonging to our experiential world. We come therefore to them and to much else when we ask what can be asserted of the world quite universally in its total consideration, purely as world of simple experience, whenever and wherever we consider experience as experience of a world.

What we gain in answer to such consideration forms, we can also say, the materially significant concept of the natural experiential world. The term "experiential world", which has thus far gained an all-inclusive but materially empty sense in the described correlation with all-inclusive experience, now obtains a determinate content by a more precise descriptive consideration of this correlation, though here exclusively from the side of the one correlate.

Description refers back to intuition. Therefore, we immerse ourselves quite intuitively in the world-experience and look at the experienced world. We survey all its exemplary forms which are familiar to us from our experiencing life and inquire after what is typically universal, and even so extensively universal that we find it in every world-experience.

In this connection it should be noted: insofar as the world taken as a whole, as entire and unitary, has collective properties which precisely as such are properties of the entire world and not of the contingent parts or ‹66› particulars, such properties can, manifestly, appear only if we bring the respective empty horizons to intuition.

To speak more precisely, we must begin with examples of world-experience actually set in motion, for example, with what appears to us as experiential world in a determinate now. But from the limited world-contents which were actually experienced there, we must then enter into the empty horizons which belong to the respective now as references to multiple possible experiences, possible experiences in which we would gain sight of what is now invisible, whether passively or in the activity of voluntary continuation of experience, in the familiar forms of going here or there, looking around, etc.

With regard to stretches of the past, and for every past now, that means: we imagine ourselves in the possible active or passive experiences which we could have gained beginning with that now and with what was actually seen in it, if we had directed the course of actual experience thus or thus, if we had gone somewhere else instead of there, etc. Thus, at every place we hit upon already familiar objects to a small extent, that is, upon all those which we had to expect from the respective now and here, according to the course of still prior experiences, with the objects and objective connections with which we had already become familiar, and which we had to hit upon or must have been able to hit upon by appropriately directed activities of perceiving. For the rest, there are objects which are neither familiar nor individually fixed, predelineated also by previous expectation, but in undetermined universality. The style of previous actual experience includes for every possible experience to be put into play, an undetermined universal expectation of future givens of a similar style; and to make this horizon intuitive means then to present any determined continuation by a representing "fantasy," which has merely the character of an illustrating possibility, of "something like that has to occur or had to occur."

In clarifying the style of expectation which a world-experience has for ‹67› arbitrary transformation of this actual experience into possible experience, we transcend this one selected world-experience by considering it as a mere example for the typically universal. For, surveying our entire world-experience thus far, whatever it is and whatever it was, we lift out just that universal feature which is indicated by its style as something which will presumably remain for every arbitrary transformation of experience into possible experiences: remain just as long as we have a world-experience, and thus an experiential world of the same universal sense, which provides us with the concept "world," but further, this experiential world which, however it proceeds, still is individually this one, but as such, has everywhere the same sort of style.

What we bring to recognition thus must be: *on the one hand*, the universal form of connection which in spite of all infinity (which is itself already a formal determination of the world) makes of the multiplicity of single realities proceeding into infinity a connected whole, one which is unitarily formed as a whole which has properties of unity which are not themselves properties of the parts but precisely of the whole; but it imprints upon every part and every singlemost member of the world a correlative form, precisely that of being a part of a whole of such form. But, *on the other hand*, in turning our glance toward the constituting single realities, it becomes apparent to our all-inclusive consideration that they have their particularly typology which holds for the entire world and in all the provinces, nexus of things, and connected systems of things which can be delimited within it: a typology which holds all-inclusively for the sort of contents and of internal structure.

Every particular whole has its form, in which only contents of a particular sort may fit; and the all-inclusive whole, the entire world, has an all-inclusive form and accordingly a restriction with regard to contents, whereby precisely only parts, members having a particular content, can fit into the total form.

But that is a second universal feature, insofar as this particularity is to be a universally valid norm for every possible real entity in the experiential world.

That yields partly universal properties which *every* single real entity without exception must have as universally common inner properties or forms of properties; partly, differentiations of the most general types of realities, as realities of different categories which refer to one another in the world as a world of a universal experiential style and which always occur together, which therefore we must always expect as long as we are to think at all of the world as experienced.

The most cursory glance at the style of totality of the experiential world leads us at once to space and time as all-inclusive forms which must belong to it, however we imagine our experience continued, and whatever the world might turn out to be amid arbitrary interventions of active experiencing. Beyond this form of distribution we immediately hit upon the all-inclusive form of causality as a form connecting all realities, as an all-inclusive mutual relatedness in affecting and being affected. On the other hand, in detailed consideration of possible realities, we hit upon most universal and regional constitutive properties: e.g., every real thing as temporal object and spatial object has its duration as a temporal form; and it has its particular spatial form, changing or not changing during its duration. It has changeable extensional qualities which stretch over its spatio-temporal form and thereby over a duration; it has persistent causal properties related to those qualities (as changing causal states), and it has its real identity in the persistent total style of its possible causality, etc. Here we had directed our glance toward what offers itself only in the orientation

‹68›

toward the all-inclusive extensional form; and thus the multiplicity of universalities of pure form to be established first is included in the proposition: every concrete single reality within the entire concretion of the world always has "physical nature", though it may also have many additional sorts of other properties which, as mental in various senses, extend beyond this physical structure. This, as an example of universal properties of *all* single realities – in contrast to that, we find in our survey of the realities appearing in the experiential style of the given experiential world a regional typology, which surpasses everything else that is empirically typical. Our experience shows us duck-billed platypuses, lions, etc. With the progress of the cultivation of the earth, they are about to become extinct. That alters nothing of the universal style of the experiential world. ' 69' The mineralogical and geological typology, as something local and variable, belongs here also. On the other hand, however we imagine experience continued and however changed, to its universal experiential style belong lifeless things, physical organisms, animal beings with their psychic life. We enter no further into details here. Enough.

We could go on in this way. In an ever further penetrating disclosure of the generic style included in our world-experience, we could procure the *materially significant concept of the world* which brings to scientific expression the universal structural form of the world, as a world merely of simple experience. And I remind you once more of what I said already today: all sciences of the world which can possibly be grounded must refer to this structural form and to all particular forms which are copiously included in it, just because experience precedes all experiential thinking and thus whatever the experiential world purely as experienced must exhibit of universal determinations of sense, must necessarily serve as foundation for every science of the world.

We can also say: since the exploration and descriptive formation of the sheer experiential concept of the world is itself a scientific performance, a first world-science precedes all world-sciences which, as rigorously grounded, want to master their deepest ground (want to satisfy the demand of genuine scientific method by clarity concerning their own foundation), precisely the descriptive science of the world as sheer experiential world, as to its generic character.

8. The Science of the All-Inclusive World-Structure as a Priori Science.

It is time now to subject our entire procedure thus far to a critique, and to bring ourselves to see that it has been pursued with an empirical restriction which can and must be removed. In other words, it is not difficult to see that this world-science of the all-inclusive structural form of the experiential world as such, this science which is first in itself, has its pure form as pure a priori science.

‹70› All our considerations began with the fact of our experience and of the world experienced in it and wanted also to refer only to this fact. How does our experiential world look most universally? What all-inclusive typicality permeates it everywhere? This was our question. Of course, we went beyond the individual facts in each case, in considering what pertained to anything real at all, wherever and whenever we might find it in the world. But we imagined these possible individual realities precisely in *the* world, and we grasped the typical universal in each case as required by the factual style of anticipation of the experience of the world. Things had always such and such universal characteristics. The preexpectation of the further but not fully determined course which pertains to the stream of experience implies that things will again appear, in some way similar, and therefore in just such universal characteristics.

The same holds for the all-inclusive structures of the world as a whole. The endless total experience of the past world prescribes its style of similarity for the future. This itself, as it is factually, allows us to consider what may then occur and how it may look.

Following experience's own train of sense, we can do nothing but project the indeterminate future world in the universal style of the past.

But in this respect one consideration is striking: however much the expectations which are connected with actual and with hypothetically assumed facts (in the latter case, hypothetically limited expectations) may guide us, we feel here something of a strict necessity, such as we do not find in concrete empirical procedure and its expectations. Empirically we expect that the dog will snap at the bone tossed to him. But it does not *have* to be; it is no strict necessity. However, that the world can never be non-spatial, that everything is restricted to its generic structures – this seems necessary to us. Every felt necessity is an indicative sign of an a priori in the sense of an unconditioned, so-called apodictic universality, which can be seen as such. Showing it is the test whether the felt necessity is a genuinely apodictic one, and not a confusion with a merely empirical indication.

‹71› Every attempted transition to an a priori in this determinate sense (of an unconditioned universality obtained by looking and seeing) demands liberation from the fact. The fact in our case is the world actually and factually experienced by us, with these factual things. Let us drop this fact.

Not as if we wished sceptically to deny or to surrender the facts of our experience and the existence of the world which is experienced in it. We do not alter our conviction at all; we have no motive for doing so, and therefore no possibility. But nothing prevents us all the same from quite arbitrarily imagining this fact otherwise, from letting our fantasy range as it pleases, and from producing as pure fantasies what, compared with the fact, are in every way thing-fictions and world-fictions.

I say *pure* fantasy. I can in fantasy imagine the brown bench as painted green; then it remains an individual existent in this lecture hall, only imagined as changed. But I can as it were transform each and every fact into a fiction in free arbitrariness. I can imagine as a pure fiction a bench with a mermaid sitting on it, in no place and no time, free from all weight of actuality, free from any restriction to the factual world. Instead of preferring the factual world by placing myself on the ground of its factual acceptance; instead of finding every instance of imagining it other than it is, a nullity in connection with its existence and in conflict with its empirical nexus – I can instead let every fictional transformation stand as equal to it and let it itself stand only as one possibility next to these other possibilities. By doing so, I abandon the ground of its acceptance and put my experiential acceptance out of play, so to speak. Then factual experience gives me only an exemplary beginning for the style of free fantasies which I shape from it, without otherwise employing it as something to be accepted.

Following it as a model, I shape multiple fancied copies as things and fictions concretely similar to it: in doing so I can systematically guide my free arbitrariness. I systematically vary the form of the experience which serves as a beginning, or rather what is experienced in it, whether by following one single moment or all its single moments.

I fancy everything as varied and in every possible manner; for instance, I let the factual figure extend and stretch quite arbitrarily, let the color ‹ 72 › change into other colors, rest into movement, movement into ever new movement, etc. "What use is that?" you will ask.

I answer: it can be very useful indeed, if it is pursued correctly. For, what I just described is the way in which all intuitive essential necessities and essential laws and every genuine intuitive a priori, are won.

Thus, also, what interests us here: the all-embracing a priori, that of this experiential world, since it is what is apodictically universal and necessary to any experiential world at all, thus to a world which, as experienced, should be able also to be merely imagined.

9. SEEING ESSENCES AS GENUINE METHOD FOR GRASPING THE A PRIORI.

Let us at first disregard for a while the question concerning the essence of a world as such, in order to describe the way in which fancying arbitrariness taken universally brings about this great performance which is called the seeing of an a priori.

a) Variation as the decisive step in the dissociation from the factual by fantasy –
the eidos as the invariable.

Let us be guided by a fact as a model for the systematic shaping of pure fantasy. Thus similar images are continually to be won as copies, as fantasy images which are all concrete resemblances of the original. Then a unity pervades this multiplicity of copy-fashionings, namely, that of the essence which grounds the similarity. Differently expressed, we face the question: what holds up amid such free variations of an original – let us say, of a thing – as the invariant, the necessary, universal form, the essential form, without which something of that kind, like this thing as an example of its kind, would be altogether inconceivable?

‹73›   That is, by employing free, arbitrary variation, we produce variants each of which appears in the subjective mode of lived experience of the "optional", as does also the process of variation itself on the other side. But here we can at any time direct our regard toward the fact that an invariant necessarily pervades. it or pervades all the variants, an invariant which, as we can see and understand, is itself absolutely invariable. More precisely described: we can see, in absolute certainty, that in the exercise of arbitrary variation during which what differs in the variation is of no concern to us, a continual coincidence so to speak of the variants is preserved, and, as the "what" or the content which remains necessarily invariable in the coincidence, a universal essence is preserved. We can therefore direct our regard toward it as toward the necessarily invariable in such a variation exercised in the mode of the "optional" and to be continued in any way at all. This universal essence is the eidos, the "*idea*" in the Platonic sense, but apprehended purely and free from all metaphysical interpretations, therefore, taken precisely as it becomes given to us in immediate intuitiveness in the seeing of ideas which arises in that way. In this case experience was thought of as the beginning. Manifestly, even a mere fantasy, or that which we have in mind as intuited object in it, could have served just as well.

If we follow this procedure by starting, e.g., with a tone, whether we actually hear it or have such a tone "in mind by fantasy," then we win thereby the eidos "tone" grasped in the change of "optional" variants as that which is necessarily common here. But if we then take a different tone-phenomenon for our starting-point, as optionally varied, then we grasp in the new "example," not a different eidos "tone," but in surveying the new one and the prior one we see that it is the same and that the variants and variations on both sides join together to make up one single variation and that the variants here and there are in like manner optional singularizations of the one eidos. And it is even evident that, in advancing from one variation to a new one, we can give this advancing and this forming of new multiplicities of variation itself the character of something optional and that in this advancing in the form of optionalness the same eidos must result "again and again:" the same universal essence "tone" taken universally.

A pure eidos treats the factual actuality of the single cases attained in ‹74› the variation as completely irrelevant; an actuality is treated as a possibility among other possibilities, and even as an optional possibility for fantasy. But the eidos is only then actually pure whenever every restriction to the actuality given beforehand is in fact most carefully excluded. If we vary freely but secretly stipulate that the variants must be optional tones in the world, tones heard or able to be heard by human beings on earth, then we have indeed something essentially universal or an eidos, but one related to our factually actual world and restricted to this all-inclusive fact. That is a "secret" and even unnoticed restriction, of course for comprehensible reasons.

In the natural development of all-inclusive, always unified experience, the experienced world falls to our lot as all-inclusive abiding ground of existence and as all-inclusive field for all our activities. In the most stable and most all-inclusive of all our habitualities, the world is accepted by us and it remains in actual acceptance for us, whatever interests we pursue; as all interests, so also those of eidetic knowledge are related to it in every play of fantasy and thus also in every variation by fantasy. With the intention aimed at a seeing of ideas, the world is co-posited; every fact and every eidos remains related to the factual world, belonging to the world in some way or other; for instance, in the natural attitude we do not notice this world-positing and restriction of existence, concealed just because of its all-inclusiveness. Only if we become aware of this restriction and consciously put it out of play and thereby also free the most extensive surrounding horizon of the variants from all restrictions, from all experiential acceptance, do we create perfect purity. We stand then so to speak in a pure fantasy-world, a world of absolutely pure possibilities; every such possibility can then become the central member for possible pure variations in the mode of optionalness, and from each there results then an absolutely pure eidos, but from every different one the same eidos only then results whenever the series of variation of the one and of the other connect to comprise one series in the manner described. Thus a different eidos results for colors and for tones; they are of different kinds, that is, with regard to their pure kinds.

b) Variation and alteration. ‹75›

Another point requires clarification. We are speaking of variation and variants, not of alterations and phases of alteration. These two concepts are in fact essentially distinct even though there is some connection between them. An alteration is an alteration of something real, apprehended quite universally as something which exists temporally, something which endures, which lasts throughout a duration. Everything real is alterable and exists only in alteration or non-alteration. Moreover, precisely considered, non-alteration is only a limit-case of alteration. Alteration signifies continually being different or becoming different and yet being the same thing, being individually the same thing while continuously becoming different, e.g., alteration of a color. Non-alteration, for instance of a color again, signifies at bottom also being the same thing while continuously becoming different, but in addition continuously remaining self-identical in every phase of the duration. In alteration, becoming different signifies being different in every new phase, but at the same time not remaining self-identical.

In the focusing of regard upon the phases of duration of something real and upon what occupies these phases, we have a multiplicity, always something else, therefore a plurality, and something identical or non-identical as the case may be, from phase to phase. But in another, correlative, focusing of regard we experience the unity, the identical thing which alters and sometimes does not alter, which lasts and endures on throughout the flow of the multiplicities.

This unity is not, as might be supposed, the universal of the single time-phases, as these are not variants. It is, of course, precisely the one individual. On the other hand, it pertains to alteration that the phases can also (though in an altered attitude) be treated as variants, and then it becomes apparent that no alteration is possible in which all phases of alteration do not belong together according to genus. A color can only alter to another color and not, for instance, to a tone. Every possible alteration occurs, as can be seen then, within a highest genus which it can never transgress.

But the genus can become seen as pure eidos only if we do not ask about something real and thus not about actualities, but raise all actuality to ⟨76⟩ pure possibility, to the realm of free optionalness; but then it becomes evident that free optionalness also has its own specific restriction insofar as every variation includes its eidos as a law of necessity. We can also say: whatever admits of mutual variation in the optionalness of fantasy (even if it is not connected and does not come together in fantasy to the unity of an imaginable reality) includes a necessary structure, an eidos, and thereby a law of necessity.

c) The moments of ideation: starting with an example (model); disclosure brought about by an open infinity of variants (optionalness of the process of forming variants); overlapping coincidence of the formation of variants in a synthetic unity; grasping what agrees as the eidos.

In the last lecture we sought to describe the complex mental activities, ‹ *› with their determinate characters, as the end result of which the eidos, the Platonic idea, the essential-universal, steps into view in such a way that we have it quite immediately and retain it henceforth as a lasting mental acquisition, just as well as any other objectivity which has come to our cognizance. We call this complex mental activity the seeing of ideas, or else ideation. Let us recapitulate, at the same time articulating the single steps or levels of ideation more sharply, in order also to add important supplementary remarks.

The fundamental performance upon which everything else depends is the shaping of any experienced or fancied objectivity into a variant, shaping it into the form of the optional example and at the same time of the guiding "model," of precisely the first member of an openly endless multiplicity of variants, in short, a variation. Of course this open infinity does not signify an actual continuation in infinity, the nonsensical demand *actually* ‹ 77 › to produce all possible variants – as if we could only then be sure that the eidos which subsequently becomes grasped actually accords with all possibilities. Rather, what is meant is that the variation itself as the process of forming variants has a character of optionalness, that it is to be carried out in the consciousness of optionally forming further variants. Therefore, even when we discontinue, we have not meant the factual multiplicity of intuitive single variants converted into one another as this factual series of objectivities which are presented in some way or other and are arbitrarily referred to, or which are produced purely fictitiously from the start; rather, just as every single moment has the character of being exemplarily optional, so also an optional character pertains continually to the multiplicity of variation, since it makes no difference what might join it, makes no difference what I might lay hold of in the consciousness, "I could continue thus." Therefore, the remarkable and extremely important consciousness of "and so on optionally" belongs essentially to every multiplicity of variation. What we call an "openly infinite" multiplicity is given only in that manner; and it is evidently the same whether we go on for a longer time producing or optionally referring to what is suitable, and thus extend the series of actual intuitions, or whether we discontinue sooner.

The seeing proper of the universal as eidos, which we can apprehend as a higher level, relates to this multiplicity (or to the foundation of the open process of variation which constitutes it, with the variants which actually appear to intuition). What we are hereby bringing to prominence as something new is this, that we do not merely pass over from the starting example which gives guidance and which we called the model to ever new "copies," whether we may owe them to the aimless favor of association and to what comes to mind in passive fantasy and appropriate them arbitrarily as examples, or whether we might have won them from our original model entirely through our own fantasy activity of imagining it as different. As we were saying, we do not merely pass over from copy to copy, from similar to similar. What counts is that all the optional single cases come in the sequence of their appearance to *overlapping coincidence* and thereby ‹78› pass into a *synthetic unity* in which they all appear as variations of one another; and then, in further consequence, as optional sequences of single instances in which the same universal as eidos is singularized.

Only in continuous coincidence is there an agreement of something the self-same which can be singled out in intuition purely by itself. On the other hand, of course, difference of various sorts is usually combined with actual agreement: as whenever in the sequence of optional tones of C, along with the identity of the eidos C, the different intensities and timbres stand out as conflicting, instead of agreeing in the coincidence. But we leave that aside at first.

Therefore, both belong to the process of ideation: multiplicity and unitary connection in continuous coincidence, and in addition as a third moment, the identifying of what agrees over against the differences by intuitively singling it out.

It should be noted here that the multiplicity must be an object of consciousness as multiplicity, as plurality, and must as such never be let completely out of one's mental grip. Otherwise we do not win the eidos as ideally identical, which precisely is only as the ἓν ἐπὶ πολλῶν [one over many]. For example, if we are occupied merely with imagining a thing as different, or a figure as optionally new figures, then we always have something new and always only one thing, precisely the last one imagined. Only if we hold onto the previous fictions and thus a multiplicity in the open process, and only if we look toward the agreeing and what is purely identical, do we win an eidos. Here, to be sure, we did not need subsequently to carry out an overlapping, since a continual process of change of this sort produces at once what differs and what agrees in the overlapping.

d) Distinguishing between empirical generalization and ideation.

Now, one might think that our description of the seeing of ideas makes its task too difficult and operates superfluously with the multiplicity of variation which was emphasized as allegedly fundamental and with the functions of fantasy which participate in it so distinctively. Surely it would suffice to say that an optional red here and there, an optional plurality of red objects already given to experience or to other presentations would ‹79› furnish the possibility of seeing the eidos "red." All that would have to be described would be the perusing in overlapping coincidence and the intuitive singling out of the universal. Nevertheless, it should be noted well here that the "optional" in such locutions must not signify merely a locution or an incidental behavior on our part, but that it belongs to the fundamental character of the *actus* itself of seeing ideas and that it must be traced in its distinctive performances, as we have done.

But if the opinion in such locutions is that a determinate plurality of similar objects would already suffice to gain the universal through a comparing coincidence, then it must be said: we may well gain for this red here and that red there something identical to both and a universal. But only a universal of just this and that red. We do not gain the pure red taken universally as eidos. Of course by bringing into play a third or several reds whenever they are presented we can recognize that the universal of the two is identically the same as the universal of the many. But thus we gain always only common characters and universalities in relation to empirical extensions. But as soon as we say that every optional like instance which can be newly brought into play must yield the same, and say further that the eidos "red" is one over against the infinity of possible single instances which belong to this red and to any red which coincides with it, we have precisely an infinite variation in our sense as the underlying basis. It furnishes us what belongs to the eidos as its inseparable correlate, what is called the extension of the eidos, of the "purely conceptual essence," the infinity of possible single instances which are included in it, which are its "singularizations," which, to speak Platonically, stand to it in the relation of participation, related as single instance to the eidos as its essence, and it furnishes us the conviction that every instance without exception participates in its essence and its essential moments. To be seen here in correlation is on one side the universal itself, on the other side the extension as the totality, but also any single instance at all.

Also, all concepts and relations otherwise belonging to the same context of producing the ideation are easily to be made clear in their intuitively original peculiarity. Thus I would like to point to the relation of likeness, ‹80› in distinction from that of participation. One must not think that the identity of the eidos is merely an exaggerating locution. By overlapping, that which is here and there alike would stand out from what differs. But just as the concrete single objects are separate in the multiplicity, the plurality, a condition which the mental operation of bringing them to overlapping coincidence would not alter at all, so also would the moments of likeness, and likewise the differing moments, which become noticeable thereby, be separate; every object would have its inherent moment, of red for instance, and the many objects which are all red would have each its individually own moment, but in likeness.

But one must see that likeness is only a correlate of the identity of a universal which in truth can be singled out intuitively as one and the same and as the "counterpart" of the individual. This identical moment is "singularized" in many ways and can be thought of as optionally singularized in an open infinity. All these singularizations have a relation to one another through their relation to the identical moment and are then called alike. The concrete objects themselves as containing eidetic singularizations are then by transfer called alike "with regard to red" and in an improper sense are even called singularizations of the universal.

The idea of the difference in its combination with that of the identically common as eidos likewise becomes clear. In the overlapping of the multiplicities, difference is what has not joined the unity of agreement, in the agreement which has become visible, thus has not contributed to making an eidos visible. It does not join the unity of the agreement – that means, therefore, it is a difference, an overlayed difference in conflict. The color is identical, but at one time the color of this, at another time of that, extension and shape. In the overlapping the one enters into opposition with the other and supplants it.

But on the other hand it is clear that nothing can enter into conflict which has nothing in common, and not only that here the identical color is already presupposed as something common; rather, if the one colored thing is round and the other angular, then they could not clash if they were not ⟨81⟩ both extended figures. Therefore, every difference in the overlapping with other differences as clashing with it refers to a new universal to be singled out intuitively, here shape, as a universal of the mutually superimposed differences which in each case have become united in conflict.

e) Bringing out the sequence of levels of genera and gaining the highest genera by variation of ideas – seeing of ideas without starting from experience.

The entire doctrine of genera and of the sequence of levels of genera and species can be grounded here, on the basis of original sources of clarified ideation. Only a little of that can be touched upon here; and it must be touched upon because otherwise unclarity would remain. We can very well arrive at different eide from the same example as model, while we let ourselves be determined purely by free variation. That is so even though we had said that all productive multiplicities of variation in which an eidos becomes originally seen by us are connected in one single multiplicity of variation and are, as it were, only aspects of what is in itself unique.

But the connecting of series of variation in one unique series can have a different sense, as can be shown. Starting from an optional red and progressing in a series of variations I gain the eidos "red." Were we to have another red as exemplary starting point we would of course intuitively gain another multiplicity of variation but we would see at once that this new one belongs in the open horizon of "and-so-forth" of the first one, as the former belongs in the horizon of the latter. And we see that the eidos is one and the same. Likewise of course if instead of an optional red I had varied an optional green and had arrived at the eidos "green." Nevertheless it can be seen on the other hand that in a certain manner the different series of variation, namely, the ones which yield red and the ones which yield green can be connected again in a more comprehensive multiplicity of variation – in one unique multiplicity which then no longer yields the eidos "red" or "green" but the eidos "color" taken universally. How is ‹82› that to be understood?

The answer is: whenever I am to arrive at the seeing of red by varying, I must maintain the direction toward red, or, amid all other arbitrariness of the varying, I must restrict myself in one way. Namely: if when I am commencing the variation a common red shines before me, then I can immediately hold it fast and mean and want to mean nothing else than red taken universally as what this commonly identical moment would yield in optional further variation. Therefore if green appears before me I reject it as not belonging, as clashing with the red which has been seen and continually intended.

But on the other hand if I direct my attention to the fact that the variant of green just rejected is in conflict with every variant of red and yet has something in common, thus also a point of coincidence, then this new common moment apprehended as pure eidos can determine the variation; now the multiplicities of variation for red and for green as also for yellow, etc., belong together; the universal therefore is now color.

Thus I could from the start be oriented toward varying in completely unrestricted fashion, therefore without restriction to any universal already lighting up, and toward seeking the universal which is higher than all the universalities which can be singled out intuitively and then restricted – in our example, which is higher than the universalities "red," "blue," "yellow," etc., as the highest universality. Here then the only demand is that the variation – no matter how – moves on, as long as it is a variation at all, thus is at all combined in a synthesis of pervasively unitary coincidence with a pervasively universal moment. That is the way therefore toward the constitution of highest essential universalities as highest genera which in particular, if they are concrete genera, are called regions.

It is clear then that this universality can no longer have a higher one over it. And on the other hand it also has the property of being contained as something ideally common in all particular universalities which could be obtained in this total variation – because they belong to limited provinces of variation of the same. The ideas "red," "green," etc., have ideal ‹ 83 › participation in the idea "color." Manifestly we can also say: ideas, pure eide, can also themselves function again as variants, and then a universal can again be singled out from them at a higher level, an *idea out of ideas* or of ideas, an idea whose extension consists of ideas and only mediately of their ideal singulars.

This is the place to add immediately an important amplification of the doctrine of ideation. We were interested in the experiential world and in the eidos of experience; therefore, we began with the experiential givens or with variations whose guiding models were unqualified experiential givens, as is good and natural for other reasons also. But as soon as the first step of the eidos has been climbed, the first step above pure and simple experience, we became attentive to the fact that an eidos can also be varied. In other words, the seeing of ideas is itself an analogue of pure and single experience, insofar as it is a consciousness – admittedly higher and actively producing – in which a new kind of objectivity, the universal, becomes itself given. The same thing that we can accomplish under the title of ideation by beginning with experience we can also do by beginning with every other kind of consciousness as long as it performs the same function, namely, that of bringing to our consciousness a kind of objectivities in original selfhood. Every ideation itself does that; the idea seen is here said to be seen because it is not meant or spoken of vaguely, indirectly, by means of empty symbols or words, but is precisely grasped directly and itself. Therefore, from the basis which any kind of grasping and having by seeing furnishes us, we can always exercise ideation again, in essentially the same method.

Thus we can not only vary experiential things, that is, final substrates for possible experiencing and higher actions, and thus gain concepts of things as essential universalities; but we also "experience" sets which we have collected by our own activity, real states of affairs, internal and external relations the seeing of which requires relating activities, etc. In this way we also gain pure and universal ideas of collections, of relations, and of all sorts of states of affairs, insofar as, starting with the seeing ‹ 84 › activities in which they become given, we form multiplicities of variation precisely for all such objectivities and single out intuitively what is essentially universal and necessary. Then we can proceed in just the same way with ideas thus gained, and so forth.

Designating activity with its names belongs here also, and the activity of stating with its statements. That is also something which can be brought to light, something that can itself be grasped; and we gain universal essential concepts, the pure idea of a statement and the meaning of a statement, of a name, of a connected discourse and the sense of a discourse, etc. The eide which fall to our lot at every level we make our own, we name them, express them in statements, and a universal statement becomes possible which shares in the essential insights and essential necessities of the seeing of ideas, insofar, namely, as the statement is a faithful expression of what has been seen and insofar as it is even itself an eidetic insight that, as long as the statement has the same statement-meaning, necessarily the seen affair that it expresses can again be established by seeing.

Finally, just one more universal remark. Whenever we speak of universal essences and essential (eidetic) cognitions, we do not mean thereby empirical universalities, which no doubt have a similar origin, but differ from the pure essential universalities in that an acceptance of existence occurs, whether it be with regard to the objects of the sphere of comparison or whether it be with regard to the total province to which they are thought of as belonging. We have therefore actuality and *real* possibility and not sheer, pure fantasy-possibility.

f) Summarizing characterization of the seeing of essences.

In the last lectures before the Pentecost vacation we spoke about the ⟨*⟩ method of ideation; under this title we carefully described a certain purely mental activity and therein a chain of purely mental products, as the final product of which an eidos becomes our own in pure seeing. We understood by this that it is a universal like the species "red" or the higher genus "color" taken universally, but as a pure universal, something transempirical, raised above all factuality of existence, if it is gained in such a ⟨85⟩ way that every presupposition of any factuality at all is thereby cancelled. The species "red," e.g., or the genus "color," is an eidos, an essential universality, but as pure universality. That is, pure of all presupposition of any factual existence at all, therefore of any red, or any colored, factual actuality.

In a related but so to speak impure method of universalization, a universal which is empirically laden can become seen. As, whenever in an empirical comparison of this red here and that red there, when both of them are accepted by us as existing actualities, we see what is common to both of them.

Also, whenever geometrically we designate the circle as a type of conic section, or grasp it eidetically, intuitively. Accordingly, a purely eidetic universal judgment, such as a geometric one or one about ideally possible colors, tones, etc., is not restricted in its universality to any presupposed actuality. In geometry the discourse is about conceivable figures; in eidetic color theory, about conceivable colors which have purely seen universalities as their extension.

To be noted: to see does not signify here to *speak* about vague presented affairs and their similarities or common elements, to have some opinion or other about them from some vague source, but to have affairs themselves experienced, themselves seen, and on the basis of this itself-seeing, precisely to have also the similarity before one's eyes: to perform on that basis that mental overlapping in which the common moment, the red, the figure "itself" appears, itself becomes grasped, becomes seen. Of course it is not a sensuous seeing. One can not see the universal red as one sees an individual, single red; but the expansion of the locution "seeing," which is, not without reason, customary in common speech, is unavoidable. In that way is expressed the fact that quite analogously to the way in which something individually single becomes our own directly and as itself in sensuous perceiving, so also something common and universal of optionally many single seen exemplars, but of course in that more complicated seeing, involving active comparative overlapping and agreement. Therefore, that ⟨86⟩ holds for every sort of grasping by seeing of common elements and universalities.

The seeing of universalities therefore has a particular methodic shape wherever the point is to see an a priori, a pure eidos. For example, it is then a question not of something common to this and that factual color and possibly of optional colors which might ever confront us in this space here or even on earth, but of the purely ideal kind "color," which is common to all colors which are at all conceivable without the presupposition of any factual actuality. Therefore, it belongs as a fundamental part to the mental method of ideation that it views the actualities which might serve it as guiding beginning examples, as mere and pure possibilities; in other words, an indifference toward actuality is put into play in a free activity, and thereby that which stands there as actuality is, as it were, transferred to the realm of free fantasy. The further method of variation in conscious optionalness, the forming of an open optional multiplicity of variation of single variants, of which each has the character of an optional example, is grounded on this basis. This multiplicity is then the support for the "comparative" overlapping and the intuitive singling out of a pure universal which is singularized exemplarily in this optional varying. In accord with this methodic origin, the universal as eidos and something eidetic has not at all an extension of facts which restrict it, but an extension of pure possibilities. On the other hand, the eidetic universality can at any time be set in relation to actual occurrences. For, every actually occurring color is also one which is possible in the pure sense; that is, every such color admits of being regarded as an example and being transformed into a variant. Everything that belongs inseparably to the pure universality "color," e.g., the moment of brightness, must also belong to every factual color. The universal truths in which we merely explicate what belongs to pure essential universalities, precede in their validity all questions concerning facts and their factual truths. For that reason the essential truths are called a priori, preceding in their validity all establishments based on experience.

The description of the method of ideation (as also of empirical general- ‹87› ization), which was understandably felt as quite difficult by you, was the description of a certain purely mental doing from which a mental product results in evident intelligibility. It itself offers an example of its own kind of descriptions which a radical psychology, which is directed toward mental living and mental doing itself, has to supply, a descriptive inner psychology which we still want to become more familiar with as phenomenological psychology. Everywhere its difficulty lies in the fact that we are indeed always mentally active, but must first learn laboriously to reflect upon this being active and bring it tangibly to sight. In carrying on our active life, only the step by step results are in our apprehending view.

In just this way the seeing of the a priori, the inner doing of ideation, is not foreign to us all, insofar as we have all learned at least a little mathematics and thus have gained mathematical insight through our own activity. But we have never learned to look into the inwardness of mathematizing activity and to witness how universalities arise out of necessities there. In this respect the beginning is difficult, but soon one becomes more familiar with the marvelous world of inwardness and one overcomes the toils of the strange, inwardly directed seeing.

10. The method of intuitive universalization and of ideation as instruments toward gaining the universal structural concepts of a world taken without restriction by starting from the experiential world ("natural concept of the world"). Possibility of an articulation of the sciences of the world and establishment of the signification of the science of the mind.

Meanwhile, I have introduced the description of the method of ideation, not as a first exemplary portion of the new psychology, but as a means for arriving at a radical division of the sciences of the world or at a radical conceptual articulation of the world into the essential provinces of the world; in just that way the mental in all its fundamental forms in which it is a universal and necessary structural element of the world, had to emerge;

‹ 88 › therefore, in that way also the sure clue had to be gained for projecting systematically all directions of problems which present themselves for a fully statisfactory science of mind in accordance with these various fundamental forms.

Only by proceeding in such a radical fashion can we liberate ourselves from all traditional prejudices, one-sided views and unclarities, which have led to ever new psychologies but never to *the* psychology, the one genuine psychology which draws the necessary method and the necessarily interrelated system of problems to be solved from the necessities of its clearly grasped theme and for that very reason can be only *one*.

Therefore, for now we need know nothing of the fact that the description of the method of ideation is itself a psychological description. We had to present it because we need this method for our present purpose and could in no way be satisfied with referring to mathematical procedure; as a purely eidetic procedure historically arisen for quantities and numbers and exercised exclusively on them for millenia, it has given occasion to the firmly rooted prejudice that an a priori method of that sort could be exercised only on mathematical subject matter (and the subject matter of formal logic, closely intertwined with it). But our description makes it evident that wherever and at whatever level objectivities become given to us in original intuition, the method of ideation can be exercised on them and essential universalities can be singled out in purely intuitive fashion, universalities which can then unfold in further essential cognitions.

First it is necessary to disclose what is experienced as a world only in a narrowly limited way and with unclarified horizons, in such a way that we put possible experience into play, progress from possible experiences to ever new possible experiences and, so to speak, form for ourselves a total picture, an actually explicated though also openly progressing *total intuition of the world*: namely, as how it would look all in all and would have to look if we would fill out the open indefinite horizons with possibilities of experience which fit together harmoniously, whether it be by actually experiencing or by immersing ourselves in any experience by fantasy. And also of course with regard to the open horizons which belong to every stretch of past experience reawakened by memory.

‹ 89 ›   But then we would also see clearly that these horizons are infinitely indeterminate, that whatever we present to ourselves as the unfamiliar or unexperienced world, that is, as the world outside the boundary of experiential familiarity, always presents only a possibility to which we could very well juxtapose other optional possibilities. But on the other hand, it is also clear that whenever we arbitrarily bring to full clarity several such possibilities in synthesis with the actuality partially secured by experience (and to be continued *in infinitum*), immediately the typically common had to become apparent. In other words, it is clear that we could now consciously put into play the method of originally intuitive universalization and do so in such a way that by proceeding in the evident consciousness of optionalness, comparing, and freely varying, we would gain something necessarily common and something unqualifiedly invariant in spite of all variation of possibilities. Therefore, the horizon of open indeterminacy which surrounds the realm of actual experience is itself a realm of possibilities subject to variation, though restricted in this, that they are real possibilities. They are continuations of the experientially familiar into the unfamiliar, which however does have partial predelineation by experience, and on occasion an incompletely determined anticipation.

Thus the method of intuitive universalization, even before it is developed, leads to a pure ideation, to *structural universalities* as absolutely intuitable necessities, necessities which here signify: I do not know of course how things look, how the entire world looks, where my actual seeing does not reach; but no matter what, it must have some appearance, and starting with what has been seen the *universal* style of what has not been seen is necessarily predelineated. Every continuation of the seen in really possible experience, and further in experience which can be continued harmoniously, is indeed indeterminate, but it can be made evident by intuitive universalization that the realm of possible experience and thus the entire world has such and such *necessary structural forms*. Manifestly time and space belong to them. However unfamiliar the yet unexperienced world-region may be for me, however arbitrarily I might occupy it with ‹90› possible objects of experience, I am restricted; universally speaking, they are necessarily enduring objects, dispersed in space, etc. (that is an absolutely evident demand).

Therefore, if we exercise this method concretely and systematically, then we gain determinate generic universalities as invariant structures; but for just that reason, definitely originally procured structural concepts, not word-concepts, but concepts whose corresponding ideal essence has been procured in self-actively intuitive fashion. Therefore, that holds also for nature and mind, as for all structures. Therefore, all vague word-concepts actually vanish and require replacement by ideas formed originally and evidently and by essential concepts which express them. Therefore after all that, you will now understand that we gain by this method taken universally the sure clue for articulating in advance the possible sciences of the world, for grounding them upon the essential structure of the experiental world, for supplying them with originally procured essential concepts. But for our purpose this should be kept firmly in mind: within the all-inclusive and intuitively rooted articulation of sciences we gain the essential place of the science of mind and the possibility of creating the essential articulation within the mental itself: pursuing the basic forms in which it has to function for the world. What a fully satisfactory science of mind has to do would be projected thematically in advance. For, a genuine science must have a clear and determinate theme in view; its all-inclusive goal and system of goals must guide it, not as a vague and empty concept, but as something universal seen in its essence.

Therefore, only by proceeding thus can we be liberated in any case from the traditional prejudices, one-sided views and unclarities which for centuries led to ever new psychologies, but never to *the* psychology, the one unique psychology which procures out of the distinctive necessities of its clear theme the necessity of a method suited to it and the necessary articulations of the problems to be solved, thus also its disciplines. But for that we need, as will be readily intelligible, not only the intuitive method of ‹91› original universalization, but the method of pure induction[1] which taken universally is the method of all insights into principles.

But the fact that our entire procedure and, included in it, the method of originally intuitive universalization and of the inductive[2] method, is itself a preliminary exercise in this psychology toward whose intuitive possession we are steering is a portion of the reference of every conceivable kind of knowledge back upon itself, of which something will still be said later.

I now add still one more important remark, connected to a possible objection. Would not the mere allusion to the experience of the a priori sciences familiar to all, namely, the mathematical, suffice in our context? Therefore, could the difficult description of the inductive[3] procedure as the method of the a priori be spared?

Meanwhile, I am speaking here as if the description of the method of ideation had been introduced by us with the aim of clarifying with it as a first example the manner of an internally psychological analysis and description. But, as you will remember, that was in no way our guiding aim. Rather, this method was supposed to be merely an auxiliary means for sketching a systematic way by which alone a guiding idea of a psychology as all-inclusive science of the mental, a guiding idea sharply circumscribed conceptually and illuminated by its necessity, as well as every narrower concept of psychology, can be gained.

This way goes via a radical articulation of the sciences of the world, or via a radical and simultaneously all-embracing analysis and description of the experiential world as to the most universal structures fundamentally essential to it: thus I mean by this, structures which persist without variation

---

[1] "Ideation" was probably meant. *Tr.*
[2] "Ideative" was probably meant. *Tr.*
[3] "Ideative" was probably meant. *Tr.*

over against all change in content of real existence and real happening in different times, places, and particular contexts. Indeed, let us assume that it could be shown with cogent evidence by a fitting methodic procedure that an all-embracing invariant typology pervades the whole of the experiential world, purely as experienceable. To speak more precisely: let us assume, there is an evidently demonstrable invariant typology to which all realities to be attributed to the world in possible and actual experience must be subordinated, with regard to their fundamental genera as well as with ‹92› regard to the forms of their combinations in wholes, and no less for the all-encompassing orders and relations or combinations which establish the total unity of the world. Then plainly this all-inclusive typology would have to be a systematic theme for an all-inclusive science of the world, precisely as all-inclusive structural science of the experiential world. An all-embracing framework, ever more deeply to be pursued, would be expressed in it, one which manifestly predelineates an infrangible norm for all possible particular sciences, and prescribes for them their essential demarcations, those of their provinces and problems as well as of the intertwinings of their problems.

Therefore, in looking back at what is universal concerning the ideative method we can say: every object has its eidos or is subsumed under concepts of essence. And, what is of special interest to us here, every object of experience, everything that exists individually, has its essence, its total idea, which unites in itself the ideas of all its determinations. An ideal object is itself already an essence, namely an ideal essence, an eidos; it may in addition be subordinate to higher eide, higher pure genera. But whatever is itself a "this here," and not an essence, *has* an essence – we can proceed to seek it. The universal description of the method of ideation is manifestly itself a description in essential universality; for, in free variation we can let every exemplary object on which it is exercised become an optional object taken universally, a variable in the mathematical sense, as it were. Therefore, it is properly itself an insight into essence that the ideative method is everywhere applicable. But "applicable" does not yet signify "applied." The a priori knowledge which we have in advance for a determinate given object, that an essence belongs to it and, explicitly, a multiplicity of essential universalities, is only a task for a practical effort, it is only aim-giving. The task can perhaps be a quite enormous one while in other cases it may also be dispatched quite easily and without further ado. Pure concepts of essence such as "color" or "tone," "brightness," "timbre" as a moment of a tone, etc., we will grasp easily. But if we speak of a ‹93› thing taken universally, in pure universality, of a body taken universally, an animate being, a human being taken universally, then it may be that pure universality occurs only in the word-meaning, emptily, nonintuitively.

But if we want to actualize the empty meaning, solve the problem which is here to be posed, actually to establish the pertinent eidos which no doubt can be established, then it becomes apparent that we move forward only with difficulty. Indeed, penetrating deeper: that each of these concepts claims many dimensions of intuitions to be produced, and that the advancing establishment of the eidos, e.g., of a thing of nature taken universally, of a human being taken universally, and the unwrapping of its eidetic elementary necessities demands in each case an entire infinite science.

But at the peak so to speak of every such science stands the guiding preliminary concept and the most universal essence to be produced through intuition and articulated only according to its most universal essential structures. For our task that alone will count.

11. CHARACTERIZING THE SCIENCE OF THE NATURAL CONCEPT OF THE WORLD. DIFFERENTIATING THIS CONCEPT OF EXPERIENCE FROM THE KANTIAN CONCEPT OF EXPERIENCE. SPACE AND TIME AS THE MOST UNIVERSAL STRUCTURES OF THE WORLD.

‹ * › In our last explanations we sketched the idea of the science of the "natural concept of the world," that is, the idea of the all-inclusive descriptive science of the invariant essence of the already given world and of every possible experienceable world. Thereby we sketched the universal frame which must include the a priori of every possible science of the world. All possible objectives which such sciences pose externally, all problems which can be raised in them, have an a priori type. Therefore, they are included within essentially universal problems, of which the respective sciences must be conscious in order to work with ultimate clarity concerning their objectives and method – thus, to be able to be sciences in the strictest sense.

Of course, our present task can not be to trace out this great science
‹ 94 › explicitly ourselves. Nevertheless, we can gain very much from pursuing this idea further in just some fundamental lines, enough to acquire a guiding and essential idea of the possible all-inclusive science of mind, as an idea which is necessarily included in the full universal idea of that science of the world.

In accordance with what has already been explained, our beginning must be a disclosure of the experiential world, and it is first a disclosure of this fact of this actually experienced world. To begin, let us assume that this has already been done; we have then, already actively occupied ourselves with that disclosure. We know what that means. The world is experienced; in every moment of our waking life it is an actuality existing "bodily" for us. But only a narrow perceptual field of actually perceived real things and connections is "properly" bodily there, that is, directly perceived; this near field is surrounded by a ring of unperceived known things mixed with unknown things, and finally, we have the distant field of open unknown things. The same holds for every point of the past. In the progress of actual experience, much that was not experienced is disclosed automatically; but possible experience, which we always set into play as motivated by actual experience, also immediately discloses to us in the image of possibilities, the consistent style which belongs to our experiential world, and its necessity already indicates the possibility of discovering eidetic necessities.

In addition, if we are to acquire universally descriptive knowledge concerning the style of the experiential world and eventually of every possible experiential world, intuitively performed universalization – empirical and then eidetic – belongs here.

Here we should add an important remark which concerns method but which also carries the subject further. We can best do so in connection with an objection which will naturally emerge for those with a background in Kant's transcendental philosophy. I can not go into the close relation of our problem to Kant's in *The Critique of Pure Reason*. We are not concerned with any philosophical interests at all, in the sense of a transcendental philosophy. But, however far our objectives and even our paths differ from those of Kant, nevertheless the essential affinity of the problem of the ‹95› evident structure of the world of possible experience with the problems of Kant's transcendental aesthetic and analytic, and even his dialectic, is unmistakable.

Kant insists that the world is not an object of possible experience, whereas we continually speak in all seriousness of the world precisely as the all-inclusive object of an experience expanded and to be expanded all-inclusively.

I can not acknowledge the Kantian proposition, no matter how the concept of experience is formed, if it is to remain serviceable. For us, real single things are experienced, but the world is also experienced; and the two are even inseparable. We experience a physical thing, for instance; we perceive it and return to it in recollections; in the concatenation of these recollections we have a synthesis of many single experiences into the unity of one experience as an experience of the same thing. But also: someone else can experience just as well what I experience, and not only do my experiences link together to the unity of one experience, but my experiences and those of others also link together to the experience of the same thing.

Our concept of experience reaches as far as a harmonious synthesis in the unity of one experience is possible – which is precisely then a harmonious experience. An experienced object holds for us as an actuality of experience, as an existing real thing, which we designate afterwards as a member of the real and actually existing world, insofar as it holds for us as something harmoniously experienceable by ever new experience – one's own and others', actual or to be made possible – as what is continuously confirmed for us, or possibly, what could have been consistently confirmed. In this connection I remind you of our previous fundamental determination of the concept of sheer experience.[1]

Only what is passively given or able to be given to us beforehand, and what we can make our own merely by the activity of grasping, by "receptivity," is purely experienced. Therefore, every activity of specific thinking is excluded, an activity which procures for itself new objects in logical formations, though this be done on the basis of experience —which for that very reason are no longer mere objects of experience. E.g., a predicative formation "Gold is yellow" is not experienced, but the gold is ⟨96⟩ perhaps experienced, and likewise the yellow. No longer yellow *as a predicate of the subject* "Gold:" judging, relating thought accomplishes the forming of the subject and the forming of the predicate; only in such thought does the *is*, the *is-relation*, the "relation of affairs" arise also.

In this sense the world is experienced just as well as a single thing, a single qualitative moment or member of the thing, a process of movement, a causal occurrence, a connection.[2]

Granted, in order to grasp the world as an object of experience, we must have previously grasped single realities of the world. Therefore, in a certain manner the experience of single things precedes the experience of the world, that is, as grasping, noticing experience. We have to turn our regard away from the experienced thing and turn it toward its real background, the horizon which inevitably surrounds it as a horizon of experienceability.

But in just that way it is also said that, while any single real thing is given, its surrounding world, or the world which contains it, is also always and necessarily already given with it. It is given as something toward which our look can be turned at any time and which it can transform into noticing experience just as it can anything else already given.

Therefore, whenever something singular is grasped, it is grasped in the world, without any necessity of turning our grasping interest toward the universe. *On the other hand* and to the contrary, if the world is grasped, singulars *must* be grasped, first from the near field of singulars. The grasping of singulars must come first and must already possess in advance its ungrasped but already given horizon.

---

[1] See above, p. 57 ff. [English, p. 41 ff.].

[2] To be emphasized especially! An experience is experience only as long as it is in play, unbroken. The experiential world is the correlate of consistent harmony; the eliminated, cancelled perceptions, etc., count only *as* cancelled, as experiences of non-existents, but not as experiences simply of real things of the world.

The process of disclosure which is possible and necessary for the one world, by progressing to possible experiences and to continued acquisition of illustrative pictorializations of what is openly unknown (but as presupposed by it) is a process of sheer synthesis of experience. The activity which may play a role here is not a practical activity, not one which produces so-called categorial formations, thus, formations which ‹97› are never intuitable in a passively proceeding synthesis of experience.

If we were to deny that the world as world is experienceable, then we would have to deny exactly the same for every single thing. For, on its part, it is always perceived, but, disregarding its worldly environment, always only with horizons of ignorance. Every experience leaves open the possibility that something new might still become experienceable concerning it, the same real thing.

It is clear that we have thus gained a highly significant and most all-inclusive structural cognition for the realm of possible objects of experience. Everything objectively experienceable as objectively existing in harmonious experience, thus intersubjectively showable, is conceivable only as existing in a world; it is situated in the milieu of a possible all-inclusive experience, whose object is the world. Or, in other words, whatever experience gives us factually as real, in a world-environment factually experienced in whatever manner, is only conceivable as real in a world, in its world to be experienced more closely.

Now we also understand immediately the all-inclusive necessity of time and space as forms to which every real thing is fit. The necessity of a world-environment for every real thing signifies the necessity of a certain form of existence: the world to which the individually experienceable real thing must belong is not determined more closely; only that such a real thing is not otherwise experienceable except in a disclosable horizon and in the form of existence of an individual thing of a surrounding world to which it must be adapted – that is a priori.

Now if this form of existence, a world, as the disclosure shows, is further conceivable only as a world of the all-inclusive forms, space and time, then of course every real thing is necessarily a spatio-temporal reality. World itself is nothing but concretely filled time and concretely filled space. Of course, it remains possible that, besides the abstract structures of space-time, other all-inclusively material structures for a world, in which every real thing must also participate in its own way, may become apparent.

12. NECESSITY OF BEGINNING WITH THE EXPERIENCE OF SOMETHING ‹98› SINGULAR, IN WHICH PASSIVE SYNTHESIS BRINGS ABOUT UNITY.

A result of the priority of the experience of single real things to the experience of the world is the methodic requirement that every empirically descriptive (and all the more so subsequently every eidetic) analysis of the structures pertaining to the totality of the world must start with the consideration of exemplary real singulars, of course accompanied by a continual surveying reflection upon the horizons which have been opened up or are to be opened up, thus upon the world as a whole.

It is also clear now that every supreme universalization which begins with an exemplary singular by itself must already be very significant for the theme of the all-inclusive structure of the world, e.g., if concerning this human being here we form in intuitive variation the supreme universality, human being as such or animal being as such. For the single instance is not something that exists or is possible in actual isolation. The supreme universality of the single instance is manifestly a form which must be closely related to the all-inclusive form of the world. It is evident that even every mere fiction, a pure possibility of something real, and thus also every universal, every pure eidos which we conceive, as an eidos of a reality as such, must have an indeterminate horizon. It is an open question in what possible world a real thing of such a nature may fit. Eidetic consideration does not inquire into that at first, but a problem is always left open in this regard.

It should be noted in this connection that the scientific concept of the world which we seek, the scientific description of the world of pure experience, itself creates and should create a logical formation, but one which only exhibits in exactly logical fashion the essential content of the givens of pure experience. To disclose the experiential world beginning with this now or with any time, and so taken universally, does not mean: to know what this world which has come to be known experientially, is essentially or must necessarily be according to its universal structure.

Certain universalities as experienced are found also in the sphere of mere experience; they are those which the philosophers of the seventeenth century manifestly had in view under the title "*experientia vaga.*" If in experience alone we skim over several trees, then each one is experienced
‹ 99 › singly, and the grouping, the group as group, is also experienced; finally, in the skimming through, an overlapping of the perceptual givens takes place passively, and each given becomes an object of consciousness passively as a single moment of what is one common thing for sensuous passivity. But only a synthetic activity of comparing, of bringing to congruence, of distinguishing between what is identically common and what is different, yields synthetically constituted universalities and logical universal concepts. Then we have in our designation not vague universal words but universal terms, expressing logical universalities.

As long as we constantly have sheer experience as our basis, and continually keep in view the unity of an actual or possible thing as harmoniously agreeing, and of an actual world as experienceable in consistently maintained harmony, then we are constantly guided by that passive synthesis in which precisely the multiplicity of experience yields a unity of an experiential object as something consistently existing. Passive synthesis which itself belongs in its various forms to experience and which is fundamentally its unity, is everywhere our support for putting into play the activities of relating and of constituting logically universalizing universal concepts and propositions. But this in such a way that the concepts, the universal states of affairs and nexus of states of affairs, gain their logical intuition, that they become intuitive knowledge.

13. DISTINGUISHING BETWEEN SELF-SUFFICIENT AND NON-SELF-SUFFICIENT REALITIES: DETERMINATION OF REAL UNITY BY MEANS OF CAUSALITY.

If we now survey the real singulars upon which our considering glance may rest within a world which is still unknown as to its structure, and if we seek most universal and even a priori necessary distinctions, then a first and perhaps the most fundamental distinction is offered between:
1) real, "concrete" individuals, things in a certain broadest sense,
2) the modifications, the modes of individual reality, which are merely modifications of things, but not themselves things.

For, within the experienceable real singulars, certain ones confront us which have the form so to speak of primal realities. They are characterized in this way, that in accordance with their own sense they are perceiv- ‹100› able without their presupposing the experience of other real singulars; e.g., a house, a human being, a mountain does not require for its experience the prior experience of other realities. Here the experience is independent as experience. But if we consider the experience of the color of the house, the shape of the mountain, the play of features of this human being, then these experiences are non-self-sufficient, and indeed as experiences of these objectivities, color, shape, etc. I can only gain color if I have previously, however fleetingly, grasped in my notice the concrete individual of which it is the color. Therefore, such real singulars already presuppose others for their experience.

Here I would also class sets and configurations of every sort. Of course, in order to grasp a row of trees we do not need to grasp tree by tree in successive single grasping. But even when we become aware of the group, the row, at the first glance, this collective notice includes along with it a noticing of every single tree by itself. Nevertheless, this is different from the prior examples insofar as they presuppose a noticing of the founding singulars by themselves, in the sense of being exclusively directed toward them, and not a mere noticing along with something else. But if we take both together, then real singulars are in fact separated into "things" and modes of things which finally trace back to single things, collections of things, configurations, moments of things, or perhaps of groupings of things, etc. Therefore, I named the things, the realities in the strict sense, primal realities.

‹*›   In the last lecture we attempted to distinguish between the concepts "self-sufficient or concrete reality" and "non-self-sufficient reality" (merely non-self-sufficient moments of concrete realities) and then to elaborate the concept of a thing, a real individual in the strict sense of the
‹101› word.[1] Subsequently it seems to me that older determinations, as I have given them in prior years, and which place the *concept of causality* in the focal point, are indispensable for the concept of a thing. I hold fast to the guiding thought that a mere configuration, a mere plurality of concrete singulars, which offers itself unitarily to intuition is still not a thing, even though taken together it is included in the concept of what is experienceable self-sufficiently. Whenever concrete objects are situated in the unity of a surveying experience, they form *eo ipso* an intuitive unity, they form a "sensuous" configuration. But they are not thereby really unitary.

If we ask what specifically makes real unity and what makes anything experienceable in a mundane experience a thing, something real in the specific sense, then it is best to answer: real unity is such a unity that its inner determinations not only preserve a unity universally in their non-alteration and alteration but such that they preserve a stable causality in the change of these determinations; or, as we can also say, stable causal properties make themselves known in their temporally changing determinations as in causal conditions. Things, for instance, material things, have,

---

[1] The world is world as totality of realities. Here I get into confusion in the attempt to introduce the correct concept of reality, and even in the "improvement" I did not find my way out.

Is it necessary from the start to explain the concept of reality by that of causality in the multiplicity of changes, real and possible?

Is it not better at first, and all that is required for the beginning, to introduce in a primitive way the concept of the logically formal "substance," as the absolute substrate of individual determinations of what exists individually?

The real existent is what it is in and of itself: i.e., it is first an individual, temporally irrepeatable, the substrate (predicative subject) of possible predicates valid (intuitable, able to be confirmed) for all times and for everyone, but it is not itself a predicate. A concrete individual is an individual existent in its individual determinations, in its totality of determinations. The determination itself is individual but as such precisely existing only in the substrate, which is itself no longer determination but determinable, etc. The real world is the totality of concrete individuals. The real world is not a single individual but a totality of individuals, a total unity – what comprises the unity still remains open. In any case, the world is on the one hand a unity and as that, existing, and on the other hand by its basic structure a totality of individual realities, each a concrete thing in itself. That will do.

e.g., changing conditions of movement, but in them determinate mechanical properties make themselves known; they have changing conditions of warmth or electrical, magnetic conditions, in which stably determined thermal, electrical or magnetic properties make themselves known, belonging stably to the respective things amid the change of those conditions. This implies that the immediately experienceable determinations of things, of material, sensuously perceivable things, are dependent in their processes ‹ 102 › of transformations on their environment of things, or on the sensuous determinations of these surrounding things, and likewise vice-versa. These dependencies are experienced in their way; and every thing itself is from the start apprehended as such a lasting individual which has its familiar style of causal behavior, its familiar style of behaving in such a way in its momentary real conditions, of comporting itself in such and such a way in lighting, in warming and cooling, in pressure and impact, etc., of changing in such and such a way with the change of the sensuously experienceable determinations of the circumstantial realities. That every thing has its surrounding horizon of things means still more precisely that it has its causal horizon; it is constantly dependent on its environment concerning its determinations, but in such a way that this dependence has its stable style; it depends determinately upon the sort of its environment and momentary determinations thereof. That is just what is expressed then in causal laws, from the point of view of universal scientific consideration. Every thing is not only universally a unity of changeable determinations, but it is subordinate to causal laws as rules according to which things of every category in all their possible environments, behave in a determinate and foreseeable manner. Of course the law is not itself directly experienced and experienceable, but only recognizable by thought on the basis of experiences. But it belongs to the sense of experience itself that what is experienced there has its causal style and horizon. For to know a thing means to foresee how it will behave causally, e.g., to have experienced, to know, a glass plate as such means always to regard and know it as something which will shatter if it is struck hard or thrown down; a spring will vibrate in a known way if it is struck; a moved rolling ball, striking against another ball, will exercise such and such effects of movement upon the struck ball according to the direction of the impetus, etc.

When several things are given together, they are not therefore one thing simply as the unity of a sensuous configuration. They are combined to make up one thing only if they bring about a whole which is an identical substrate of causal properties, which has a stable style, recognizable by dis- ‹ 103 › closing experience, of behaving causally in the respective conditions of its existence.

In this sense a stone is a real thing, or the sun, or even our entire solar system – even this, for however much every single member of this system is a real thing by itself, the system is nevertheless also a real causal unity. Likewise a human being is a real thing, but also an association and a people. An association is a unity of causality within its real social environment, as is a people in its environment of peoples.

14. ORDER OF REALITIES IN THE WORLD.

Within the scope of the world of sheer experience, things of higher and lower order are distinguished. We arrive finally at things of the lowest order, singular things which are no longer given as a system of things, as pluralities of single things joined in each case to make up the unity of one thing; as, e.g., a heavenly body, a human being, etc. But that leaves open the possibility that in the causal process an explosion of a thing into several single things might appear and that therefore, universally and in advance, a singular thing can be thought of as something divisible, divisible further into things.

If accordingly we make a survey of the entire world of pure and simple experience, then it is clear that it is articulated throughout into single real things, which can then be further united in real complexes of things, as things of a higher order. Every such reality in the specific sense is a causal unity related causally to its real environment and a substrate of stable causal properties in this play of changing causal transformations, therefore stably preserving its causal *habitus*.

Within this pervasive structure which belongs to the form of this world and of any world at all, a great distinction confronts us at once. Real things break down into living things, in the everyday sense of the word, into animately, psychically living and acting things, and on the other side into things lacking psychic life. Of course human beings and animals present an example of the first. We do call plants also living beings. But only if they would seriously be experienced as psychically living things, as sensing,
‹ 104 › perceiving, feeling, striving, in the manner of psychic subjects, psychically affected or psychically active, only then might we class them among psychic beings, among those things which are subjects and live as subjects. Otherwise we class them with things that are not subjects, things that lack psychic life, like stones, mountains, houses, architectures, works of art of every sort, machines, books, etc.

Thus, one of the most proximate distinctions, therefore one which emerges already for the most superficial consideration, presents us with mentality as a structural moment in the experiential world. Beginning there, we must attempt to advance to the pure distinction between the physical and the psychic and then the mental as such, and also to the fundamental insight that in the concrete world of sheer experience, physical nature and mentality are everywhere inseparably intertwined, though each can nevertheless be pursued purely on its own as a self-enclosed nexus.

15. CHARACTERIZING THE PSYCHOPHYSICAL REALITIES OF THE EXPERIENTIAL WORLD; GREATER SELF-SUFFICIENCY OF THE CORPOREAL VIS-A-VIS THE PSYCHE.

What first impressed us as a difference between subjects and non-subjects was a difference in the species of things. In that way, subjects alone were defined by a positive characteristic, i.e., as living psychically, while other things were only negatively defined as non-subjects, by the lack of psychic life. What psychic life means in this context we have clarified in a manner which suffices temporarily, by examples which we can multiply abundantly. Thus, for instance, feeling sensuously, perceiving and other forms of experiencing, carrying out thought activities such as: considering together, comparing, distinguishing, exercising universalization and ideation, concluding and proving; but also passively feeling joy and pain or else actively taking pleasure or displeasure in something, instinctively striving for something or else actively setting oneself goals and being directed toward them by desiring or willing, but also achieving those goals by acting.

What is psychic in the sense of such examples is immediately comprehended in psychic subjects, precisely as their psychic life, by correspond- ⟨105⟩ ingly directed experience which is called "psychological." It offers itself as something changing incessantly and necessarily, as if it were a stream with waves which fleetingly rise up and flow away again.

But we also experience equally well subjects with abiding psychic characteristics, as characteristics, that is, which manifest themselves as remaining during the multiple change of psychic doing and living. Thus by experience we are acquainted with some persons as nearsighted, others as farsighted or as having normal vision; some as deaf, others as somewhat hard of hearing, still others as having an especially fine musical ear. In this way, permanent habitual properties of the visual or acoustic sense-life of the people in question are expressed. Again, we ascribe to people a normal, weak, or extraordinary memory, in particular, a memory for numbers or names, etc., or an active and rich imagination; in another respect, a certain temperament, perhaps melancholy or choleric, such and such character traits, a resolute will, a weak disposition prone to melt into sentimentality, etc. These are all habitual dispositions of the subjects concerned; they are not momentary occurrences or series of occurrences. Rather, they designate experiential unities which manifest themselves in the typical manner in which the psychic life of the respective subject runs its course, the sense-life, feeling-life, active thinking-life and willing-life, etc.

Now, it is clear that the distinctive characteristic of those real things which we call subjects, the distinguishing feature of living psychically and, in doing so, of manifesting an abiding psychic *habitus*, can not have the sense that subjects should and could have no other characteristics at all, other than psychic properties of that sort. Subjects – animals and people – are concrete real things, but only if we take their psychic characteristics together with their underlying *extra-psychic* ones.

⟨106⟩ We experience people and animals as bodily-psychic beings; we distinguish their psychic life and their psychic species from their corporeal body which, considered separately, no longer includes anything psychic and yet really belongs to men and animals.

⟨ * ⟩ In the previous lecture we were involved with the analysis of the experience of concrete real things like people or animals. We easily separated in them their psychic life, or the habitual characteristics of the psychic subjects which were manifest experientially in it, and, on the other hand, their corporeal body. In such a contrast, their corporeality no longer included anything psychic at all, while in each case it still belonged *realiter* to the human beings and animals. Universal experience also shows us a universal possibility of transformation of these realities, whereby they can be reduced from psychic subjects to psychically lifeless things – in a word, whereby they can die. Every animal being can be reduced to a mere body, which, when it originates in this way, is called a dead body, a corpse. Every animal being is also apperceived in experience with this change even foreseeably coming.

Accordingly, the analysis of experience shows that realities of this sort are two-layered; they are "psycho-physical" beings. Their physis as well as their psyche can be considered abstractly by themselves in the concrete wholes; each has its own course of change, but they are not indifferent to each other. Human corporeality and the corporeality of each kind of animal is restricted to its specific style.

But, whatever particular type of change may be predelineated within the concrete experience of human beings or experience of horses (of course, that pertains then to the respective horizon of experience which indicates the empirical possibilities for the sense of the experience of human beings or of horses) one thing is certain: whenever the always open possibility of bodily deterioration sets in, whenever the possibility and the shape of a unitary organism passes over into the shape of an organically non-unitary compound or even into merely inorganic matter, then the psychic life is annihilated. Nullity means non-existence in the real world as world, that is, within the unitarily experienced and experienceable multiplicity of things and modalities of things, processes, and the like.

If we question all-inclusive experience and the possibilities for an ‹107› experience of the psychic – possibilities conceivable on the basis of its empirically universal style – the situation is quite different from that of the experience of the corporeal. The latter can be experienced as inanimate. In the shape of the inorganic, or at least of the organically non-unitary, which it can assume at any time, it lacks animation. But, on the contrary, wherever the psychic is experienced or should be experienceable, there an organic body must be the substratum; in possible experience, its animated body presupposes such a substratum.

The state of affairs is more profoundly illuminated if we point out that every worldly experiencing individual who, as such, experiences in an originally perceptual manner an experiential world as his surrounding world, finds in it his own body as so to speak the central member of his corporeal surrounding world, and especially as his presenting organ of perception, by means of which alone he can experience things of all sorts, among them, other human beings and animals.

One's own body functions in this respect also as so to speak the originary body, insofar, that is, as the perception of one's own body is distinguished as the most original experience of a body, and is the apperceptive presupposition for every possible experience of the type, "someone else's body." Since one's own body is perceived as body, it is perceived as animated, and indeed in originally proper and self-perceived animation. My body is given originally to me and to me alone, as that in which my psychic life governs. My psychic life is for me quite directly and in the strictest sense of the word perceived, and directly perceived not alongside my body but as animating it. Here alone I experience in an originally perceptual manner this unity of body and psyche, this intermingling of bodily and animating happening. Therefore, this is for me the most original source of the sense of body and psyche and animating. It is also clear that only as long as my body has its typical form, its division into organs, in which I can rule accordingly – perceiving, moving, pushing, etc. – only so long is it possible that an experiential world of things is there for me. It is perceivable only in activities of perceiving, which are always bodily activities – seeing, ‹108› touching, etc.

As to others' bodies and the others' psychic lives which belong to them, it is easy to see that they are experienceable for me only in *this* manner, that I can interpret the other's corporeal body which I experience sensuously, and interpret it, to be sure, in accordance with the analogy with my own as the only originally perceived body and with my life which animates it alone in a perceivable manner.

As soon as this analogy is lacking or, where it was effective, as soon as it is shattered – as it is whenever the other's body loses the style of an organism, such as mine still displays – then that body loses the ability to indicate experientially an animation belonging to it. The other's psychic life then ceases in principle to be experienceable. Whatever is in principle not experienceable for me does not belong to my experiential world, is nothing in it, is not something existing in the world.

Now, an objective world is an intersubjectively experienced and experienceable world. It presupposes, therefore, that first every subject by itself has its experiential world with things, with animals, with human beings, and that there are, experientially, possibilities of exchanging our experiences by mutual understanding and in this exchange, of establishing an intersubjective harmony of the reciprocal experiences. Accordingly, the presupposition of an objective world means this presupposition, upon which we stand as natural human beings and as representatives of the objective sciences: already this much, that we each have as given our own body as original locus of our own animating lives and likewise, have others' bodies given in analogising experience of others, as the locus of others' psychic lives. Now, in whatever way we can think this presupposed experiential world as changed, with whatever changing determinate content in the progress of actual and possible experience – it is clear in this state of affairs that the conditions included in the apperceptive sense of psychically functioning bodies, one's own and others', must always be fulfilled. In other words, it is clear that neither one's own nor another's psyche can ever become experienceable except as animating one's own or another's body, ‹109› restricted in its typicality, and that every sort of psychic existence already experienced and established must become nothing as soon as the apperceptive presuppositions of psychic experience are cancelled, therefore, whenever a body ceases to preserve that sort of organic style which is the condition of the possibility for its being capable of an animating function, or of indicating animation. Therefore, death as a real event in the world does not have the meaning of a detaching of the psyche to its own reality within this world. From the point of view of the world, death is the annihilation of the psyche, *nota bene*, as psyche in the world. The doctrine of immortality, therefore, if it is not to contradict the sense of the world which is fixed by all-inclusive objective experience, would have to have quite a different meaning. And it can actually have a different meaning if it is true that the natural consideration of the world, that of all natural and world-cognizing life and of all science, need not and perhaps must not have the last word. In other words, if it can be shown that this entire universe, the totality of the objects of possible objective experience, does not hold as that which exists in the absolute sense and that the absolute which the world already presupposes is mind, but then by no means as mundanized mind, and especially not as psyche.

In any case, without being allowed to go into such questions here, so much can be seen: that real subjects of the sort of animals and human beings are, taken concretely, two-layered, but in such a way that these layers may not be taken as completely equal. Corporeality has greater self-sufficiency inasmuch as it can furnish by itself something fully concrete, though by a transformation of its real form as organic body, while the psyche can never become a real thing in the world in concrete self-sufficiency.

In these considerations we have questioned the experiential world according to the universal style in which it gives itself to all possible experience. In doing so we have found necessities which are structural, permeating the entire unity of possible experience. To clarify the extent to which these necessities are a priori intuitable as purely eidetic, therefore as absolute and evident, would be a particular task which would require a ⟨110⟩ much deeper structural analysis of the experiential world, a task for which we are therefore not yet prepared.

16. THE FORMS IN WHICH THE MENTAL MAKES ITS APPEARANCE IN THE
EXPERIENTIAL WORLD. THE SPECIFIC CHARACTER OF THE CULTURAL
OBJECT, WHICH IS DETERMINED IN ITS BEING BY A RELATION TO A
SUBJECT.

It would be a natural development now to pursue descriptively the structural distinctions which we have made, thus merely by following experience, to study on one side what comprises the essence of mere matter, which in part has a reality on its own as that which lacks psychic life and in part has to function as the support for a psyche, as its body.

It would surely become obvious here that all the matter of the world is situated in one single corporeal nexus in which it can be considered on its own and which is governed throughout by the closed unity of an all-inclusive causality.

It would become equally obvious that spatiality and spatio-temporality belong in a distinctive manner to matter and that everything psychic participates in objective extension only mediately by its matter and the spatio-temporality belonging to it.

In the direction of the other layer, that of the psyche, corresponding descriptive problems would ensue: questions concerning the fundamental descriptive characteristics of everything psychic, concerning its elementary types, concerning the connecting forms of unity, concerning what makes necessary the unity of *one* psyche purely as psyche, and how, further, several psyches can gain unity by purely psychic relationship and connection in spite of all concrete separation, and how in this way mental association among human beings and animals, personal unity of a higher order, becomes possible.

‹ * ›   But a closer consideration soon shows that our structural distinction between physis and psyche is not yet a fully pure one; and a still deeper analysis is needed, to prepare the idea of a pure and sheer nature, as it has become the foundation of modern natural science.

‹ 111 ›   And likewise, on the correlative side, the idea of a purely psychical mentality should be determined in a parallel manner by way of a corresponding purification. This purification is the separating out of something "merely subjective".

For our purpose, it is especially very important to mention the various meanings which discourse about the *subjective* can have in a consideration of the experiential world, or: in what forms, taken universally, the subjective and mentality can play a role in the experienceable world.

Mentality in the form of psychic life and psychic habituality of animal subjects is a basic form, indeed so to speak the original form in which mentality has existence in the world, whether it be in the form of singularity or of community.

But we must also note that things, even lifeless things, if we take them as they are experienced by us, can include or embody, as it were, a mental endowment, even though they are lifeless things and therefore not organic bodies in which the mental is embodied in the form of animation proper. Most of the things of our life-world, as the world which constantly surrounds us as our experiential world, can serve us as examples: desks and other furniture, houses, fields, gardens, tools, pictures, etc. They are immediately experienced by us as mentally significant things; they are not seen as merely physical, but in their sensuously experienced shape, in their spatial form and every turn of this form, and in their other sensible features, a mental sense is expressed. This sense, in its often very complicated mental structure, has its counterpart in the structure of the formings and divisions of the sensuously experienced matter in which it is embodied by way of expression. The sense is not found next to the matter which expresses it; rather, both are experienced concretely together. Thus, a two-sided material-mental object again stands before our eyes.

Therefore, there is an analogy between the way these objects are experienced and the way in which, in experiencing a fellow-man, we experience a unity of body and psyche. In the experiencing perusal of the play of features, of gestures, of word-sounds uttered, etc., it is not something ‹ 112 ›   merely physical that is experienced, but the animated physical: and that is precisely the manner of an expression, of an expression which by continuing, agrees and confirms. As such, of course it is not capable of making psychic functioning itself perceptually given, as is the case in the self-perception of our own bodily-psychic unity; but it can do so in the manner of an originally lively and fitting indication, as what is expressed in the expression.

But, in the present sphere of experience, of culture, what expresses is not a body and what is expressed is not a psychic life, nor a disposition which makes itself known in it. A tool or a work of art is a physical thing, but not merely that: in it a rich mental sense is embodied; in it a formation originating from a subjective performance is objectified. The multiple material articulation of the thing, e.g., of a Gothic cathedral, is not an arbitrary articulation, but one which is senseful and which is comprehended in its sense.

Every component has its particular form or even its multiplicity of particular forms and contains in its entirety and according to every form-element a mentality which is expressed in it, which is – literally or figuratively – uttered in it. It is not associated in a merely extrinsic fashion but is intrinsically blended in, as a sense included in it, and expressed – we might even say "impressed" – in it.

A separation between the matter of the sense and the sense itself, which is possible at any time, is an abstractive distinguishing of layers. In the concrete contemplation of a work of art, as of any cultural object, of any tool, of a machine, of a building, of a speech or a text, we experience not duality but unity, which can then only afterwards and abstractly be considered according to two sides: of that which expresses and of the expressed sense, the cultural significance.

The genesis of such mentally endowed realities manifestly refers back to activities of a creative subjectivity. The sense refers back to a sense-forming subjectivity which creates the expression as an expression of this sense, and the concrete work as a work of this form of purpose.

At the same time it is evident that whatever is already given in community experience as such a mental formation (in the broadest sense of the word), whatever is already given as a cultural object, can serve again and again ⟨113⟩ for new purposeful activity and can take on ever new cultural sense. Quite universally, there is nothing objectively real which can not take on some determination of purpose or contain a sense impressed by a subjectivity; it can then eventually be subsequently understood in just that sense by everyone who belongs to one and the same community of those who can mutually understand one another, and be experienced as a constant article of the surrounding world. Even human beings themselves, however much they function as subjects creating culture, are at the same time cultural objects for one another. For example, they are simultaneously educated and capable of being educated. Educating is the performance of an art, and one can recognize good or bad education in a person. Scientific, artistic, or technically practical training is a cultural performance, which gives human beings a form of sense embodied in them. Thus, human beings have culture in many sorts of possible forms. They have determinations of purpose impressed upon them and experienceable in the context of experience, for example, as government officials, officers and other state functionaries, or as functionaries of ecclesiastical or other communities.

The experiential world as cultural world has a perpetually changeable historical countenance, and in this change it is, as is well known, a proper theme of theoretical interest, a theme for different sciences, the socio-cultural sciences in a particular sense. In these sciences, research has continually a double direction, since culture and culture-creating subjectivity are inseparably related to each other. Every experience of a cultural object, therefore of a reality which includes a mental sense which it expresses, has its way of being endowed with open horizons, thus also its way of disclosing that sense which is expressed but which is nevertheless at first only imperfectly grasped, merely indicated. The disclosure demands a corresponding intuition; it requires projecting oneself into the corresponding purposeful striving, the determination of purpose, and the ways of fulfilling the purpose – for example, in the case of a weapon, an intuitive understanding of the universal purpose, but also of the particular way of handling it in the corresponding circumstances for which it is calculated to fulfill its purpose. Manifestly, that always refers back also to the corresponding ‹114› subjects, to the weaponsmith, to the warrior, in the circumstances of their temporal surroundings and the broader systems of goals within which the making of weapons is included, not to the isolated persons, but also to the personal communities in whose communal living all the aims of the time are rooted.

Inasmuch as mentality objectified as culture refers back by way of origin to personal mentality, if we follow this reference back, we are situated again in psychic life. For, what makes a human being a personal subject is not contained in the physical, in his matter, but in what animates that.

Let us look somewhat more closely at the disclosing illustration. Through it we shall gain clarity as to what sort of a "mentality" it is, which, properly speaking, we ascribe to the "cultural objects" under the title "mental sense," or as to what relation this mental aspect has to the psychic, which we designated as the *originally* mental, therefore, as the place of origin of all mentality.

Cultural sense, objectified mentality of every sort, is on the one hand objectively experienced, as we had emphasized, that is, experienced as a sense belonging to certain things, inhabiting them as expression, and endowing them with mentality. On the other hand, we said already, and the disclosing clarification of the expression leads us immediately to the same result, that every expressed sense and the object entirely endowed with sense, itself refers back, in its disclosed experiential content, to a psychic subjectivity, universally speaking: to a human being or a human community out of whose personal performance it has arisen. It is the product of a subjective fashioning, arisen from intention, aim, setting of goals and means, realizing action – and finally the total performance, therefore, in the broadest sense, a product of work. Thus, originally having come to be by creation, as a production in producing activity, it has its original form, its actual originality, for the producing subjectivity and only for it. It unfolds in or from his intention and realization in a series of shapes, in which continuously his momentary sense of purpose and sense of work dwells perceptually and thus finally in the completed work itself, which is something not only for the worker, but is there for original ‹115› intuition in the form of the work intended and purposefully fashioned. Of course, this sense of the purpose of a work is not something sensibly perceived or perceivable as, e.g., the shape of an arrow, if an arrow is carved. The physical shape is sensuously experienced, to be seen with the eyes, to be felt with the fingers. But the form of purpose which the word "arrow" expresses has arisen non-sensuously from aim and will; yet, wherever it becomes actual in goal-conscious producing, there the sensuous shape produced according to the guiding purpose is also seen precisely as purposed and effected; here the work as work has its most original mode of givenness, accessible to perception in an acceptably broad sense.

But whatever has come to be this way can be repeatedly experienced and can be experienced by any number of subjects; but it is no longer originally perceptual in the same sense. The same individual thing can not be produced, but at best something similar or like it can be produced. However, that which is individually the same can be repeatedly experienced, and eventually by any number of subjects, as this product of work, for instance, this arrow. But this is the case not merely in so far as spectators, by watching the fashioner of the work and putting themselves by understanding in his place and that of his purposeful effecting, have their co-experience of the work as such: even after the work has come to be, it is universally experienceable. The purpose and sense of the work which accrued to the object in its original production is something permanently appropriated to that material object. The corresponding experience has therefore the basic form of an interpretation; physically the arrow is sensuously seen and is at the same time, as we say, understood in its final sense as an arrow. It shows itself to be that in possible and actual experience whenever it is shown and demonstrated as having been produced for the sake of this sense and as corresponding to it.

In this way, on the one hand, an object endowed with a purpose, a cultural object, has an original realization in personal life and has for the personal subject the mode of givenness of perception proper, on the basis of the original producing. On the other hand, it can be repeatedly expe-

rienced in the form of intuitive and continually self-corroborating interpretation by every other subject within the understanding community.
‹116›   The cultural object itself or its *cultural sense is accordingly not, for
*instance, something psychically real in the manner of real psychic states or real
psychic properties making themselves known in them.* Universally speaking,
a real thing is a unity of change; it is a unity of changeable states which
extend throughout a duration, which as states of a changing thing are subordinate to causal regulation. In this sense, a material thing, but also an
animal or a human being, has the unity of a real thing—but not a discourse,
a text, a literary work, a work of the plastic arts, etc. The cultural sense
insofar as it belongs to the material body, so to speak, of the work, and
belongs to it in an enduring manner, is not something belonging as a layer
of reality to this material body. This material body taken on its own does
have its unity of material reality.

The sense which makes it a cultural object is certainly time-related, and
in a certain way we also have to speak of a duration in its regard. But here
we find no variable circumstantialities spreading over the duration, no
proper temporal extension with an extending temporal fullness, and no
possibility of now changing, now not changing, as long as the cultural
object is identically the same. And of course, since there are no proper
changes, neither will you find any proper causality of changes. The unity
of the work, its identity, determines its invariant sense of purpose.

If a picture, through the darkening or spoiling of its colors etc., not
only changes physically, but as a consequence is experienced differently as
to its sense, then the work of art as such, as this esthetic picture, has not
changed; rather, a different picture is now experienced. And the experience
is a false one, one which will not persist harmoniously in the event of an
appropriate disclosure.

Even the universal change of interpretation of past cultural creations,
a change grounded in the essence of all that is historical, is not its
change in the sense of reality in which we speak of the change of a physical
thing or a human being; rather, there is a series of historical declensions,
‹117› in accord with which an original work with its original sense passes over
into a multiplicity not of actual works but of immanent ones, a multiplicity
which exhibits a particular type of unification, that is, as a multiplicity of
mutually conflicting interpretations of the same.
‹*›   Attention should be drawn also to the fact that diverse things can never
have identically the same states or real properties; each has its own, they are
individual. But diverse cultural formations in spite of really separated individual matter can very well have identically the same sense. Thus, a mathematical proposition which is objectively embodied in the German language
and is thus a German cultural formation, can become embodied in other

languages with fully identical mathematical sense; and everyone can also grasp this identity.

The sense is therefore a peculiar irreal layer of a material reality; through it, it gets a position in the real world, a kind of temporal duration, of spatial restriction, even something like spatial extension; and again something like efficacy in the world, insofar as, just as it arose from subjective producing, it can also influence the subjectivity which subsequently understands it, motivating it to new personal performances.

We must take this peculiar species of experienceable objectivities just as they are experienced and experienceable, as they are given to disclosure and experience and within the scope of possible harmonious experience, and as they show themselves eventually to be actualities in the world. Therefore, we must not push them aside because they are not real things like natural realities, nor may we simply regard them as psychic objects on account of their "subjectivity." Going back to their locus of origin we find them as personal products and find nonetheless that, according to the sense thereby appropriated to them, they are not anything psychically real, but intersubjectively identifiable actualities in and with their sense, reiterably experienceable in the manner of an interpretative subsequent understanding and eventually even experienceable in a universal acceptance of purpose, as purposefulnesses in the sense of a universally held ⟨118⟩ system of purpose. – They are existent in their manner, of which we can change nothing.

Whereas realities are what they are in themselves without question of subjects to which they refer, cultural objects are subjective in a determinate way, springing from subjective doing and on the other hand addressing themselves to subjects as personal subjects, for instance, offering themselves as useful for them, as tools utilizable by them and by everyone under fitting circumstances, as determined and fit for their esthetic pleasure, etc. They have objectivity, an objectivity for and between subjects. The relation to subjects belongs to their own essential content itself, with which they are meant and experienced at any particular time. A physical thing or a human being is of course a priori, like any object at all, referrable to a subjectivity, as experienceable and knowable by it; but in its experiential content itself, in its sense as an object, a thing includes nothing of a subjectivity related to it. To explicate a thing – we may pursue the disclosure as far as we wish – leads always only to the properties of a thing, but never to a subjectivity creating it according to a purpose or relating the created object to itself as purposeful, useful, beautiful and the like. But the relation to a personal community belongs to the proper meaning of all cultural objectivity.

And precisely for that reason, objective research must here be directed partly to the cultural sense itself and its form of efficacy, but partly and correlatively to the multiple real personality which the cultural sense pre-supposes, to which it itself constantly refers.

17. REDUCTION TO PURE REALITIES AS SUBSTRATES OF EXCLUSIVELY REAL PROPERTIES. EXCLUSION OF IRREAL CULTURAL SENSES.

a) Once we have clarified this point, we recognize that the concrete experiential world admits of a purifying reduction by means of which we attain a closed realm of pure reality as an all-inclusive structure which pervades the experiential world everywhere. Though the experiential world may be furnished almost everywhere and ever so abundantly with cultural sense and though it is continually being so furnished as a result of the
‹119› culture-creating performance or bestowal of sense which we human beings have accomplished individually and in narrower or broader communities – nothing prevents us from abstracting from these predicates of the expe-riential world, these subject-related irreal characters of such things, and directing our regard exclusively toward the universe of pure material realities which are united with them. Then we have, as pure material real-ities, human beings and animals in their concrete double-layered reality and likewise the realities which lack psychic life, in their exclusively real characteristics. This material world is manifestly prior in itself to the world of culture. Culture presupposes men and animals, as these in turn presuppose matter.

b) Once we have thus attained the pure world of things, we can mani-festly go one step further back abstractively. For, if we abstract from the psychic characteristics of the animal realities, thus, if the originally mental is also disregarded, then only pure matter is left over everywhere, as that which is absolutely mindless.

If we proceed in this way with regard to the entire experiential world, we gain nature in the precise sense of physical nature as a universal nuclear structure of the world, and plainly a purely self-enclosed nuclear structure. It is composed exclusively of material realities, from whose sense as objects all psychic meaning as well as all cultural meaning has been excluded by our abstraction; therefore each material reality is taken purely as a unity of physical states and purely physical causality, while they are all interwoven with one another in the all-inclusive unity of one nexus of purely physical causality. Here is the realm of originally spatio-temporal extension. It was not without reason that Descartes defined the physical thing as *res extensa*, though he may afterwards have fallen into aberrations in doing so. And here is the spatial and temporal locus, or here are space and time as a system of places, to be distinguished as the indi-viduating factor or the form of all physical individual things, from the material "what," the qualitative, that which is concretely localized. The latter, as something identically repeatable, is a universal down to its last specific differences. It becomes an individual unique *this* only through localization. Note well that we are not saying here that a pure physis ‹120› ever exists or could exist on its own, as if a world were conceivable as pure nature.

We need not take any position in that regard here; we merely claim to have carried out an abstraction by means of which a proper nexus to be researched in its own way appears as a nuclear structure, as an all-inclusive, though also perhaps abstractly dependent, structure of the world. Just as we can keep on experiencing purely at the level of physis, as we can continue to keep our regard away from the mental in every sense, while we notice, disclose, and confirm, so also we can be active in researching and theorizing exclusively in this endless layer of experience.

Modern natural science does that. What comprises its radical uniqueness in contrast to ancient natural science and what defines its method through and through is precisely the just described abstraction from everything subjective in the two-fold sense designated above.

Only thus has the essentially distinctive connecting unity of all-inclusive physis appeared as a self-enclosed spatio-temporal causal nexus of physical things, stretching into infinity; and only thereby has a science of this pure nature, breaking down into many disciplines, been grounded.

18. OPPOSITION OF THE SUBJECTIVE AND THE OBJECTIVE IN THE ATTITUDE OF THE NATURAL SCIENTIST.

The method of excluding everything subjective, by means of which natural science gains its all-inclusive province, takes on a special sense by the way *in which this method necessarily passes over and must pass over into the method of natural scientific work itself.* Science is constituted first by an unfolding of the horizons of experience, by an exposure of the harmonious real possibilities, but also of real acutalities – the latter by actively expanding actual experience in the interest of theory, thus by opening up the horizons of actuality in experiment and observation.

Theoretically conceptualizing and defining thought operates on this ‹121› basis, therefore in relation to exposed actualities and possibilities of natural existence – exposed in continuous harmonious confirmation. But in this procedure the establishing and defining activity is to be directed toward what is purely objective in experienced nature, which is to be elaborated and defined in a theoretically productive manner in its pure objectivity (in opposition to subjectivity).

What does this "purely objective" mean, and with what sort of a

"subjective" is it contrasted, as with something which so to speak continually disguises it, something which must accordingly be abolished?

The abstractive elimination of the psychic from the experiential world
already includes, properly speaking, the elimination of all that is merely
subjective, if one actually does abstract from the psychic on all sides and
in every place where it may appear. Then all cultural mentality is automatically omitted. For, if we adopt a purely natural focus and abolish everything
psychic, not only in the present but also in the entire past and future
experiential world, as the natural scientist constantly wants to do, then
the entire experiential world loses *eo ipso* all cultural meaning as to its
genesis and thereby all assertable cultural predicates. They are omitted *eo
ipso* from the theoretical province of the natural sciences.

The same holds for that sense of the subjective toward which we will now
especially direct our remarks, and which plays such a great role in the natural scientific struggle for pure objectivity.

In all natural scientific method, and finally in all experience, in which
alone there is talk of an experiential world (whether concretely or in any
abstraction), the natural scientist and universally the one who is experiencing and theorizing is of course always there, too. What is experienced is the
experienced of his experiencing, and in this experiencing it is always given
to him, to speak in popular terms, just as it looks for him at any particular
time. And then further, in his thinking, just as he takes it into consideration,
just as it gives itself to him in concept and judgment.

Now, whatever varied sense the usual discourse about such subjective
intuitions, interpretations, opinions, varying in multiple ways according to
the momentary peculiarity of the respective subject, may have, as well
as discourse about varying interpretations of the different scientists who
‹122› experience and theorize together – the *difference* between the *objectively
true* being to be determined out and the merely *subjective* as what merely
appears to the respective subject in his respective subjective attitude, what
is merely meant by him – in his merely subjective interpretation – is generally intelligible even in a vague and distant consideration.

The one who experiences and notices, notes this or that object as existing,
as now there before him or by way of memory as previously having faced
him; the one who is experiencing as a natural scientist notices therefore
the thing observed at any particular moment. But how could he experience
it otherwise than in subjective modes, e.g., as here or there, as near or far,
as to the right or to the left, above, below? In the progress of experience the
orientation varies, but the experienced thing does not change for that
reason; and even if it does, change of orientation is not itself alteration of
the thing.

In intersubjective communication and collaboration, each individual has the things in his own oriented modes of givenness; but also, a unity of the experience of the same thing pervades this change, with the characteristics belonging to that thing itself, though they present themselves as subjectively varying, now in these, now in those modes of orientation.

Of course such subjective modes are not the theme of the natural scientist, even though, whenever he has things in experience, he has and can have them only in these modes. The attending regard and also eventually the theoretical interest can at any time be directed toward the latter. But the so-to-speak *straight direction of regard* toward the thing itself and the inner characteristics belonging to it itself and again the relations to other things belonging to it, as they themselves are – is a different direction of regard; it is the directedness toward one and the same thing which is harmoniously experienced in the running off of various modes of orientation, as this thing having such and such characteristics.

It is plainly possible to be thus directed without the respective modes of appearing becoming thematically considered, although they are necessarily in the field of consciousness. The one and the other direction of regard – ‹ 123 › we could also say, the one and the other experiencing notice – can also enter into a synthesis (and that happens quite commonly already in ordinary life): as when we notice and accordingly assert that this same thing appears in our field of vision at one time near, at another time far, at one time to the right and at another time to the left, and as a consequence has still further characteristics of subjective appearance, such as perspectival displacement, shortening, pulling apart, etc. But all such subjective directions of regard and syntheses yield nothing constitutive for the theme of natural science. Of course, the investigator of nature must carry them out in his method but only with the aim of arriving at his own proper theme and of consciously exposing it in its purity. The turning of regard toward the subjective modes of giveness of things does not serve toward including them in his theoretical interest, but toward excluding them from it, thus in order for him to say to himself: that does not concern me; I need not make any descriptions and theorizing definitions, nor to pose any theoretical questions, concerning them.

Thus, the objectivizing of the objective scientist is accomplished "abstractively," and the objective entity itself that he grasps and investigates is something abstract. For, although it is itself grasped in the experiencing, it is nevertheless inseparable from the subjective "how" of the givens. None of that is changed by the fact that the thematic goal is what is objective, as the identical thing itself, not only of those experiences which are actual at any particular time, but of all future and all possible experiences.

This thing itself remains always and necessarily subject-related, a pole of identity for an openly endless multiplicity of my experiences and those of all other subjects, experiences of actual and possible subjects who are to be able to arrive at a harmoniously confirming synthesis with my experience by possible mutual understanding.

But the natural scientist does not have to reflect on that fact. It is his manner and intent, simply in the attitude of experience directed straight-forwardly toward the thing itself and nature itself, and in collaboration with a community of thus oriented scientists, to define what is true for nature as such in its existence and its being such and such, according to fact and even-tually according to eidos. What is objective is as something objectively ⟨124⟩ true the theme of experience and investigation. Here we can point toward another difference between the merely subjective and the objective, i.e., what is objectively true.

That abstractive orientation toward what is objective gives us as a result the object itself, here nature itself. And it is *actually given*, exper-ienced in the strict sense, as long as experience proceeds in the form of harmoniously self-confirming experience. As long as that is the case for me or for us, so long do we assert obviously, following precisely the un-broken certainty of experience, or certainty of existence: we experience such and such things, we experience nature. But, as is well known, it often happens and, properly speaking, it happens again and again in the further extended course of experience, that harmonious experience does not remain permanently harmonious.

What was certain as existing and as being such and such in just those objective properties and was continually confirmed as such, often loses its certainty, its character of simple actuality, of unquestioned harmoniously confirmed existence. The character of dubiousness, of discordant clash, of being "questionable whether thus or thus," takes its place; eventually, the character of the merely likely, or in a negative decision the character of nullity, for instance, of being "not thus" in connection with an "instead of that, rather such and such."

If it has gone that far, then the originally certain actuality is degraded to a merely subjective opinion now shown to be null. But at the same time it has its correlative in a new certain actuality. Thereby the harmony of ex-perience as a whole and the pertinence of this new actuality to now uni-tarily accepted actuality as a whole is re-established.

Thus the difference appears here between what holds as objective actuality for the subject in his experience, but which is nevertheless *not* given *conclusively*, rather as ready for a possible correction, *and* what is precisely conclusive actuality, insofar as it remains safe from correction in arbitrarily extended experience.

Plainly, this can affect existence itself, with all its ways of being con-

SYSTEMATIC PART 95

stituted; but it can also affect single characters only, the existence of which can become doubtful and need to be surrendered or corrected, while the ⟨125⟩ object persists continually as actually existing.

19. THE TRUE WORLD IN ITSELF A NECESSARY PRESUMPTION.

However much what is given us in experience as existing actuality always and everywhere leaves possibilities of correction open for thought, and however often the surrender of experienced actuality becomes necessary in fact, nevertheless in natural life we are governed by the certainty that in spite of everything there is an objective, conclusively true world, *the* true world, as we simply say. That holds for us constantly as a matter of course which is beyond doubt. Considered more closely, this implies a presumption which transcends every actual experience.[1]

For it implies that the harmony which is established at any particular moment in our entire experience will not and can not turn out afterwards to be illusory *in infinitum* and with regard to all actualities which present themselves, and that endless experience could not continue forever and everywhere in the form of corrections. Rather, however many corrections may become necessary in single instances, and even though, as a matter of fact, such corrections might never be lacking with regard to single items in our experience, we are certain that this Way of the Cross of corrections leads at least in progressive approximation toward the knowledge of an actuality which is not further corrigible. A conclusive, true actuality (*the* world in its actual truth) must come to light in the endless process of experience, or at least must come to light ever more purely, ever more completely. It must then be theoretically determinable as conclusively true. Every break in certainty concerning experienced actuality, every transformation into discrepancy, doubt, into empty appearance, all corrections, are taken by us as mere cognitive bridges into the realm of conclusive actuality. Behind all these doubts and semblances lies the true actuality, merely subjectively hidden and disguised, but in itself without question and not subject to cancellation.

This presumption which belongs to the natural style of all-inclusive experience in its never questioned certainty governs also the objective ⟨126⟩ sciences. To elaborate the true actuality definitively by observation, experiment and theoretical thinking, thus to draw up conclusively true predications and theories concerning it, that is its goal, and in particular the aim of all objective natural science. Accordingly it conceives of its scientific

---

[1] Better: in natural life, practical certainty of something true for practice. Presumption of the scientist, that of truth in itself.

struggle for pure objectivity as a battle against what is merely subjective in an experienced and yet only supposed truth, against every "merely subjective" illusion, against all merely subjectively experienced conflicts, doubts, and merely provisional conjectures.

Discrepancy, illusion, etc., are indeed subjective occurrences; they appear in the domain of consciousness of individual or of communally collaborating experiencing subjects. To be sure, this is no less the case concerning harmony, or the experienced actuality itself, insofar as it is present to consciousness in the one experiencing, as certainty of such and such unities of appearance. The natural scientist, of course, has nothing to do with all these subjective elements. But we have to say again as before: what is subjective is not his theme; it is not his affair to research descriptively how it appears, how agreement, discrepancy, illusion, etc. look, and what defines them theoretically as such. His theme is rather straightforwardly experienced nature itself in its true actuality, while the striding through illusion, doubt, etc., is a method he practices, which takes place in this subjective domain and yet does not have the subjective itself as its theme. The same distinction is to be made eventually in all sciences. If the mathematician speaks of counting, of computing, of his designating something and making a note of it, etc., mathematics is not therefore a science of such subjective activity, but of quantities, numbers, etc.

It is useful to heed still one more thing here. To experience simply, that is, to experience in the normal attitude, is to live unreflectedly in the carrying out of a continually proceeding synthesis of experience or even in syntheses which link discretely interrupted experiences to newly beginning experiences. I say "unreflectedly," for it is a change of attitude if the one experiencing turns his glance back from the experienced object to the experience and the experiencing subject; if he does that in the unity of a ‹127› synthetic regress, then he finds on one side the object and eventually the entire world as what is experienced straightforwardly and harmoniously and what is continually experienceable, and at the same time he finds on the other side that this object was unnoticed in his field of experience as something of which he was conscious and afterwards, by becoming an object of consciousness in a particular way, enters into his field of notice. Here are two actualities related to each other for the one reflecting, and both given in the unity of one acceptance: the objective, worldly actuality and the actuality of the experiencing as "having or acquiring that which is objective in its subjective field."

But if we take the case of an illusion, then in the straight direction of regard in which the one experiencing, in his devotedness to the object, is not aware of himself and his experiencing, there is found something experienced at first as actuality but which later turns out to be an empty

illusion; consequently, instead of something existing, something not existing. This illusion turns out to be surrounded by the rest of the experiential
surrounding world, which is not challenged in its actuality. For, in its
steadfast certainty this experiential surrounding world is what votes against
it and assigns nullity to it. This is found, then, in the straight direction of
regard. On the contrary, if the regard is turned back once more toward the
subjective experiencing, then from this side something actual is again given,
namely the actual subject and his actually having grasped something as
actual, as well as his actual cancelling of this actuality as an empty illusion.
Now the illusion is given not as an objective existent, but as a subjective
occurrence in the field of consciousness of the actual subject and, in
reference to the rest of the experiential surrounding world which is not
challenged in its actuality, as a subject which falsifies it at this objective
spot, a subjective occurrence which has its species of acceptance only in
the form of cancellation or nullity.

The carefulness with which we are pursuing the subjective element which
the natural scientist excludes by his method in order to attain to pure
nature freed from each and every "merely subjective element" has of course
a double purpose for us. On the one hand, to bring the idea of these natural
scientists to clarity and to recognize it as a mere product of abstraction;
on the other hand, to survey gradually the entire subjective field in all its
experiential forms. Only in this way can we acquire an original understand- ‹128›
ing of what a universal science of the subjective can have in mind, and of
what groups of problems are fundamental, which though connected with
one another, are to be distinguished again in special disciplines corresponding to the forms of the subjective, the disciplines of the socio-cultural
sciences, universally speaking.

20. OBJECTIVITY DEMONSTRABLE IN INTERSUBJECTIVE AGREEMENT. NORMALCY AND ABNORMALCY.

But in this respect some other modifications of what exists merely subjectively come into question for us. For we have to distinguish between what
is pervasively confirmed for the single experiencing subject and what is
intersubjectively confirmed as actuality. Both need not coincide, what is
confirmed as actuality merely subjectively, can turn out to be an appearance which does not hold objectively.

It can also happen that several or many subjects agree in their experience
and accordingly have and express one and the same objectivity, while that
is not necessarily the case for all subjects. Especially important here is
the distinction between the community of normal human beings, or the
normal world experienced in intersubjective experience or understanding,

the world of those with normal vision, normal hearing, etc. – and the community of human beings which includes besides the normal also abnormal human beings: those who are color-blind, those born blind, the tone-deaf, those born deaf, etc.

The nature of everyday life is plainly the normally experienced nature, but the nature of natural science is by no means this, the normal nature, but wants to be the "objectively true" nature. The single subject can find his way in the harmony of the nature given him in subjective truth, in subjectively-related objectivity as it were; human beings in community life restrict themselves to the nature of the experience of those with normal senses; and those with abnormalities have then their ways of helping themselves with indirect analogies and are in touch with the circle of normal people in other ways. However, there are not many natures, but there is one nature.

‹ 129 ›   The subjective-relative natures deviate from one another, but in mutual understanding and in community experience a core of commonness permeates them all and is established or can be established in spite of all multiplicity of subjective deviations, a core by which just one world is experienced as the same for all, which "appears" thus to some, differently to others.

As is well known, natural science attempts to determine theoretically the one objective nature which is elevated above all actual and possible subjective differences, as opposed to these "appearances," which now means the same as subjectively appearing, though subjectively harmonious, natures.

But in this respect a further subjective aspect comes into consideration. Everything experienced in subjective modes has together with reference to these modes simultaneously reference to the respective physical body of the ones experiencing. For the locutions concerning blind, deaf, and the like refer us back to that. Thus we come to the psycho-physical connections and the embodiment of the psychic. E.g., the eye of a normal human being has this much in common with that of an abnormal individual, that as an eye it is a functioning organ of the psychophysical subject. But in spite of all commonness of the psychophysical function directly experienceable by the respective subject, the eye of the normal individual and the eye of the abnormal have organic differences in a purely physical respect, differences with which eventually other differences in the central nervous system, etc., can be connected. But only what is purely physical is the theme of natural science, not however the psycho-physical function, nor the psychic in itself, which is interwoven with it. Natural science, in the first sense of a science of purely physical nature, abstracts from all that.

The natural scientist, oriented physically, interested in the world of the sheer *res extensae*, excludes from the domain of his judgment the subjective in all its forms.

The scientists of the mind, taking the word quite literally, make precisely the subjective their theme. That everything subjective which makes its appearance in various shapes belongs together is clear; but how it belongs together and how it can determine sciences, that is not yet clear by any means. Here are difficulties, concerning which the centuries have toiled.

21. HIERARCHICAL STRUCTURE OF THE PSYCHIC ⟨130⟩

The cognitive direction of the natural scientist is toward the external world, toward the universe of things, of "externality," of things which are ordered spatio-temporally and exercise and undergo external causality. As pure physicist, he moves about, as we showed, specifically in the nuclear structure of this spatial world, of which the physical things are the primarily, originally spatial things, those by which absolutely everything which is otherwise called spatially real gains its localisation in spatiality and thereby participation in natural causality.

Let us now, proceeding upwards from physical nature, follow the subjective insofar as it is spatially real and let us then consider how everything else subjective has a relation to the spatial world.

Therefore we begin our considerations with the psychic life which stands out as spatially real in human beings and animals, in the world of universal experience, and with the habitual psychic properties which manifest themselves in it.

Here an *essential distinction of levels and layers* was already suggested in our prior explanations, a distinction which we want to make somewhat more precise now, namely, between the psychic of the lower levels, psychic passivity, and the specifically mental, namely, the life which proceeds in I-centered acts, acts of: I grasp, compare, distinguish, universalize, theorize, or I exercise acts of doing, of purposeful shaping, etc. Likewise, the affections directed toward the I, of being attracted by something, etc., with the habitualities belonging to them. That holds for animals (at least for the higher ones) as well as for human beings. In human beings this higher level includes the entire personal life and, based upon it, the entire sociohistorical living and producing which transcend the single persons. We have had to speak somewhat in more detail about that in the analysis of the origin of the specific cultural predicates as arising entirely from personal activity.

Unfortunately we lack a most broad concept of "person," which is indispensable, one which includes also the higher animal life and which designates only a being which is active or affected in spontaneities pertaining to an I and as such an I has enduring I-properties.

‹131›   As regards the psychic life of the lower passive levels, it is everywhere the presupposition for personality. Already mere receptivity, namely, again every "I notice, I grasp, I consider" which starts from the I-center, presupposes that what is to be grasped already previously lay ungrasped in the field of consciousness of the grasping I and exercises an affection, an attraction upon the I, to turn attentively toward it. Thus as we see, prior to the noticing experience there is already an unnoticing experience, with appropriate syntheses of agreement and eventually of disagreement, before every participation of an I. Likewise, a passive feeling in contrast to every pleasure or displeasure, fond devotion or aversion, and the like, which radiate from the I-center.

The most immediate and most original animation of the physical body clearly belongs to the lower level, as that which an I looking at its own body can see as directly localized in his body, as immediately animating it uninterruptedly.

Thus, the body is seen at this level, as well as every specifically bodily process, every specific bodily member, and seen in its two-sidedness, at the same time in its physical externality and its animating internality. Only if we abstract from this internality co-existing in every normal experience of the body do we have the purely physical body-thing. Thus, e.g., the foot as material spatial body. But as my foot in the experience of my body it is more; the field of touch-sensations and contact-sensations governs it, is localized in it. Its movements as movement of the body in the experience "I move" my foot is two-sided in contrast to, e.g., a merely mechanical being shoved. It is simultaneously a physical movement in space and (in continual coincidence with that) a subjective movement of the foot, etc.

The experience of the body as body is therefore already a psychic or rather two-sidedly psychophysical experience. Here is the psychic of the lowest level: the somatologically psychic, the directly embodied, directly animating, and as such experienced in unity with the physical.

That holds for the entire body as well as for the single parts of the body,
‹132›   the single bodily organs: as organ of perception, organ of subjective actualization of physically-objective occurrences such as hitting, shoving, kneading, hammering, etc.

All higher mentality clearly comes to be experienced as animating this physical body only mediately. That means that all psychic acts (and residues of psychic acts) are indeed built upon an immediately embodied psychic, somatically "sensuous," support, therefore always include the sensuous, in such a way however that they are not themselves localized in the proper sense. Only as interwoven with what is localized and as indicated by it in the manner of expression are they co-experienced "at" the body. Anger, but also an energetic character, a noble sense and the like, is "noted" and yet not seen as actually embodied.

Manifestly, one can also apprehend the matter in this way: there are two concepts of animation which belong together as layers.

1) The animation which makes the body be a body, a system of subjective organs fused with inwardness; or all together a two-sided being, in which something else that is psychic is embodied uninterruptedly.

2) The higher animation, as it for its part animates in a higher sense this two-sided body. This higher animating moment is above all personal subjectivity, mind, which holds sway by its I-acts in the body and through it in its surrounding world, and manifests itself as co-existing with the body, in bodily expression. Therefore, in the first case the physical corporeal body is said to be animated and in this animation it is called a body. In the second case the body itself is said to be animated by the governing I-subject.

Animation designates the way in which mind acquires a locality in the spatial world, its spatialization as it were, and together with its corporal support, acquires *reality.*

Reality, namely, insofar as the mental in its co-givenness with the physically natural is not only co-existing with it but is united with it by real causality.

In accord with the sense of the experience of animals there is not only a purely physical causality, or, not only is the physical body a substrate of causal properties and interwoven with causal dependencies which connect ‹133› it with all the rest of the physical surrounding world. Rather, causality connects (that belongs to the proper sense of the experience itself of animals) the physis of the animal with its psyche and vice-versa.

Accordingly, the objective experiential world as spatial world is not merely a unity of physical causalities, but of psychophysical causalities. Psychic effects pass over into the physis and thereby into the entire physical world.

Or, to speak concretely: there appear in the spatial world animal and human animated realities, which actually function on both sides as substrates of causal properties. The effects proceed partly only in the line of the physical side, they go partly into the psychic side, or are two-sidedly psychophysical, etc.

22. CONCEPT OF PHYSICAL REALITY AS ENDURING SUBSTANCE OF
CAUSAL DETERMINATIONS.

But admittedly there arises the question whether the concepts of causality and of reality are not differentiated in the expanded sphere; and that leads to important considerations. Therefore, let us consider somewhat more closely the concept of causality in reference to concrete animal realities as members of the spatial world and especially by deliberating upon what is universally common with, and on the other hand what is different from, the concept of purely physical causality. If we recall what we have already said in a most universal way about this concept in its correlation with the concept of reality, then causality signifies experiential dependence of individual changes, i.e., of the changes of individual objects changing regularly with one another and in dependence upon one another, in fact, as a dependence which is included in the experience of the respective objects themselves as determining their sense. In the realm of the spatio-temporal world structurally simplified by the abstractive attitude of the natural scientist, the world of the sheer *res extensae*, it means, more closely, the following: every such *res* has a persistent being, it has its stable character of properties, in spite of its continual variability in a likewise continually variable surrounding world of things. All changes of a thing are restricted to a stable style of change in their relation with the changes of their surrounding things, and the sense of experience as experience of things even includes from the start this attunement of things with one another in their changes, this being able to see in advance more or less definitely how the things will behave in given circumstances, but also the presumption that one can pursue this and can learn to know more closely this "specific character" of the thing.

⟨134⟩

If we grasp objectively and conceptually what is included everywhere in the sense of experience, then we say: every thing as a reality has its stable causal properties, each one related to its universally possible environments of things; every such property is then an index of a stable causal regularity in the dependence of changes. Of course we transfer that, and did so previously, to animal and human realities. They are objectively recognizable experiential unities in the spatial world and are included in this world by their physical bodies which are already realities considered in and of themselves. But as animated they have a psychic element not simply hovering over them somehow but interwoven and combined with them, not externally tied on but interwoven in the particular manner of unitary realities, having two sides, as animals, as human beings.

An animal, a human being, has its stable causal style in the multiplicity of its changes, not only as to its sheer physical body but, as we said, psychophysically and psychically – in the last respect, e.g., the psychic total character, individuality in the mental sense.

23. PHYSICAL CAUSALITY AS INDUCTIVE. UNIQUENESS OF PSYCHIC INTERWEAVING.

Here it is of the greatest importance to consider what one connects with realities of every species as common to them all; also in particular what one may attribute to reality in common and what one may not.

Causality in physical nature is nothing other than a stable empirical regularity of co-existence and succession, always given in objective experience in the form of certainties of expectation, as expecting "now this must happen" or "now this must be there too," that is, according to how this ‹135› or that already is now in experience or how it happened previously.

The empirically necessary co-presence and succession is here continually only a presumption which must be confirmed by further experiences. This is the type of physical causality; it is, we may say more precisely, through and through inductive causality, and this determines entirely the distinctiveness of real properties of physical things.

If one is in the pure attitude of directedness toward physical nature, then, under the title of physical properties there is nothing further to investigate sensefully, than whatever presents itself descriptively as inductively causal regularities in extensional states and changes of states, and beyond that, in investigating the properly real sphere, so-called material properties, for instance, physiological properties. Hence, the descriptive method governs all empirical disciplines of natural science in their theorizing.

But what is the case in the domain of animal beings, and in the domain of the psychic which confronts us together with them in the spatial world? The psychic comes into the spatial world only through a species of annexation; it is not extensional in itself, but acquires secondary participation in extensionality and locality only by a physical body.

Now, what if it had a real proper essence with its own species of causality, which would indeed be interwoven with inductive causality and would have to be interwoven through spatial objectivization, yet in such a way that the inductively real were only its external aspect as it were, the external side for a different sort of principle of unification of changes, namely, of mental properties to persisting mental properties, mental characters? And so it is in fact, as a consideration undisturbed by historical prejudices teaches.

Here, everything depends on the manner in which and the extent to which the psychic, which within a consideration of the spatial world is a mere stratum of the physically real, can be considered purely in itself and for itself, according to its own essence which is perhaps absolutely self-contained. And it depends on what kind of unity of process, to be obtained

‹136› from this proper essence itself, the psychic displays as I and as lifestream and what unique higher unification it includes under the titles of various abilities and habitualities of a different species, under the title of a personal I, thus as substratum of these abilities with permanent properties pertaining to an I; and thus to obtain by immanent analysis the unique concept of psychic reality which can be procured here.

Insofar as the proper essential closed nexus of psychic being and life is incorporated in the natural being of the spatial world, and has unitary existence as bodily-psychic in the spatial world, the connection of an inductive causality must *eo ipso* extend beyond mere physis and inductively encompass the psychic also. In a word, the entire spatial world, just as it is given as a unity of an externally experienced world, must be an inductive unity of everything which has its spatialized existence in it, even if it be secondarily.

That, I say, is obvious. For, only what necessarily dwells originally in space as *res extensa* can be objectively experienceable in it. It is originally experienced in it by pure external perception, that is, as presenting itself bodily, in harmonious certainty of existence and simultaneously certainty of expectation amid the change of harmonizing perspectival appearances – as something appearing bodily and certainly in sensuous appearances.

But whatever is not itself *res extensa*, not itself originally perceivable as extended, such as something subjective or psychic, can only be objectively experienceable in the spatial sphere as belonging in its being to such *res extensae* and annexed, by this belonging, to the realm of spatiality. Therefore, it must either be co-perceived with something directly extensive, co-perceived as existentially belonging; or it must be indicated in a more mediate manner as so belonging, thus by way of an indication, an expression, something non-physical co-existing in the perceptually given physical thing.

But now it is clear that every such experience of the non-physical as belonging in its being to the physical (whether in simultaneity or temporal succession) is nothing else but an experience of the non-physical as induc-
‹137› tively belonging to it. To perceive immediately the existential belonging of the non-sensuous does not mean merely to perceive its existence together with [the physical] and its proceeding together in succession; rather, it means to be referred, in the perception of what exists physically or in the course of the physical process, to the non-physical given simultaneously in the perception as co-existing and co-proceeding: as something which *must* co-exist and co-proceed. Again, this signifies nothing else but that a unity of referring expectation passes over from the sensuously existing to that which co-exists; and this expectation is fulfilled of course in the

perceptual co-givenness of the psychic. Thus, in the perception of my own body, the evident belonging of the internal "I move" to the externally experienced physical hand-movement is nothing else but the internal process in its expectant "must co-exist" with the simultaneously starting external hand-movement. However, this expectant "must" is evidently explicated as having arisen from repeatedly having been perceived together as existing together and thus as the force of an inductive "must." Every expectation is "induction," and correlatively every such belonging together is an inductive belonging together.

Thus, therefore, the most original mode of givenness of the psychic in the realm of spatiality, namely, the mode of givenness which my own body, or its immediate body-psyche-layer has for me, is already an inductive givenness, and likewise then the belongingness to my body which the rest of my psychic life acquires.

The same holds of course mediately for the mode of givenness of every other psyche as belonging to another's body; induction leads in this case to something psychic which is non-perceivable for me, therefore as an "inductive inference," as it were. But here there is no talk at all of an inference in the usual sense of an *activity of thought*. For, according to its sense, induction as a logically conceived type of argument clearly has its sphere of validation only in the realm of that experience which we have here designated and described as "inductive," which constitutes associatively expectant connections of sense. We are dealing with structures of mere experience or with structural connections of objectivities of possible experience purely as such. With regard to these, however, thus objectively, ‹138› this existential belonging is called inductive causality. Already the connection of the *res extensae* in nature, the connection of their conditions and changes of conditions, is inductively causal. And now also its connection with the annexed psyches and psychic states. The annexation is inductive; unity of body and psyche is inductively causal.

Plainly the embodiment of psychic being in the spatial world – in accordance with its structural division into single things which maintain a real unity amid all changes of states – presupposes that parallel ordered complexes of states and lapses of states of the physically corporeal things on one side and of the corresponding psychic on the other are connected with one another by inductive causality, by coordination. Therefore, the psyches considered purely on their own must include an inductively effective typicality. Whatever psychic states appear together in any psyche and whatever proceeds in it universally in succession, must have a typical regularity which grounds a style of expectation, therefore a belonging together for inductive expectation. For, otherwise no regular inductive coordination with the regular physical processes of the thing qualified for embodiment would be possible, and it would then be incapable of expressing the psychic life in itself in an inductively causal manner.

But here one must beware of an egregious error, which has played a disastrous role long enough. The fact that each of the two strata of reality which are inductively connected in the unity of one spatially objective reality – the physically corporeal and the psychic – considered on its own, has the style of an inductive unity and even of a certain parallel structural form, which alone makes possible at all the total unity of parallelistic body-psyche structure, by no means signifies that what is combined in the real unity of an animal being, under the titles of material body and psyche, actually is thoroughly parallel, that is, actually of thoroughly parallel structure of being. To speak more accurately; the physical thing in which as body a psyche is embodied, is as physical thing nothing at all but a unity of induc-
‹ 139 › tively belonging together; considered on its own and in its connection with universal physical nature, it is merely a real unity arising from inductive causality. By no means does the parallelism of the psyche which belongs to it signify that the psyche is also a merely real unity arising from inductive causality. One can be of such an opinion only if, instead of immersing one-self in what is properly essential to psychic being itself, one lets oneself be guided by the prejudice, as was psychology already in its first beginnings with Descartes and Hobbes, that the new science of nature is the prototype for every genuine objective science and that therefore every objective science must be of the same style, and correlatively, that every objective being, and that means every objectively spatial reality, must have precisely the properties of physical reality. This conception determined the fateful parallelistic doctrine of Spinoza. According to it, the physical world and the psychic world were two exactly parallel worlds of absolutely identical structural form, form of being as well as form of law, only constructed from fundamentally different material.

But, considered exactly, this is flatly absurd. Not only because – as would already suffice – psyches do not have a properly psychic space which would have its own psychic geometry, but also because according to this inter-pretation, it would be just as proper to say that bodies must be spatialized in the parallel psychic space, present themselves by expression in the psyches, etc., just as the psyches are embodied, physically incarnate and expressed in physical space. All that is absurd, just as the entire metaphys-ical ontology of Spinoza which is behind it, is to be rejected.

When we are further along, we shall be able to learn to understand the true relationships more deeply, simply because we do not construe any-thing metaphysically, because, rather, we do and must do nothing further than to disclose the sense of the experiential objectivities which is itself included in the natural experience of the world, and with it the sense of the psyches which appear in it as animating bodies. What has to count here in our eyes as the decisive point and what has been sharply characterized in advance was this, that the psyche indeed must necessarily have *also* an inductive structure in experience, but that it is and can be nothing less than a unity construed in and for itself as purely inductively causal.

24. THE UNITY OF THE PSYCHIC.   ‹ 140 ›

On the basis of the last expositions we can grant psychological naturalism   ‹ * › only this much, and only this much is a priori certain: in a mode of observation of animals which takes its point of departure from their purely physical corporeity, from their analogy with the physical and from their physical-chemical explanation, a view which therefore lives of course in the purely inductive [attitude], and which then ascends to the observation of the psychic and psychophysical, a rich field of inductive research and of the exposition of inductive properties of mental being must be possible. Provided that one does not become blind to the fact that at the higher level the inductively causal does not comprise the real essence of mind, and that here indeed the inductive research itself must advance beyond what is graspable in a merely inductive manner. For, without a description of the psychic in itself, it does not get far. But if one is serious about describing the mental in its own essentiality, then one must soon become aware that the psychic (disregarding what gives it unity by its connection with a physical body, that is, as the unitary animation of a body) is a self-contained unity which is subordinated to totally unique essential concepts. Let us bear in mind that every psyche is the unity of a streaming psychic life, and what streams in it as a psychic state or act is subordinate to fully unique principles of this stream-unity. The marvelous time-structure of the streaming transformation in the forms of an "ever new now," with the form of streaming away "just passed," and on the other hand, the form of anticipation "just coming," pertain to it. However, the psyche is not just streaming life, but a life in which, inevitably, distinctive new unities, habitualities, are constituted, that is, the passive and active abilities, abilities of perception, abilities of feeling, abilities of memory, intellectual abilities, etc. With these constantly variable abilities we are already referred to the properly essential unity belonging to every psyche, the unity of an identical I as substratum for ability-characteristics pertaining specifically to an I, for personal characteristics which are variable and in fact never resting, and which eventually, in a collapse, can change totally; among them are ‹ 141 › the strictly so-called character traits; the unity of mental individuality which persists even through character changes, permeates all that.

Mere allusion to such characteristics and a deeper penetration into their sense lead to the recognition that in the pure regard for the psychic in its own essentiality, novel principles of the unification of multiplicity appear. The concepts: real flowing state (here lived experience streaming away), real characteristics, real process, reality which lasts amid the causality of real alterations – these are concepts which here gain a totally novel sense, one which above all has nothing at all to do with empirically inductive formation of unity. In particular, therefore, psychic causality, and specifically personal causality as causality of mental motivation, is something totally different from inductive causality.

To be sure, the inductive, as we said from the beginning, plays its role also in the psychic sphere. And it makes possible the embodiment of the psychic sphere in the first place, its incarnation in the unity of the inductive spatial world.

Since the psychic lived experiences are also temporally formed in their manner, that is, as experiential data running on in the temporal unity of a stream, and thus have their regularities of co-existence and succession, they also form, of course, a field of empirically associative unification, a field of anticipative, inductive connections. But this inductive causality need not first establish that anticipative unity which is quite external in its manner. Here, whatever is unified inductively, is already unified intrinsically according to unique essential principles, and has its intrinsic modes of creating ever new and higher synthetic unity. The externality of the inductive – I mean the inductive connection of purely psychic contents (therefore, an externality to be understood non-spatially) – appears here internally as something secondary. Indeed, perhaps it will turn out later that all externality, even that of the entire inductive nature, physical and even psychophysical, is only an externality constituted in the unity of communicative personal experience, is thus only something secondary, and ⟨142⟩ that it therefore requires a reduction to a truly essential internality. But this is not the place to speak about that.

The consideration which we have just carried out is of significance insofar as it removes a historically understandable natural-scientific prejudice which governs psychology, led by the development of natural science. The methods of thought customary to the natural sciences are transferred to psychology; what was in the former a method suited to the subject matter, had to become here finally a harmful inhibition. In a completely onesided fashion, one attempted always to continue proceeding exclusively in the mode of natural science and to reduce all research concerning reality to inductive research. Inductive science and empirical science of fact stood and still now stand for many as equivalent expressions. Connected with that is the unclear transfer, one which is as a rule even false in principle, of the idea of a *science of nature* to the science of mental essences and of the psyche itself.

25. THE IDEA OF AN ALL-INCLUSIVE SCIENCE OF NATURE. DANGERS OF THE NATURALISTIC PREJUDICE.

There is a justified expansion of the idea of the science of nature, namely, one which takes it as the all-inclusive science of all realities of the spatial world in their all-encompassing unity as one unique world which connects all realities in real causality in the framework of the all-inclusive form of the spatio-temporal world.

In all-inclusive experience and in the all-inclusive presumption proper to it *one world* is posited as continuing and ever accepted actuality in its unitary spatio-temporal form and encompassed by a unitary causality in such a way that *all* things of this spatial world are unities of stable causality.

Then "nature" expresses precisely by extension, the full natural external world, whose mere structure is physical nature. But then the extension itself suggests a direction of progress for research, from physical nature to the concrete spatial world, a direction very natural to us externally oriented moderns. Whether this direction of progress is actually the only ‹ 143 › possible one, and therefore necessary, for making personal subjectivity our theme, that we shall still have to ponder seriously. But precisely this point of departure and acquired habituality of beginning with it, includes a compulsion to understand the concept of natural science in such a way that on the basis of physical natural science and proceeding further, beyond its inductively causal region of being, it investigates the whole of being as interwoven with it in inductively determined reality, in all inductively causal properties.

This is just where the prejudice gets inserted that the entire spatial world is nature exactly in the sense of physical nature, and very closely connected with it, [the prejudice of] sensualism in the interpretation of psychic life and the interpretation of psychic life as a proper realm of elements which form a physically real nexus by exclusively inductive regularity of their alterations, a nexus which in turn is again interwoven with physical nature or physical corporeality in the mode of a merely inductive natural causality to form a unity of real causality.

We do not deny that much can be investigated purely by induction here, even much that is very closely connected with physical nature. Physiology, which in great part is psycho-physical somatology, shows that.

There we actually grasp a closed natural side of the somatic psyche, insofar as pervasively inductive connections join *this* somatologically psychic [layer] of sensation and sensuous feeling with the physical body. But the concrete and full world does not have the mere style of a nature.

The naturalistic prejudice must fall.

That determinism which mechanizes the natural world, which makes of the world a machine unintelligible in principle and running on senselessly, originates only in this prejudice. A prejudice which at the same time makes naturalists blind for the distinctive performance of the entire historical and generalizing sciences of personal mentality and culture.

‹144›   26. THE SUBJECTIVE IN THE WORLD AS OBJECTIVE THEME.

‹*› What we have just presented in preliminary sketches and in fundamental guiding doctrines will gain its grounding content and concrete clarification if we first direct our regard toward the subjective occurrences which are excluded in the natural-scientific method of access to nature, subjective occurrences which we have not yet considered more closely under the aspect of a science of mind.

At the same time I must call your attention to this, that the method of exclusion of the merely subjective is shown again as necessary *mutatis mutandis* whenever we want to investigate, beyond physical nature, the animal-human world in pure objectivity, even if we take it as nature in the extended sense, that is, with a one-sided direction of interests toward the inductive.

For it can be made evident a priori that whatever is given and is to be able to be given us objectively must be given in subjectively changing experiences in changing subjective modes. Perhaps the locution of objectivity and its knowledge has a good sense even where a spatial world is not in question. Even there it might all hold. In any case it holds concerning everything experienceable as objective in the naturally given experiential world and thus also concerning human beings and animals, and not merely with regard to their physical corporeality.

A human being can be given by experience in many modes, in differences of orientation and of perspectival modes of appearance. If we take these words in their customary sense, then they regard exclusively the physical body of the human being and him himself, just insofar as he has a body. But even his psychic side, though with different content, has the same sort of differences, with regard to the somatological *as well as* with regard to the higher layer, and thus with regard to the entire psychic layer. Thus, my body is experienced and experienceable differently for me and for everyone else; but it is objectively the same and recognizably the same over against such subjective modes of givenness; just as the specifically bodily-psychical layer, so also the higher psychical layer is given in varying
‹145› "modes of appearance," namely, according as it is experienced originally by me as my own or by others through expression, eventually even mediately (as whenever someone speaks out the window). The concept "mode of appearance" has admittedly an essentially different content here in con-

trast to the multiple physical modes of appearance in which a physical thing is presented perceptually as the same.

Of course in the objective experience of what is animal or human (and not only with regard to the physically corporeal and somatological aspects) there are also breaks in harmony and in the existential certainty experienced in it; there is doubt, error, mere anticipating presumption, the subjective in the shape of illusion which is null and of correction. Therefore, here also as wherever objective science is to be put into play, there is the battle against the subjective in these shapes.

Accordingly it is clear that even where animality and the animal psyche and whatever else comes under the title of the subjective is to become a theme for objective knowledge, a methodic distinction and separation has to be made, namely, between the respective objective element itself and the multiple "*merely* subjective" element which pertains to it but is not intrinsic to it. Wherever the intrusion of the merely subjective into the objective content poses a threat, it must be excluded from the theme by a conscious method.

For physical natural science no particular difficulties are connected with such an exclusion, precisely because it excludes anything and everything subjective, thus even what is embodied as *psyche*. But difficulties arise immediately wherever a species of the subjective and of what is subjectively laden becomes the objective theme and in particular whenever the theme is not only all-inclusive physical nature but universally the entire concrete spatio-temporal world with animals and human beings, then further with human societies and their cultures.[1]

For here the difficulties arise that the merely subjective moment to be excluded at any time, all the subjective modes of orientation, perspectival variations of appearance, modes of dubiousness, nullity, correction and ‹146› the like are not foreign to psychic life, that they belong necessarily to the psychic or personal domains, precisely to those domains in which they appear; therefore, that they can not drop out of the thematic domain so simply as out of the thematic sphere of natural science, which is in principle subject-alienated.

All the subjective modes which the investigator of physical nature excludes are his appearances or those of his fellow human beings or fellow animals, as appearances (or illusion) about or of the objective, appearing in his or others' psychic domain.

---

[1] In a "pure psychology" we would have the situation the reverse of that in natural science: everything "objectively physical" would have to be excluded here. But does it not still lie hidden within the psychic sphere again as an idea, in the intersubjectively psychic connection of confirmation?

They are nowhere within physis, but they are nevertheless and are in the domain of animal or human "consciousness." Everyone that has them can find them in himself by a reflective turn of regard and eventually describe them in their own changing descriptively graspable specific character. But if we want to be not merely physicists, but investigators of the psyche, then of course we can not avoid including all that is subjective in that way within our theme; and then not only that subjective moment which belongs immediately to the mode of givenness of the physical but also every other subjective moment including what we ourselves at any time exclude as psychologists in order to obtain a human being in pure objectivity. Of course, if I have as particular theme the psyche of an ape, with which I am just now experimenting as an animal psychologist, then every subjective mode of apprehension with which he is given to me belongs in *my* psychic domain and not in that of this ape psyche. But if I intend an all-inclusive psychology and universally an all-inclusive consideration of the world, within which every particular consideration and particular science of the objective is classified, then I can not entirely discard any such subjective moment. Every one belongs in some psychic domain and perhaps in the psychic domains of many simultaneously. Therefore, can a psychology be possible which does not include in its consideration everything and anything subjective, and can it not be foreseen that this must hold for all conceivable groups of subjective moments which can be made visible for us in the experiential world?

But that is only a pointing of the way to enter into the proper and deeper difficulties.

‹147›　In connection with the perspectival appearances and the sensuous illusions let us consider this: in unqualifiedly outwardly directed experience we know nothing of subjective modes of appearance. Such and such things simply stand there for us, as bodily actualities, of course incompletely; in the progress of experience ever new characteristics of them enter the luminous circle of what is actually grasped bodily. All subjectively significant words which were used by us here, such as: the things are there for us, in the progress of our experience, etc., express by only indirectly indicating, *what* was experienced. In the unqualified experience itself of a thing nothing subjective as such is found. Our entire subjectivity remains so to speak anonymous to itself. It loses this anonymity by reflection, by an eventually multiple turning of regard away from the experienced thing and its determinations as a thing toward the subjective modes of appearance of the thing and then eventually toward me myself, toward the I which finds this subjective moment already there, toward the I which is at all active there, e.g., as experiencing this thing, considering it more closely, relating it to other things, evaluating it, desiring to enjoy it, etc.

27. DIFFICULTY THAT THE OBJECTIVE WORLD IS CONSTITUTED BY EXCLUDING THE SUBJECTIVE, BUT THAT EVERYTHING SUBJECTIVE ITSELF BELONGS TO THE WORLD.

In the last lecture we were engaged in a transitional consideration. A ⟨*⟩
turning is being prepared. We all live within the natural world of experience; all our doing and suffering was related to it; to it is related every
thematic attitude in which we establish any object or any region of intersubjectively agreed upon experiential givens, in order to be active with it in
theoretical work and finally in order to produce sciences of whose intersubjectively confirmable truth we can convince ourselves. The universe
itself encompasses all such objectivities, anything and everything that is
experienceable and knowable in intersubjective agreement as actuality.
But each objectivity is given for each of us in a subjectively varying manner.
This subjectively varying factor is excluded in order that we can single out
for experience and determination what is objectively identical and true.

This already implies quite universally a difficulty which I would have done ⟨148⟩
better to emphasize right away in this universality in the last lecture. For,
if the universe includes, as was just said, everything and anything which
is in objective truth, then what is the status of the subjective factor of
the manifold subjects, which has been put out of play? The universe itself must also contain these subjects as objects belonging to it. We can
single out for experience and determination the subjects and all their subjective characteristics as objective, by excluding such and such subjective
modes of givenness. The objective universe – is that anything else but all
that is brought to harmony of experience in the subjects which experience
together, and all that is subordinate to the presumption common to us (and
a presumption which is itself confirmed empirically) that it will continually
admit of being singled out for experience as a harmonious unity, with corrections necessary on occasion (then, as a further consequence, will allow
itself to be known in theoretical harmony)? Therefore, the world-sphere
seems to swim in a milieu of the subjective; indeed it even seems to be in it
and to be possible only as a unity-formation related to subjects and constituted in the combined subjects.

On the other hand, do we not have an objective science of the subjective,
and is not everything subjective, even the experiencing and knowing of the
world at any time, with all its excluded subjective element, itself to be
described objectively again, and universally to be made a scientific theme
within the world? Does it not, therefore, belong also in the universe as a
constituent part?

The natural scientist experiences no difficulties here. He excludes anything and everything subjective from his theme and thus actually acquires physical nature to be investigated as self-contained. But by an abstraction. His nature is something given or rather something to be worked out as a thematic unity only in his milieu of subjective appearances and inter-subjective mutual agreement and correction. The natural scientist simply does not concern himself about this; nor does he need to, insofar as in his subjective milieu he wants to pursue only one single line, that of the unities of experience of what is physically objective.

But then if a psychology is to be pursued and the psychic becomes ‹149› spatially objective only together with the physical, then we have the un-comfortable situation that everything subjective, which must become excluded here too for the sake of pure objectivity, still must plainly belong in some domains of psychic subjects; and we are now unclear in advance as to how the subjective is to become objective by exclusion of the subjec-tive, which nevertheless itself must have its place again in just such an objective domain, namely, in the domain of some psyche.

We take this consideration here as a means of making ourselves quite sensitive to this, that the correlative titles of objectivity and subjectivity include a profound sort of unclarities, and that it is not so simple as one who is naïvely directed toward the external world might at first suppose, as for instance according to this schema: the spatial world lies given before us as of course the existent totality of things. And in it the physical on the one side is separated from the psychical on the other side – in some way or other joined to the physical as a second something of quite a different sort – for the rest, including within its sphere everything that is to be called "subjective."

For us the point is radically to overcome such unclarities. The point is to become clear about the subjective as it is already pre-thematically related to objectivity, and how then, once it itself becomes the theme and object, it combines in concrete unities in its own essential manner, and poses distinctively closed, universal tasks for research.

The point is for us to come to clarity as to how it is all connected in its own essence – the spatio-temporally objectivized or non-objectivized subjective – finally, how it all acquires its position in the spatial world in a natural attitude directed toward what is natural in the broadest sense, toward what is extensive and what is spatialized in what is extensive, and how it can be investigated from the point of view of spatial reality; but how, on the other hand, an essentially new attitude and mode of observa-tion is possible, in which the subjective is investigated as mind and in all its purely subjective occurrences, investigated in a manner in which no question of natural science in the narrower or extended senses is asked – no question in the manner of physical natural science, none in the manner of psychophysical natural science, concerning for instance the physically natural consequences of psychically real occurrences, or even personal acts, or vice-versa. In a word, the distinctive character of the socio- ⟨150⟩ cultural scientific attitude of experience and method of investigation must be established, in contrast to that of the natural sciences in the extended sense, directed toward spatial realities.

Finally, the possibility of a boundlessly all-inclusive, purely subjective mode of consideration must be clarified, one which consistently recognizes as subjective *all* producings carried out in subjectivity, including the objectivizing ones – by means of the inseparable unity of producing with the produced formations – a mode of consideration which thereby includes in ultimately encompassing subjectivity all objectivity precisely as a product to be shaped in subjectivity.

But that requires surrendering the natural standpoint, therefore rising above the idea of an investigation with regard to an experiential world given and accepted beforehand. Therefore, it transcends the task we have set ourselves in these lectures and leads over into the ultimate philosophical mode of consideration.

28. CARRYING OUT THE REFLECTIVE TURN OF REGARD TOWARD THE SUBJECTIVE. THE PERCEPTION OF PHYSICAL THINGS IN THE REFLECTIVE ATTITUDE.

Let us begin with the experience of the spatial world with which every scientist starts – the natural scientist in the narrower sense, who is directed toward merely physical nature, but no less the natural scientist in the broader sense, which includes in its theme the universe of realities interwoven with one another in spatio-temporal causality. Here, the direction of progress from the narrower to the extended sense of nature is predelineated; everything mental as something real within the totality of nature traces back to the individual psyches as animations of physical bodies. Accordingly, the investigation of reality must be founded in physical research.

Let us begin therefore as physicists (in a very broad sense of the word).

We have discussed how the physicist acquires his theme *nature* by the access-method of eliminating what is merely subjective, in order precisely to be fully conscious of nature as pure nature. Clearly, unreflecting *straightforward-experiencing* comes first, and above all, the straightforward-perceiving of the *res extensae*. Reflective conduct has no other function ⟨151⟩ than that of habitually fixing the regard on that which already stands before the eyes in the straightforward direction of experience: the purely extensive.

First, we must deal with one's own perceiving and only subsequently with communication with others. Experience and research in the first form of immediacy are carried on in the individual subject on his own; communicative research presupposes this immediate form. Let us act as if no one else were in our field as co-experiencer. Now, if one who is focused purely on objective nature busies himself in perceiving straightforwardly, he grasps the natural directly as it itself, in its natural properties and relations. At first there are no motives here for distinguishing between merely specific sense-qualities and those which are truly objective. We need not take account of this distinction here since, as is easy to see, it appears only at a higher level. In any case, if we are experiencing in a straightforwardly noticing manner and are looking purely at what is and is such and such in space, everything which comes to be laid hold of in this manner offers itself just as pertaining to spatial things, the shape as shape of the thing, a quality pertaining to it in movement and rest, in change and permanence; likewise also, color as spreading over the spatial figure and thereby over the thing itself, qualifying what is objective in space. Nothing at all subjective falls within our mental sphere of vision. Thus, nothing concerning the entire subjective aspect of modes of givenness, about which we spoke earlier, and which doubtlessly does already affect this pure perceptual thing and its pure intuitive objectivity with a plethora of distinctions – even if, in a more inclusively extended experience, especially an intersubjective experience, it should turn out to be a merely subjectively laden and not yet final, pure objectivity.

My perceiving is a continuity of noticing this spatial thing by grasping it, stretching out to see and touch it, etc. This continuity is one which changes multiply and which includes multiple contents. Already the fact that I see this thing here at one time from this side, then and even in continually changing manner from another side and ever new sides, that I am continually directly noticing it, this same thing, and yet notice now these, now those characteristics of the surface, or of the inside of something that opens
‹152› up, etc. – those are already subjective modes of the manners of givenness, to be characterized as a closed group of such modes. In every phase of perception I have perceived this thing, but more exactly: this thing from this side, with these marks. It is perceived and perceivable only in this *how*.

Thus, we have before us not something unchangingly identical, but a multiplicity. But a multiplicity which in its running off yet includes something identical in its own way, namely in such a way that I who am directed straightforwardly toward that thing "itself" have the consciousness of noticing something one and the same.

In this straightforward attitude, I know nothing at all of this multiplicity. Only by a reflection do I gain the multiplicity in my now new direction of regard. Thereby I also acquire in my grasp the unity which permeates the continuity of this multiplicity, the distinctive coinciding in the same thing, the same thing now given from these sides, now from those sides.

Now in this reflective attitude I can also directly grasp that the thing itself is never to be found as something on its own in this multiple series, but that it is always and necessarily to be found only as offering itself in these subjective modes. Now, if I reach back to the still conscious experience (in so-called retention) and possibly the experience again realized in repeating recollection of my direct perception previously put into action – in which I had not noticed these subjective modes at all – then I must evidently say: all these subjective modes were there as lived experiences, only not in the subjective form of being consciously grasped. The purely objective, the thing, could not, a priori, be an object of consciousness without these subjective modes. Reflection discloses therefore what was a subjective mode in the domain of lived experience of the perceiving subject prior to reflection; and thus that inseparability of the objective and its changing subjective mode can always become recognized.

The same thing holds if we cite the oriented modes of givenness of space and of everything spatially objective, the modes of givenness of here and there, right and left, etc. Changes of orientation, we already pointed out, are not changes of the object, since the same spatial object ‹153› perceived as unchanged can appear as varying in its orientation.

As long as I am perceiving straightforwardly, I know nothing about that either; I notice it only in reflection; again I find the unity of what pertains to the thing not as something to be detached for itself, *alongside* such modes, nor as a real portion to be separated off *within* them, but once more as the unity of appearances which becomes an object of consciousness in a distinctive synthesis, amid the variation of these modes. Every subjective mode of orientation is again in its way an appearance *of* the thing, *of* the process and the like; each contains this subjective form of the *of*; and the same appearing object stands out in the coinciding, in the distinctive synthesis of appearances *as* appearances *of* – as a pole of direction, as it were, found in the appearances themselves, in which, as an ideal point of intersection of the directions, they coincide. But of course that is merely a methaphor.

Again, we must say: in straightforward perceiving, everything of that sort was already there, only our notice was not set toward it. Indeed, we lived through the appearances, but our attending notice went through them exclusively to the pole, to the thing itself and then to its pole of properties, to the color of the thing, shape of the thing, and the like. The reference of reflective givenness back to the synthesis arisen unreflectedly for recollection teaches that too.

Again, the same holds for the varying perspectives in which, always according to the oriented givenness, the shape of the thing appears, and with the shape, the color.

In reflection upon the perceptual stream of the adumbrating presentations, we can then also study how the constitution of a pole-unity takes place as determining itself, so to speak. And when we have learned to penetrate into the further course of consciousness, then we can also study how it comes to genesis with these its marvelous horizons of anticipation into infinity.

Just to emphasize one thing, pay attention to the particular manner of the unity of lived experience which characterizes the momentary stable phases and segments in the stream of the perspectival appearances. Not ⟨154⟩ only to the fact that a unitary stream takes place at all and that the conditions for the unity of such a stream must be fulfilled. The single appearances (and already every phase in the streaming is appearance *of*, and so is every segment of the stream) have a particular unity, a "synthesis," in which precisely one and the same objective thing appears and can appear. The appearances must fit together as such; one can not arbitrarily feel them together or even arbitrarily bring appearances snatched out of the perceptual series of different objects, together in one perceptual series.

Precisely considered, the visual data belonging to the object and universally to any perceptual object, have a hyletic unity of lived experience, the unity of a closed sensuous field-form [*Feldgestalt*]. Likewise the tactual data, which are ready to function for the same object, as presenting it in the field of touch, and similarly all other functioning hyletic data. But the data of the different fields have no hyletic, no purely sensuous, unity with one another.

It is different if we take into account the characters of apprehension and thereby acquire the perspectival appearances themselves. In those characters of apprehension, in those which establish intentionality, is grounded the synthesis by which all these genera of different data of separated fields also acquire intentional reference to the same object, the same intentional pole-unity. By it the visual appearances come to synthetic connection with one another, likewise the tactual with one another, etc.; but also, all these series of appearances with one another, whereby they become mere layers in an all-encompassing synthesis.

In each layer on its own, e.g., the visual layer, a layer of the perceptual object is constituted, or rather a visual objective aspect of the perceptual object, or respectively, the tactual aspect, etc. But those are not, in truth, layers of the object itself, as if this itself were objectively to disintegrate into layers corresponding to the senses. In the *synthesis with one another* of all the series of appearances, to be distinguished according to the sense-fields, the one object is constituted in the progress of its determining itself as object in objective duration, objective space, with objective determinations, etc. *Space*, or respectively, the spatial body, is one in ‹155› numerical identity; objective duration is one; every space-locus and time-locus and the objective moment belonging to it is one in numerical identity no matter how the presentation may proceed, whether as visual or tactual, etc. I can see and touch the same shape of a thing; and if I cannot also touch the color as such, yet, that objective element which I grasp by seeing, in the aspect of color, is seen nevertheless as individually belonging to objective duration, spatial shape and spatial location. However, if the spatial-temporal something into which I can grope as well as look, is something identically in common, then everything grasped by the one sense (for instance, exhibiting itself visually) *must* belong also in the realm of the others, i.e., of that which is to be objectively laid hold of by them. It is customary in psychology to speak of the visual space, and of a tactual space; but taken seriously that is a wrong way of speaking. One numerically identical space is experienced, as well as one identical time.

Thus, there are not visual objects and tactual objects, but simply objects which exhibit themselves differently in their objective determinations by visual and tactual appearances.

In our previous lectures, in the context of our universal considerations ‹*› concerning the structural characteristics of the experiential world, and in particular concerning the methods of access by which the natural scientist singles out his pure nature by abstracting it, we had already touched several times the same themes which have now begun to occupy us in the last lecture. That should not lead you astray.

Pay attention to the new viewpoint of our considerations. Now, after we had already defined the idea of a science of nature with all sorts of reflections and preliminary gropings concerning objectivity and subjectivity, and after the task had arisen for us, vis-a-vis that idea, of making the subjective elements always excluded in the attitude of natural science our theme, our concern is no longer to speak merely allusively of the subjective as a mere means of becoming acquainted with another main theme, such as physical nature in its purity. Rather, now the subjective itself is ‹156› to be our theme, our question now concerns the tasks of a rigorously scientific treatment of the subjective.

Thus, the new beginning, as you may notice, consists in this, that we no longer stand in nature and in the science of nature, but as it were, we adopt a direction of regard which deviates from it. We do this by now turning our theoretical interest (and turning it in a pure isolation) to that which it has excluded in its lower, fundamental level of the investigation of physical nature, as merely subjective, as not pertaining to its aim, or as damaging it. We do not yet know what kind of self-contained region, and what kind of an all-inclusive science pertaining to it, have accrued to us here, nor how it may be related to the science of nature. To be sure, we know from our consideration of the experience of the external world that subjectivity as such is embodied in nature. But how that sort of subjective element which we have accepted into our theoretical interest as a little segment cast off by the natural scientist is related to the *psychic*, to what has embodiment in nature – in our present attitude, nothing can be known concerning this. Whither our studies lead (how we shall be driven on from our first directly grasped subjective theme to ever new ones, and how the circle will be closed, and what kind of countercircles it may have), must still show itself. Accordingly, the first gropings of the previous lecture, however much they may have taken up again what was already touched from another direction, are thought of as the beginning of a serious, systematically proceeding science which establishes itself as independent.

It begins with a kind of demarcation from natural-scientific research. If this begins with purely natural experience and progresses by describing real-causal determinations etc., of the natural, we begin, without any interest in the results of natural science, thus also without applying them in the least, by stepping back to contemplate what is already there before the beginning of natural science, or what always subjectively gives the natural scientist his beginnings, his natural things. Thus, we said his first concern is perceiving and what is contained in his own perceiving ‹157› admits of being separated out, if we prescind from his communicative experiencing together with his colleagues.

And now there accrued to us as the first theme of the scientific investigation of subjectivity simply the "I perceive something pertaining to a spatial thing;" I have therein my perceived object, single and many, a space filled perceptually with things, etc.

Our regard is now directed first, not toward the I and its being active, but toward what is perceived, and that with regard to the subjective *how*, just as it is thus given. In this way we are dealing, not with contingent subjective occurrences but generically with that subjective moment which can be exhibited everywhere and necessarily, wherever anything is originally experienced in perception.

There we had the straightforwardly perceived thing itself purely as thus perceived, without busying ourselves further with its description. We immediately pursued the possible reflective turns of our regard and the subjective theme which they yielded. The multiplicity of the modes of appearing, the aspects, of the continuously perceived thing were distinguished in various senses from that thing itself and what can be described in it as its properties. Thus, the constant change of its modes of appearing in ever new "sides." Then, in a new direction of reflection, but still inseparably connected with it, the multiple modes of appearing in orientation, according to which the entire perceptual space, as well as each individual thing and group of things, is given only as oriented, as to the right and to the left, ahead and behind, etc. All orientation is thereby related to a null-point of orientation, or a null-thing, a function which my own body has, the body of the perceiver.

And again, the perspectival mode of givenness of every perceptual thing and of each of its perceptual determinations – on the other hand, also of the entire unitary field of perception, that of the total spatial perception – is something new. The differences of perspective clearly are inseparably connected with the subjective differences of orientation and of the modes of givenness in sides. Assuming that the orientation is altered, then we will have reason to say, though by going beyond our present attitude: we ‹158› carry out bodily a local movement in space, or we stand still and the things move, or else both. But, whatever experiential basis such locutions may have, if we heed purely the subjective appearances of the subjective rela-tionships of right and left, of in front of me or behind me, etc., then it is clear that the things show themselves thereby from varying sides, and again, that the *perspectives* change. How completely different, for example, the surface of a cube appears, and continually different, if the cube rotates in oriented space. To rotate in oriented space is the properly phenomenal rotating, which in no way signifies in the experience itself an objective rotating. Objectively perhaps I see an unmoved cube just when it appears in the rotating change of orientation, that is, if I go around it or know that I am being bodily pushed around it, that I am traveling around it.

This subjective rotating as a phenomenon of orientation contains much continual change of the aspects of the cube's surface. These are perspec-tival changes. And if we heed the coloring, it has its own color perspectives which change correspondingly, in functional dependence upon them. The surface as perceived straight on is given for instance in the objective coloring, which I describe as uniformly red. But if I heed the changing givenness of the coloring, parallel with the change of orientation, then I have, as with the shape ever new adumbrations of shape, so here ever new adumbrations of color. The same uniform red appears to me with each subjective rotation as being different again and again. In the perspectival presentation I have as perspectival red, by no means also a uniform red, but a more or less irregular red, constantly gradating in certain modes. It is, I say, similar to the way it is with the shape. The square is seen with four equal right angles. But if I pay attention to the perspectives of the square in the subjective rotation, then I see in them the equal angles presented by unequal angles; this deviation from the equal is itself inflected in the multiplicity of perspectives. The equal exhibits itself in the irregular and

‹159› the unequal, up to an exceptional mode of givenness, in which the square, objectively speaking, is parallel to the frontal plane. Only in this case does the perspectival givenness of the square have equal angles in its appearance. Beginning there and following the continuity of coincidence, I see how equal is "distorted" in unequal, this right angle into an ever more obtuse one, this other into an ever more acute one. Of course, the same holds, *mutatis mutandis* for the entire cube, and thus for every thing, every complex of things whose content is perceived in space, within the scope of the purely perceptual.

Close attention should be paid to what is opposed as distinguished in the change of attitude: as identical spatial object, and as multiplicity of perspectival modes of appearance. One should further heed this: that both, the multiplicities in their continual change, and the unity which appears in them, which is presented in them, are inseparably united, that they belong to perception even if the perceiver, lost in his object, does not notice the multiplicity at all, just carries out no reflection.

As easy as it is to begin here and to carry out such turns of our regard, and to distinguish, nevertheless, one must *first learn to see in the right way*, in order to see, in all its essential moments, and to describe in pure seeing, what lies in the different directions and yet has a unitary relation to the same objectivity. The point is not to transgress the perceived as such in any point, but to describe it purely as such, purely in its subjective *how* of givenness, but, on the other hand also, to overlook nothing which is constitutive for it. Thus, we have to establish here, and to retain forever in view, that the objective shape, the objective extension is presented perspectivally in adumbration-shapes, in a correlative adumbrational co-extensivity: but, in such a way that these adumbration-shapes are not themselves shapes in space. These also have a diffusion, their species of extension; but the extension of the perspectives of something spatial is not extension in space. If we call what is presented the objective element
‹160› of perception (even if in other connections it should rightly be called subjective again), then in relation to it, its subjective adumbrations are not in the same space, but also not in a second space, for instance a depictive space. The perspectives which belong to perception itself are not silhouettes of the object on a board. A board is itself objectively in space and is perceivable only by subjective perspectives of it. Thus, also the silhouettes drawn on it are perceivable only by perspectives, which are not themselves silhouettes. Silhouettes are objective depictions of something objective. On the contrary, perspectives of something objectively spatial present it subjectively, non-spatially.

The multiplicity of subjective perspectives presents one and the same spatial object, the same objective shape with similar qualifications. Every division in the perspective itself, in its own diffusion, is itself again presentative for a corresponding part of the objective shape. And, vice-versa, every part has its infinite multiplicity of perspectival presentation belonging properly to it. The relationship is always that of subjective presentation and what is presented, of appearance and what appears. And they are always to be distinguished: we must not jumble together what is an affair of the presentations in the multiplicity with the unity which is presented in the multiplicity. Only one limit-case stands out – I remind you of the priviledged mode of appearance of the square of the cube.

Soon it will turn out that this is a proper point of departure for newly directed exhibitings and descriptions. But let that be postponed at first, in order to pursue one more aspect of our perspectival multiplicities and their unity. If we are at first in the attitude of one straightforwardly perceiving the spatial thing and if we describe it itself as a whole or, respectively, the perceived object in its properties, as to what can be grasped of it, the spatial thing, during the perception, then extension itself as a fundamental structure, and in fact, its extensional spatial figure, is distinguished from the color, roughness or smoothness, and the like, which qualify it. If we then carry out a reflection upon the corresponding perspectival presentations which belong to it necessarily, then a parallel structure always results for each of the perspectives: the shape-perspective corresponds to the objective shape, the color-perspective corresponds to the objective ‹161› color, etc. But in such a way that, just as the objective color is extended and formed in objective extension in an objective shape, in an analogous way every subjective color, that is, each one functioning as perspective of the objective color is diffused in the subjective shape, that is in the adumbration of the objective shape, as covering it with color. The unitary coloring of the entire diffusion of each perspective of the thing is divided throughout the partial diffusions which can stand out in it. And this division in turn sets *forth* something, namely, a corresponding division of the coloring of the thing in accordance with the parts of the spatial extension of a thing.

29. PERCEPTUAL FIELD – PERCEPTUAL SPACE.

If we begin with the especially perceived single thing and take note of this fact that whatever is offered to our notice as a single thing has perceptually its spatial background, then we remark, again beginning with straightforward perception and description, that an entire perceptual field objectively encompasses an entire field of things.

The field as field of perception is a perceptual space which includes all the things singularized in it with all their spatial shapes. The single shapes continue to belong to their things in every perceptual change and movement, but they are shapes in this space, each occupying a segment of space in it. Correlatively, every thing of perception is given in perceptual space as filling it in its place, and that by its shape, as qualitatively filled.

That the perceptual space is experienced as endlessly open space, in which we could progressively penetrate to new perceptions, is certain. But if we restrict ourselves to what is actually given perceptually, then we have the respective thing-multiplicity in the unity of an actually perceived space which however is not perceived as something separated on its own, but includes an empty horizon leading further on. That too, the entire question of the horizons, will have to be a theme for new descriptions.

If we now pass over again from the straightforward attitude to the reflec-
‹162› tive, then, corresponding to the advance beyond the singly perceived thing to the respective totality of what is perceived, the respective perspective of the single thing leads us to the unity of a total perspective, and the multiplicity of the perspectives of the single thing as continually presenting this single thing, to the multiplicity of the total perspectives of the total perceptual field.

Here we notice that in perceiving, amid the change of things and of their momentary total perspectives, a stable form persists, as an analogue of space, in which the continual, objective form of perceptual space itself is adumbrated, the space which in the progress of perceptions and their objective givens always persists as the same all-inclusive form. The continual total form of the total perspectives is nothing else but the total visual field, the visual field of sensations, which includes all visual data or all subjective shapes of the single color-data, which for their part can function as adumbrating presentations for perceived colors of things.

The colors of the things of perception are found with the *things* themselves *in* space: the colors adumbrating them and the subjectively shaped colors which we see and raise to prominence purely on their own in the concrete perspectives, are all found in the unity of the visual field of sensation.

Likewise all the shapes of the perspectives in which objective spatial shapes are presented perceptually are found as mere particular shapes in the one visual field which encompasses them, e.g., all the perspectively distorted squares in which the perceived objective square of a cube is presented, together with all other adumbrations of other objective shapes. But as perceiving progresses from perceptual field to perceptual field a synthetic perceiving of one identical objective space occurs, one infinitely open objective space continually opening up for perception: and indeed as one infinite, three-dimensional space which is the form of ever new unknown things – to the contrary, the situation is quite different with regard to the visual total field, in which space must be presented in visual

perspectives. It can never be expanded to infinity; it presents infinity
by ever new qualifications and prominences of particular shapes which ‹163›
take on the ever new subjective functions of perspectives in the mode of
lived experience as an appearance *of*. Here we never get beyond a two-
dimensional and finitely closed field.

At first we can disregard moving perception, the structure of which
requires difficult analyses.

In this way we have also gained a very marvelous distinction of two
domains of objects: the objective data which are straightforwardly perceived in the perceiving of spatial things refer back to subjective data,
the "hyletic data," the pure sense-data. These are themselves something
in their own specific character; they have their own being, a being which is
not objective. They themselves are not perspectives, but they become that
by what we also call apprehension, precisely what gives them just the
subjective function of being an appearance of what is objective. But we
can at any time grasp them directly as themselves without being interested
in the fact that together with them something else, and indeed something
objectively spatial, appears.

We can not even say that this sort of data must *necessarily* serve a presen-
tational function, that we can have them as lived experiences only in the
way in which something spatial appears by being adumbrated in them, and
so something quite different from them themselves. But note well, conversely it is an evident necessity: if something pertaining to a spatial-
thing is seen, that is possible only if hyletically visual data are sensed and
serve a certain subjective function, therefore if they include a distinctive
adumbrational character which does not at all alter them in their own
being but gives them precisely the "character of consciousness:" appearance *of* such and such.

But, to characterize more precisely this sphere of objects here exhibited
in perception, a purely subjective sphere, it is important to bring together
in a certain way our consideration of the subjective modes of givenness of
the perspectives, with what was said before concerning the givenness of
sides and orientation. The perceived object itself, the spatial thing described purely as perceived, gives us the contrasting concept in our sphere
for what is subjective relatively to it.

30. SPATIAL PRIMAL PRESENCE.   ‹164›

In the last lecture we had contrasted the perceptual givens of perception   ‹*›
directed straightforwardly toward what is spatially objective and the modes
of givenness of the perspectives which come to the fore in the reflective
attitude, and we had recognized that the respective momentary perceptual

space (the primally present perceptual field) or the spatial primal presence as stable total form of the objects perceived in this moment is presented in the visual sense-field as the invariable total form in which all visual adumbrational shapes are included.

Taken concretely we have on this side the visual field with sense-qualities which spread throughout it and form these and those concrete particular shapes in it, each concretely as a shaped quality. They are the visual sense-data. The visual field-form which persists amid the change of sense-data is, as can easily be seen, two-dimensional, while the space of objects of perception is three-dimensional.

But it would be wrong to say that objective space is presented in a two-dimensional space, perhaps even in something like a plane or other flat surface. A space is a form of real objects like things, and the possibility of movement belongs to it. But one sees easily that the concept of movement makes no sense in the field of sensations.

Of course what we have situated in the visual sphere has to be carefully studied likewise in the parallel spheres. The same thing can at the same time be seen and perceived tactilely. Now data of touch function also as bearers of objective apprehensions. If the thing is perceived only in touching so that the visual perceptual appearances drop out, then we have precisely merely tactual appearances in which the mere data of touch, as nuclear content, function as bearers of the character, "appearance of."

Here there is no perspective properly speaking.

All tactile sense data belong to the unity of a tactile field. Simultaneously various physical things are given tactilely to perception, even though I may ‹165› pay attention only to one single one. While for instance I am feeling one thing, my other hand lies upon the table; that means: the table is tactilely there for me, though not by actively feeling it. By means of various sensations of contact, the clothes touching me, etc., are present to my consciousness. Thus I have a unitary field of perception which has its unity of tactual presentations, and the tactile field belongs to it as a closed field of sensations. It is the stable field with its stable field-form for all things which are simultaneously perceivable tactually. It is manifestly a totally different field, which can never be mixed or united with the field of visual sensations to make up *one* field. All uniting takes place here by means of the functions of apprehension which make of the sense-data appearances *of*. Here, of course, a visual datum and something of a totally different kind, a tactile datum, can have unity in that the one is given in the character of the objective adumbration, as visual adumbration, the other likewise as tactual adumbration, of the same object.

But we can still distinguish clearly here, we can heed the sense-data purely on their own, here the visual, there the others, and abstract from the function of appearance, from the character of consciousness which makes them to be adumbrations of this or that.

Precisely considered, we can not even say that this sort of data must necessarily serve such adumbrating function – the possibility of data without adumbrating function is already suggested to us by the fact that we can readily find cases, e.g., in the consideration of perceptual doubt and what are disclosed as illusions, where the same or similar sense-data change their adumbrating function and then objectively present something different.

It is only evident conversely that whenever something spatially objective appears for perception, it can appear only by sense-data, namely only if such data have the subjective functional character of adumbrations.

Now if we heed merely the data, which are contents for such adumbrating functions, but disregard these functions, then we find that they belong to fundamentally different genera. We collect all genera of data suited in ‹166› this way for the function of adumbrating, to gain the concept of the sense-datum.

But we still have to go one step further. First it must be pointed out in advance that *what*, as a subjective character in the visual datum or in data of other genera, brings it about that not only this datum is given to us but something objective is experienced as presented with it and so to speak in it, is only a particular case for a universal wonderful occurrence. For, a broader class of subjective occurrences will confront us, and in many particular shapes, a class which may perhaps be characterized in these words: a merely subjective datum or a complex of subjective data is given perceptually, but (whether in the mode of an objective adumbrating function or in another mode) it makes something different from it become an object of consciousness; e.g., if a datum, say a visual or acoustical datum, reminds us of a different one or refers to a different one, then the other one is not presented in it, for it is not brought to perception *in* it by something like adumbration; but it is brought to consciousness by the subjective function of reminding us of it or of pointing ahead toward it.

31. HYLE – HYLETIC DATA AS MATTER FOR INTENTIONAL FUNCTIONS.

Certain merely subjective data, namely such as are not themselves objectively perceived, therefore perceived by subjective adumbrational functions of other data and such that in their own being they are free of all characters of consciousness, have the signal position that in multiple ways they can become nuclear contents of marvelous functional characters which all have this in common, that by means of these nuclear contents and as it were endowing them with mentality, they make other objects become present to consciousness.

All these functional characters are called *intentional characters*, characters of the consciousness of something; but the perceptual data which as
purely subjectively given nuclear contents are matters for the modes of
consciousness which transcend them, and which in their own essential content contain nothing of such characters of consciousness, are called universally hyletic data. Hyletic data are data of color, data of tone, data of
‹167› smell, data of pain, etc., considered purely subjectively, therefore here
without thinking of the bodily organs or of anything psychophysical.

The expression *hyle* suggests this being a core (being matter for functions
of consciousness). A particular case then is that manner of function in
which the subjectively perceptual datum is an adumbrating one and thus
becomes the perceptual appearance of something objective.

The universal concept of hyle offers then the broadest extension for the
concept of sense-datum, to be drawn from the purely subjective sphere, and
eliminates all confusions which emerge with the blurred, multisignificant
word, "sensation."

With this consideration we have designated in advance and brought out,
though only by way of anticipation, a fundamental structure in mere subjectivity, the purely immanent disclosure of which we are working on. For,
even in the perceptual sphere we have actually become acquainted only
with a first shape of intentionality, that one which includes objective perception as its essence.

If we restrict ourselves again to this sphere, by what we had elaborated in
it in the last lectures, it can serve in a new way toward making evident a
fundamental recognition which will also be shown to hold for all of pure
subjectivity. To designate it in advance, it deals with the fundamental distinction to be documented in it between immanence and transcendence.

The perceived spatial object, described purely as perceived, gives us in
our limited sphere of what can be shown as belonging to external perception itself a sharply determined concept for contrasting everything that
can be designated as "subjective" in relation to it.

32. NOTICING GIVENNESS AS I-RELATED MODE OF GIVENNESS OF THE OBJECT.

What we call perception of a spatial thing, and in that sense an objective
thing includes, as can be seen from our analysis thus far, a plurality of possible perceptual directions, as direction of noticing or of grasping; we even
‹168› have to say that different perceptions are here entwined in a unity, if we distinguish between grasping noticingly and perceiving, therefore, if we count
as perceiving just the fact that something is given as directly it itself, whether or not it has the precedence of being grasped noticingly. I note in this

connection: discourse about noticing, paying attention, is discourse relating to an I, but the I with its noting is not itself to be found in the directions of description which we are pursuing. Our descriptions have to do with the object and its modes of givenness. We note at once that even the difference between the object which is given and noticed and one which is given but unnoticed is a mode of givenness which is showable in the object itself as its "standing out," as its distinctive privilege.

Disregarding that, what is perceived (which implies, grasped as bodily actuality, as immediately existing) in our sphere is sundry: on the one hand, the object itself and it alone whenever we perceive it in straightforward objective fashion, e.g., this table here; on the other hand, the subjective modes in which relative to the object this is given as object from this side, as oriented in oriented space and as adumbrated in this or that manner.

The object itself is given as continuously existing, stretching out through a duration. Its duration is the form of its entire determining content, to which spatiality and qualification of spatiality belong. Duration, lasting on temporally, is given, is present to consciousness in perception, even in continuous perceiving. In that regard, we grasp in our directions of reflection the continuous streaming forth of those familiar modes of givenness, thus of the perspectives which continually follow one another subjectively. The noticing grasp can fix here on any such momentary mode or, on the other hand, can pursue the unified streaming series of these modes, the series of sides streaming on, of the momentary modes of orientation, of the perspectives, and of the species of their unification; and everything presented in this way is perceived, is given as existing. But I can bring about still different attitudes here by means of which what is perceived in the different directions of perception is shown respectively as intertwined or separated ‹169› in a certain important manner.

For, 1) if I pass over reflectively in the first and natural manner from the straightforward object-perception to the modes of givenness, then they are perceived, noticed in their subjective existence. But the object itself also continues to be perceived and noticed, although it is not what is exclusively noticed, as when I am directed straightforwardly toward it. What I now grasp is the object as appearing in this or that *how* of its mode of appearance; or, vice-versa, the mode of appearance is preferred as the main theme, but still as mode of appearance of the object which so to speak is still in our grasp and remains in its previously posited actuality.

2) But now we see that we could single out the hyletic data from the perspectives, and make the hyletic data subjective objects of attention on their own, by disregarding what makes them adumbrations, therefore also without a thematic interest in the object presented. Why should I not be able also to pursue the concrete perspectives of the purely subjective series

of appearances, without being directed thematically toward the appearing object, therefore without keeping it in my grip as something existing, having it included in my account, so to speak, precisely as an object among my objects in my field of actuality? Admittedly it always continues to appear. But, if it stands outside my experiencing interest, does it have to count also for me as existing? Likewise, in the straightforward perceiving of the object its modes of appearance are continually there also, but they are not taken account of in this purely objective attitude.

33. OBJECTIVE TEMPORALITY AND TEMPORALITY OF THE STREAM.

Here, included in the unity of my perception, I have several layers which should be well distinguished, and I can in any case let my perceiving have its way at one level alone, persisting quite purely in its nexus. Each can be taken both as a sphere of perception in its own right and as a sphere of actuality in its own right. On one side the sphere of the existing object or of the perceived spatial field and, as I can also say, the sphere of objective tempo‹170›rality; on the other side the sphere of the merely subjective appearances with their temporality which is to be strictly separated from objective temporality. We separated previously the objective duration of the spatially perceived things from the subjective streaming which is parallel to it, or the stretches of duration of this streaming of the modes of appearance.

This fundamental distinction will extend beyond the sphere of perception. Even within the restriction to spatial objectivity, it is clear from the start that it can be not only perceived but also remembered, expected, pondered, evaluated, etc. Thus we have many different subjective modes in which objects can be present to consciousness. Therefore the double temporality reaches much further.

We have infinite objective time as the form of the objective world, to which even objective space is subordinate, and subjective time as the form for all that is subjective, existing in the mode of "streaming," existing as lived experience in the streaming. It is a particular problem of pure phenomenological analysis to clarify how not only the objective content is constituted as to space and spatial shape and quantitative fullness, but also how the objective form of duration is constituted as appearances in the subjective time-form of streaming, and further in the streaming of appearances of what is objective.

One must not say in some extrinsic fashion that the subjective series of appearances is an appearance, is something like an adumbrating presentation of the objective series of the contents of objective duration. The matter is not that simple.

But it suffices for us here that we have strictly distinguished these two different forms of time and accordingly the corresponding, essentially different temporal objectivities within the scope of perception itself. In just that way we have also defined a certain distinction which can be exhibited purely within this scope, between "external" perception as perception directed toward objective space-time and internal perception as perception of what is purely subjective.

Now we can also say, internal perception is perception of what is immanent; external perception, of what is trancendent. The correlative distinction between immanence and transcendence, insofar as it presents itself ‹171› already within our scope, is clarified in the following way.[1]

34. DISTINCTION BETWEEN IMMANENT AND TRANSCENDENT, REAL AND IRREAL IN PERCEPTION. THE OBJECT AS IRREAL POLE.

If we restrict ourselves purely to internal or immanent perception, that is, to perception directed purely toward what is subjective in the immanent time proper to it, then what we here point to singly and lay claim to as perceived is something individual, something which in its temporal determination has its individuality, its character of occurring only once and, as something existing individually or temporally, has its real combinations or, as a real temporal whole, has its real parts and moments. The stream of what is subjective, therefore in our sphere, the stream of the subjective sense-data, perspectives, appearances, as a stream of immanently temporal objects joining together to make up the unity of one temporal objectivity, is also called a stream of lived experience. Everything that we pick out of this immanent temporal sphere as a singly immanent temporal object as *one* lived experience, is something existing only as streaming. Thus every sense-datum, but also every appearance *of*, every intentional lived experience without exception. Now it is clear: whatever appears here as concrete, as a lived experience, is perceived "adequately," i.e., it is given in the noticing perception not merely in one side and in ever new sides, but whatever of the lived experience is grasped in each phase of perception, that is precisely the lived experience itself in this phase in its full content, and not merely one side of this phase, not a mere part of its content.

And if the lived experience streams on in the perceiving, then it is present to consciousness in its full content phase by phase as a stretch of time

---

[1] This is an unsuitable terminology, as unsuitable as is the grounding of immanence and transcendence on it. Improved in the next lecture. What is unsuitable consists in this, that the irreal intentional object as such, the perceived as such, is understood as transcendent; therefore, the "transcendence" of the *objective sense* is fixed as transcendence instead of the *perceived unqualifiedly*, the transcendence of which consists in this, that it is what is believed in unqualifiedly, what can never be given as closed off, nor fully determined in a synthesis of perception, no matter how far such synthesis is extended.

‹172› being filled as it streams. For immanent objects of perception there is plainly no distinction between what of them is "properly" perceived in every phase of perception and what of them is merely improperly co-posited as something that could have been perceived or that could still come to be perceived in the future or in another juncture. What is immanent is grasped fully without anticipation of anything which only other perceptions might or could give. Here there just are not many perceptions of the same thing. Such a thing is inconceivable here. Here there just is not the tension between something objective which is presented only by subjective appearances and this subjective moment which presents it. It *is* the subjective, which is nothing at all other than what is subjectively perceptual and thus flowing away.

Every intentional lived experience taken in pure immanence has its real part, as, e.g., the hyletic data included in it, tone-data, etc., which are really included in it. But also the character of the adumbration of something objective is a real part, a part of the immanently concrete lived experience in the stream.

But now we have the wonderful fact that such a purely subjective moment as an intentional lived experience not only *contains* individual temporal moments in the sense of real parts, but as intentional also contains such a thing as, e.g., an object presented in it.

External perception, the lived experience streaming on, contains as inseparable from it the appearing object as such. Perceiving of a spatial thing is nothing at all other than a having it there bodily before one, but always from this or that side and, in harmonious continuation in ever new sides, having the same object as existing. Now if we say rightly, the spatial thing is something perceived in the perception, belongs inseparably to it, and is evidently to be noted in it, nevertheless this intentional object is not immanent to the perception. That means: it is not its real part, not one of the parts and moments which can be found in its immanent temporality.

To be sure the appearing object is there, and that in every phase of the perception. But in the transition of phases into ever new and temporally separated phases no real moment can be identical, whereas the appearing
‹173› object appears evidently as identically the same throughout all phases and appears in differing content.

Only the appearing is really immanent, i.e., only the hyletic data and the characters of consciousness of . . ., which belong to them and are adapted to one another, are really immanent. In the continuation of the multiplicity of hyletic data streaming on with their characters of appearance, these, the appearances taken fully, have a real unity of lived experience and a certain particular species of being bound to one another, namely, one which is called a synthesis of appearances. This implies first that in the concrete unity of a lived experience the phases and segments must not only be appearances to begin with, but the appearances must fit together in order to be able to form a unitary intentional lived experience in which one objective thing can appear. One can not throw together appearances, for instance from optional external perceptions. Considered precisely, the visual data belonging to a perceptual thing have also an immanent hyletic unity, that of a closed "sensuous" field-form. Likewise, the eventually parallel hyletic data of the tactual and other hyletic fields. But the data of different fields have no sensuous, therefore hyletic, unity with one another. But when the characters of apprehension are included, when therefore the concrete appearances are considered, the situation is different. The synthesis is based upon the intentional characters of the hyletic data, by which they become adumbrations. What becomes produced here is that unity of visual appearances with one another, the tactual with one another, but also of the visual with all others, whereby the one object appears in them continually; and at the same time the changing (coming to perception proper and vanishing again from it) features of the object, belonging to it, appear therein. To every homogenous group of hyletic data there corresponds a synthesis of its own in which a layer of the perceptual object as an aspect of the physical thing itself appears as belonging properly to it: by the visual data and the specifically visual characters of apprehension belonging to it, the layer "visually appearing object," etc. But these series of appearances with their object-layers are again synthetically *one*: the object is one, space and ⟨174⟩ even before that, objective duration is *one* in numerical identity; the same temporal and spatial place and the objective moment individuated in it is individually *one*. I can see and touch the same shape of a thing, and both at the same time; I can see and touch the same roughness or smoothness; and if I can not touch the color, the color as objective feature, as a determination belonging individually to objective duration and spatial shape and spatial location is actually objective only insofar as it is not only visual but also belongs in every other mode of givenness which can function as perception of the same object. The locution concerning "perception of the same object," which the visual perception, the tactual, etc., brings to givenness, refers back necessarily to the unitary synthesis of these modes of givenness, which brings to givenness the same individual object simultaneously visually and tactually and in other ways. And that must admit of being identified in further actual and possible experience, if the identical perceptual object is to be in true actuality. However, with this identifying we are surpassing what we have thus far seriously drawn into our consideration.

But if we restrict ourselves firmly to what is exhibited and shown within the streaming perception itself, we see, then: the synthesis of streaming appearances in the same object (singularly in the same, in the direction toward the object, as a characteristic of the object belonging to it and picked out) has the marvelous specific property on the one hand of being a real synthesis and on the other hand of containing at every phase something irreal, namely, of having "in" itself in separated phases evidently the same numerically identical object which is here called irreal in relation to the immanent synthesis of lived experience. It could also be called ideal in this relation because it is evidently identically the same, whereas the separate phases of lived experience can not really contain anything identical.

Again to use another expression, we could also say, the spatial object within the scope of external perception and grasped purely as its perceived object, is inseparable from the intentional synthesis of appearances of it; ‹175› and it is given in this synthesis as an ideally identical pole, which each of its phases includes as its intentional object and which they all include as pervasively identical. *Mutatis mutandis*, that holds also for every objective feature, for its color, its roughness, for its bodily shape, etc. Each comes forth by appearances, continues to appear as the same in different modes, precisely as long as it is visible. But these poles of properties are non-self-sufficient. They appear as determinations of the ever identical thing itself, the substrate-pole, which is determined by them. But that is a distinctive point of intentional analyses.

As will be shown further in an expansion of the description of the subjective sphere, this is the way in which multiple "consciousness" as well also as other intentional lived experiences generically bring something the *same* to consciousness in synthetic unity, even though it may not be a matter of that intentionality which is called specifically perception of something objective and even more specifically of something spatial. Whatever is present to consciousness and is present to consciousness as the same in multiple consciousness is, taken purely as it is thus present to consciousness, an ideal correlate of the synthesis really occurring in the immanence of the intentional lived experience. But everywhere this *something*, the object of consciousness, is inseparable from this synthesis as something itself exhibitable in it (in a certain broad sense a *what* directly visible in it) but as something irreal in contrast to what is immanent or, as we say also, something transcendent in relation to it.

In this connection a particular concept of the transcendent has to be distinguished. For, every object in the broadest sense of the word, therefore also everything purely subjective, is an object of possible multiple consciousness of it. Therefore, there is also multiple consciousness which in the really immanent nexus, in that of subjective time, can make present to consciousness one and the same purely subjective moment, e.g., several recollections of one prior, subjective lived experience. Then this subjective moment is transcendent in relation to the multiple and synthetically united consciousness of it. Therefore in this relative way of speaking immanence and transcendence do not exclude each other; but however important this relative concept is, we come finally and manifestly to an absolute distinc- ‹176› tion which the realm of temporal-spatial objectivity illustrates for us.

Whatever is itself in principle only perceivable, therefore can only be given in its selfhood, as a unity of appearance of the subjective, whereas a priori it can not itself appear in the immanent sphere as a lived experience, that is absolutely transcendent in the proper sense.

Nevertheless, we should note that even this "absolutely transcendent" remains in the sphere which we have opened up for ourselves as that of pure subjectivity in contrast to nature and natural-scientific investigation. The subjective in the sense of the stream of lived experiences is a concept determined in relation to the objective as absolutely transcendent, which in principle is not in the stream of lived experiences as something real; but both, stream of lived experiences or immanence and what is *unqualifiedly transcendent*, are non-natural concepts, belonging to the science of what is purely mental, as long as we grasp the transcendent purely as that which is present in consciousness and is itself inseparable from it. To that extent we can also say: all the concepts recently formed by us, "immanent" and "transcendent," "adequate" and "inadequate perception," can also be determined in a different sense, just like the concepts "subjective" and "objective." All that we now established is to be called "subjective" in this new sense, all "adequately perceived," all "immanent." For, insofar as the object of perception as perceived cannot be separated from it, even though it is not a real moment of the perceiving, it is subjective. Likewise the word "immanence" fits the object of perception, only in a correspondingly new sense.

What we recently called "transcendent" was called that as an irreal moment in the subjective sphere of the stream of lived experience; it transcends the real sphere of lived experiences. On the other hand, it was not without reason that the scholastics who became attentive to the fact that the object itself is present in the conscious lived experience, therefore that it itself as something present to consciousness belongs to it, called this object of consciousness as such an immanent object (though without deeper fundamental insight). The justification for this manner of designation is of course the same as the justification for designating it as "subjective." If I restrict myself purely to the stream of consciousness, then I find that which ‹177› is present to consciousness in it, even though as an inseparable ideal pole.

But we can even speak of adequate givenness of what is transcendent in relation to the real lived experience. For, if we restrict ourselves to each phase of the appearing on its own and if we describe what appears purely as what appears in this phase, then the description is adequate. If we describe by so to speak swimming along from phase to phase and describe what appears in an entire stretch of appearance as it continually appears little by little, then of course the description is adequate. The fact that it [the appearing object] appears as enduring identical substrate of the features which come to the fore perceptually and again vanish perceptually and that at every place it means beyond itself, in anticipation so to speak, a fuller object, belongs manifestly to the adequately graspable content. The description will be inadequate in this new sense if we go beyond that. Thus the object itself is given in every appearance and every stretch of appearance, but given inadequately insofar as in every such stretch it is more, is meant as being more than what is properly perceived of it.

But now two things are to be distinguished:

1) The perceived object purely and simply and its description as this object purely and simply; that is what I as perceiver experience as actual and bodily.

2) The perceived purely as correlate of the perceiving, namely, as what the perceiving as this determinate real lived experience includes inseparably as its ideal moment, as what appears to it and is meant, and as is again emphasized, just as it is meant in this perceiving. If in perceiving, one ideal and continually identical thing is meant and if in every phase the same thing is meant in anticipation with features which are not yet properly seen and still to be seen, with a "horizon" of what is unknown – then the horizon itself, the anticipating with a sense of anticipation belongs also in the adequate sphere. But it is surpassed if we wanted to determine as object and treat as something actually given what is meant in a stretch of perception only by anticipation.

⟨178⟩   But since the spatial object itself is not what the perceiving actually has of it, what of it actually appears, but as spatial object is without fail more, then the spatial object itself is never given adequately and it itself never is as a mere correlate of the momentary perception. It is itself transcendent to the perception in yet another sense than in that of the polar irreality; rather, in the sense of what is given perceptually, and that implies grasped bodily in a belief which – however harmoniously the perception would continue and the belief would be confirmed in this harmony – can never be completed by a synthetically expanded perception, which yields the object adequately as completely given in all that it is and with no further anticipation which would count on possible new perception and corresponding confirmation.

⟨*⟩   In the last lecture we brought out a distinction fundamental for the intentional lived experiences which confront us in our perceptual sphere as appearances of what is objective. If we remain in the attitude of reflection and restrict ourselves purely to the lived experiences in their on-flowing individual being, then each has its real parts and moments. What a lived experience really contains is individually fixed by the temporal locus, its position in this subjective stream, and can in no way belong identically to other lived experiences. And likewise two different phases of one lived experience can not have any real moment in common, in numerical identity.

But on the other hand multiple lived experiences as appearances of one and the same object have something identical precisely in what appears in them, and this commonness is something which can be noted in them themselves, is something inseparable from them. The perceived object does not enter somehow from outside into a relation to the perceptual appearances by being brought in from outside and placed into a relation to the appearances. The continuity of perspectives runs off: that itself means or implies that the respective thing appears continually, stands there, and as the case may be, with just such and such features of the thing. Therefore, we say justifiably: *in* all these appearances something appears and one and the ⟨179⟩ same particular feature appears, or appears throughout a certain stretch, but this *in* expresses no real parts, for really separated lived experiences can have nothing really in common.

All that appears and comes to be present to consciousness in the fluctuation of streaming modes of appearances, in the fluctuation of intentional lived experiences therefore belongs inseparably to these lived experiences as something irreal or as we can also say with good reasons, something ideal.

The object transcends the real content of the stream of lived experiences; only its real moments are "immanent" to it.

Yet this concept of the transcendent, of the object present to consciousness in its immanence still includes several great difficulties, even scintillating multisignifications, and demands further consideration. These will also serve to give you an idea of the marvelous implications, hidden from all traditional *psychology* as well as theory of knowledge, which are concealed in intentional lived experiences, even in a relatively simple structure such as an external perception is. Without the unraveling and exact description of these implications there is no serious psychology and no serious theory of experience and reason.

Let us resume our discussion of the ideal containment of the object in the real. It is not at all the case that this ideal moment persists as a fixed common segment through all the intentional lived experiences which it inhabits ideally and all of whose phases it inhabits, only not common to them as a real segment. Certainly, in the flow of the adumbrating perspectives this one and the same and even objectively fixed, unchanged table appears; but while it appears as something identical, it appears nevertheless with ever new features, in ever new sides. What appears constantly in the unity

of every momentary phase of perception is what we call the especially
appearing side of the table. But considered more precisely, it is not this
mere side of the table that appears in every phase; it is rather the perceived
table *as* especially seen from this side.

Also in the entire continuity of adumbrating appearances, the series of
‹180› the especially perceived sides of the table is not the ideal object; rather, in
the entire continuity the table itself, which is presented "especially" now
from this side, now from that, is the ideal object which inhabits the real
continuity of adumbrations, and that means here: the object of perception
is constructed, as we note, in its flow of lived experiences and yet not by
way of being pieced together, as the image of construction suggests. And
let us add immediately: in accord with this being constructed it has its ideal
construction, an ideal structure which expands progressively during the
constructing.

35. SUBSTRATE-POLE AND PROPERTY-POLE. THE POSITIVE SIGNIFICANCE OF THE EMPTY HORIZON.

If we pay attention not to the way it is internally constructed but precisely
to the building, the object itself, it is characterized as something identical
which appears from the start and in the entire progress of the perceptual
continuity, but as the identical thing which is determined in ever new features. Therefore, it is an ideal pole which has the character of the substrate
for the determining features, which successively come to appear in a special
way. This ideal substrate-pole is nothing without the varying determining
moment; therefore it is a non-self-sufficient pole of ideality. On the other
hand, every feature which comes to appear is itself an ideal pole, something
which appears identically in adumbrating perspectives belonging to it; e.g.,
the identical "brown surface of the table," which enters into the perceiving
and is ideally given as the same amid the alteration of perspectives until it
becomes invisible. These objective properties for their part are again non-
self-sufficient; they are what they are only as properties of the substrate-
pole. They are possible only as a determining pole.

But if we look still more closely, the perceived table, just as perceived
in this perception in the continuity of its adumbrations, as grasped as
bodily existing, is at every spot in this flow of lived experiences more
than has been described here. It is not the mere substrate-pole with the
feature-poles which are especially in view just then. Otherwise we would
have had to say that in every phase a changed object were perceived,
whereas we say in fact, as we experience: the same unchanged table stands
‹181› there. Accordingly we also do *not* say that the table gains properties and
loses them as they become especially visible or invisible. The respective

property becomes originally apprehended and cognized by becoming visible, but in becoming invisible it remains as acquired knowledge, *remains* in the determining grasp as still *proper* to the substrate-pole. *On the other hand,* not only does what has become invisible remain in our grasp and continue to determine the substrate, but at every place the appearing of the object *anticipates in advance*; the object is so to speak an object determined in advance before it has actually been determined by a special perception. It has an empty horizon of yet unknown features – which can only be brought into view by future courses of appearances or such as might possibly be put into play. This *empty horizon* is not nothing, but a character of the substrate-pole, an emptiness consciously present in it, and one which belongs especially just to it as substrate-pole of this perception. The progressing perception brings the fullness which fits into it, although necessarily an imperfect, incomplete fullness; for, even after the new determining features become visible the situation is the same: the empty horizon is always still there, except that a partial emptiness has been filled. What can fill here is not optional. Every object of different perceptions has its own empty horizon according to the perceptual sense which precisely its perception, its continuity of appearance bestows on it. What determines this table can not determine a horse. The particular perceptions which fill the empty horizon which the table has for me in a perception, can not be inserted in the seeing of the horse and further determine this horse. –

In addition, the respective horizon is indeed a character to be found in the substrate, as it is subjectively a momentary pole of perception, but of course it is *not* given as determining it objectively, as a feature. More precisely designated, it is an empty horizon *of* features still missing from knowledge.

Accordingly, when our regard is directed toward the substrate, we continually have a subjective movement in perception: continually the identical substrate as a central pole enduring continually, but continually ‹182› a movement in the content of the determining property poles, continually an empty horizon which does not persist fixedly but is changeable, shaping itself anew in the new phases as a framework within which the determinations are restricted, and to which they give fullness. This horizon is, as we also note, an indeterminately universal anticipation at the substrate, at the abiding center for the features which determine it at any time, a total intention pointing ahead toward newly determining or possibly newly determining features; an anticipation which is fulfilled and confirmed by their appearing. From the outset every visible feature is a fulfillment; e.g., the substrate as table is from the outset an intention aimed at a system of features fulfilling-determining just this object, and every given feature, while it determines, also fulfils.

In the continuity of this movement to be pursued on the ideal side, one line in the indefinite universal system of horizonal intentions is actualized in a distinctive way, namely, in the form of those actual anticipations toward the future which we call expectations and subsequently fulfillment of expectations. Whatever becomes known in special perceiving, for instance, as to shape and color, allows the subsequent moment of color and shape in this movement to be expected in varying degrees of determinacy; and what actually occurs fulfills these expectations.

This consideration was nothing other than a deeper clarification of the subjective process of the givenness of sides, in which the respective object of perception in its objective sense is constructed as existing.

Above all, in confirmation of what we had recently said in anticipation, it instructs us that the object with its objective properties is not simply something which, even as an irreal segment, is found in the process of subjective lived experiences as something thoroughly identical. The object as object of perception is not conceivable at all except as in this changeable structural context which belongs inseparably to the stream of lived experiences of perspectives; even this movement is a streaming whose temporality plainly coincides precisely with that of the lived experiences of perspectives phase by phase. But the streaming does not belong to the object itself.

‹183› In the streaming on, it is the one uninterruptedly persisting identical substrate-pole as substrate of the features, of those which surround it in anticipatory and empty fashion, as well as of those which so to speak come to the light of day in the movement, the fulfilling ones. The positing with a horizon of anticipation which can never be eliminated from the object of perception gives the concept of its trancendence a particular sense and justifies designating the object as an idea.

How is it to be understood that a perception apprehends its object as bodily existing and yet transcends it by reaching beyond it?

36. THE INTENTIONAL OBJECT OF PERCEPTION.

The external object is meant in perception as existing and bodily apprehended but not in the mode of a finished datum of perception, not even one which inhabits perception ideally. It is meant from the start and continually with a transcendent sense, with an open horizon of sense. That implies: it is not only meant as substrate for such and such perceptually actualized determinations but also meant as existing substrate for determinations yet to be actualized *in infinitum*. The transcendent object of perception is not conceivable without this horizon of what is co-meant.

We can perhaps also say that whatever is present to consciousness in transcendent perception as an object existing bodily, is as present to consciousness itself a meaning with a sense which is partially actualized but which also includes in anticipation a certainty of anticipation that further actualizations stand open *in infinitum* for the unactualized aspects of the sense. A meaning can ideally contain an infinity of meanings, or a sense, infinities of sense; infinities which are unseen, unactualized, unknown, at first quite empty, undifferentiated. They are infinities of sense which the respective meaning in the actuality of its lived experience encompasses, implies in itself ideally in the mode of disclosable predelineation, but as possible closer determinations in possible single meanings which only ever new processes of the determining-actualizing consciousness actually bring out.

In every phase of actual perception not only are the future actualizations ‹184› actually predesignated but the predesignation is a system of multiple signification of such a sort that the perception itself admits of being questioned and the open possibilities admit of being unfolded. Everything which comes to be brought out thus is evidently recognizable as an explication of the meaning originally present to consciousness. The intentional object of external perception as the first form of something which exists as intentional object shows us also for the first time how an object of intentionality, and even of a perceiving intentionality, is nothing else but meaning, meant sense, and how meaning includes in itself new meanings, even infinities of meanings belonging together as possibilities, and yet does not contain them really as segments. Belief aims at really possible actualization, it posits in indeterminate universality, e.g., that one of the infinite possibilities must result. The object of perception gains its sense of existence by the sense-bestowal which takes place in the series of appearances, in their motivations; that is intentionality as sense-bestowal. But meant sense is as such itself an intention in a correlative sense of ontic "meaning," partially fulfilled, partially transcending meaning, reaching beyond the fullness. This intentionality is the correlate of sense-bestowal. The object of perception as a meaning meant in perception therefore allows two moments to be distinguished: the object is meant in perception as *existing there*. Perceptual certainty, precisely as the unqualified consciousness of this existent, can pass over into dubiousness, can be "modalised" and, e.g., even pass over to the character of illusion, of nullity, while remaining still intuitively given.

That makes the distinction evident between the merely objective sense of perception as the object, in abstraction from the character of existing "actually there," which can pass over into dubiously existing or not existing, etc.

But in this connection the objective sense is not the object as mere substrate-pole, but this pole as substrate of the determinations attributed to it, as they comprise its known and unknown presumptive *what* of properties.

This is therefore the changing sense-content for the character of the exist-
⟨185⟩ ent and for the changing modes of existence. It belongs to the objective
sense in its entire sense-content or *what*-content; therefore, it does not belong only to the momentarily actualized property-determinations of the
substrate-pole nor to this pole as being determined in them. For these
actualizations actualize in the mode of an installment payment the total
objective sense or the co-comprehended property-essence of the object,
co-meant in the horizon of anticipation, though yet unknown.

It can be made evident that the infinity which the meaning of the being
of this table: "perceived spatial object" includes, is subordinate, by means
of this unity of objective sense, to a stable system, a stable all-inclusive
regularity for all the possible perceptions which could synthetically connect with the given perception in the pervasive consciousness of one and the
same object being determined harmoniously in them all.

Now we understand at least roughly – for greater problems are opened
up by our discoveries – wherein the transcendence of the object of perception consists, and from this point of departure, how the strict concept of
"transcendence" as opposed to "immanence" has to be understood. A
hyletic datum, for instance, a datum of the visual field, taken not as adumbration of something objective but purely in its own existence is an object
of perception in every reflection which picks it out and grasps it itself
originaliter. Even this reflective perception has its perceptual sense in its
object (in the respective visual datum), has a sense-content which is given
as certainly existing. We named such objects immanent; we said their
givenness is an adequate one, and we said also that they are real constituents in the immanent time in which they flow on.

Adequate givenness consists in this, that in every phase of perception its
sense – and in the total perception of the visual datum, its sense – is fully
actualized. The immanent stream of perception really includes the datum
as what is continually perceived in it. Here there is anticipation only as
anticipating expectation which however is itself adequately fulfilled.

⟨186⟩   On the other side: the transcendent object is characterized by this, that
it is essentially only perceivable with an objective sense which can be only
imperfectly actualized, insofar as its objective sense always and necessarily
reaches out beyond the perceiving actualization and yet is certain in anticipation as actuality-sense, certain as progressively to be actualized in
endless processes of possible perception. In just this way a concept of
"idea" has also been clarified, implied in the now intelligible contrast: the
immanent or adequate objectivity is a really immanent givenness in its perception and *is* only if its perception is. The transcendent givenness is an
idea which is originally actualized as actuality only in a transcendent perception, though necessarily one-sidedly and in anticipation, but in such a

way that it is not restricted to this perception. An infinity of actual or possible perceptions is ready, of which any selected one would also bring it to givenness. Indeed, if outside this circle of its perceptions, subjective conditions were fulfilled which could guarantee the production of such perceptions, then the transcendent object as idea would still be an actuality and would hold as existing even if no perception at all were actualized. Thus every object of the type spatial thing is in itself vis-a-vis all perception of it and as is evident, vis-a-vis every other consciousness of it. First in this sense that the Feldberg, e.g., even if no perception out of its system of perceptions actualizes it, is nevertheless accessible by other perceptions of other things and in such a way that paths of experience from their objects to it and its perceptions are predesignated in producing a subjective guarantee. My present perception and its object have a further horizon of experience which would lead to it in possible perceptions and, literally speaking, on familiar paths.

The impossibility of apodictic certainty of existence, the constant possibility of the transcendently perceived object's not existing or of not being such and such, is very closely connected with these properties of transcendent objects. However, in every adequate perception the perceived ‹ 187 › object is apodictically certain.

37. THE PHENOMENOLOGICAL REDUCTION AS A METHOD OF DISCLOSING THE IMMANENT.

Before we speak about the great problems which are opened up concerning ‹ * › the transcendence of external perception, a fundamental difference of attitudes, previously only fleetingly indicated, must be discussed in detail; by this difference of attitudes, we gain in each case where transcendent objectivity is perceived, the total stock of the immanent and thus purely subjective elements belonging to this perception. To use the term for the first time, we can exercise *phenomenological reduction* on every perception belonging here, therefore on every external, transcendent perception, precisely as a methodical operation of reduction to the purely immanent, to pure subjectivity. We are describing a method, therefore an activity carried out by us as active I-subjects, and what it produces; therefore, we have recourse to the active I. However, we must also pay attention correlatively to what stands out in the result itself.

To have a perceived object unqualifiedly is to have it just as existing; and this "possession" is, to speak from the point of view of the I, to carry out the consciousness of perceptual acceptance of being, to live in perceiving certainty. As a rule, it stays that way, as already said. In the transition to reflection, which is then natural reflection – therefore, in this natural attitude, this mode of carrying on perception – we transcend the perception itself; our existential certainty affects also the object which is irreal vis-a-vis the perception, and the infinities which we would realize only in infinite new perceivings.

If we perform a reflection upon the modes of givenness of the object, upon the streaming subjective appearances and then even upon the actively participating, perceiving I, as it directs its attending and explicating acts toward the appearing object, etc. – all that yields reflective perceptions which direct themselves to the components of the given external percep-
188 › tions, but go beyond them by the continual positing of the transcendent object. We as phenomenologists, i.e., directed purely toward the subjective, the immanent components, inhibit every perceptual positing of the object and of any sort of transcendent object at all; we take as our reflective perceptual theme purely the *perception* of what is objective; that is, only the perception of this external perception and of all the immanent components that it includes is the medium of the acceptation which we practice; or, we posit in acceptance only what offers itself in this medium.

The understanding of all of phenomenology depends upon the understanding of this method; we acquire phenomena in the sense of phenomenology only by it. And that is true whether (as I recently distinguish) we have aimed at a philosophically transcendental phenomenology, or, as here, at a psychological phenomenology which should deliver us the purely self-contained realm of psychic phenomena in their concrete total unity. The inhibition, indeed the putting-out-of-acceptance, of the spatial material perceptual object, of any transcendent object at all, does not mean to take it as unacceptable, or to doubt it, or to alter its certainty in any other way. That is not at all within our liberty. Where motives of questionableness, of dubiousness, etc., are not effective, where we lack "grounds" of doubt, there we can be conscious of nothing but the perceived object as certainly existing; at the most, we can imagine ourselves in a situation of doubting and the like, in which case we also think of motives for it, which we fancy along with the doubting; we can then also add hypothetically the dubiously-existing, not-existing, and the like. But none of that is to be meant.

We are concerned with something else, which also stands at the bidding of our discretion: simply perceiving, noticing, considering more closely, we are interested in the object perceived, thus appearing as certainly existing and being-thus – interested in its existence and being-thus, therefore, in becoming acquainted with it, the existent, in acquiring determinatively the properties which accrue to it existentially, in appropriating them habit-
‹189› ually as an abiding possession. Thus is the world our experiential theme in the natural attitude of perception.

We can also say instead, according to our analyses of external perception: to be experientially interested in the objective world is to be directed in aspiration toward this world which is perpetually posited in perceptual belief and presupposed as idea; presupposed, namely, as a goal for belief to be actualized in systematic processes of possible perceptive actualization. Being interested, therefore, is in practice an aspiring toward and eventually actively being directed toward factual actualization of what is believed, in progressing experience which is accordingly goal-directed. We can deliberately alter this attitude of naturally interested external perception and experience.

Then the perception can run off, the continuities of appearance can flow on harmoniously, with all that is intentionally united in them, without our being interested in the existing object and its being-thus (and if the perception has flown away, no such interest needs to be continually effective in the form of still retaining in one's grasp what was once thematically apprehended – whereby it continues to be an existential theme). This change of interests, this *not* having as theme or abandoning from the thematic domain, putting out of reckoning, is an essential change of the way in which the object-consciousness, the perception, is executed, and in particular of the way in which its belief is executed, the way in which its object is taken by us. The radical change of interest of the phenomenological reduction makes the proper existence of perception with all which is really and ideally inseparable from it the unique theme, or by expansion, the unique theme of subjectivity. The radicalism of the phenomenological reduction consists in this, that every interest in objective existence is consistently thwarted. If perception in itself makes us conscious of its object as substratum for actualized and still unactualized determinations, conscious of it as an existent in a transcendent sense, then this making-conscious of what is transcendent is a property belonging to it itself, belonging to its own essence: therefore, this property is thematic in the orientation of interest toward perception in its subjective, own essential being. But one must ‹190› note carefully that two kinds of thematic spheres of objects or domains of confirmations are sharply distinguished from each other by the radicalism of the phenomenological reduction. Thus, presented in more detail and in reverse order:

1) In the one attitude we live exclusively in the interest for the subjective, for external perception as lived experience and for its contents which are inseparable from it itself, inhabiting it really or ideally. The external object belongs there, but purely as that which is meant in the external perception itself, as its transcendent meaning. In phenomenology we say: the object in parentheses or quotation marks, not the object unqualifiedly.

Here then, thematic confirmations result exclusively about the subjective, and if the subjective includes transcendent intentionality as its meaning, then that too, and the analysis of this meaning as such is part of the theme. To live in the interest for the purely subjective is to live by meaning and aspiration in reflective consciousness and ultimately in reflective perception, in which the subjective is actualized subjectively in its existence and being-thus. How does the phenomenological reduction provide for this exclusiveness? Because, guided by the explicit demand for this exclusiveness, it arbitrarily thwarts the interest in objective existence, arbitrarily forbids the natural mode of executing experience and of every consciousness which presuposes experience. To speak figuratively: every experience, with its existential object, is put in parentheses.

2) In the other attitude, which is earlier in natural life and which also in itself must necessarily precede, the interest goes toward the objectively existent. That is, we live in the belief in objectivity: as quite customarily and continually, wherever an objective world is quite obviously there for us in advance. To live in this belief or to be "interested" in the world which exists certainly for us in it is to be directed, in aspiration and activity, through progressing perceptions, toward the doxic actualization of the objective, of that which in doxa is perpetually accepted in advance. Precisely this striving directedness is forbidden in phenomenology.

⟨191⟩ Whereas external perception and its existential belief are actually executed here and are the medium for actualizing the aspiration directed toward the goal of belief, in the opposite phenomenological attitude, reflective perception is actually executed, the immanent perception, e.g., of external perception.

The natural attitude or direction of interests opens the way for every objective knowledge, every objective science, as well as every objective praxis operating upon the world. In the directedness toward confirmations about the objective world, the modalisations of existential belief which transform its certainty to doubt, to mere conjecture, to negation, appear as restraints. That leads to the necessity of secondary confirmations of possibility or impossibility, of likelihood or probability, of non-existence and of what truly is in its place: but always in relation to the objective world. In the phenomenological attitude, which is kept pure of all interest in what pertains to the objective world, all such confirmations, just because they are objectively directed, are abolished.

It opens the way to a quite different science, to the science of *pure subjectivity*, in which thematic discourse concerns exclusively the lived experiences, the modes of consciousness and what is meant in their objectivity, but exclusively *as* meant. This is an important point which should be considered again and again: *that* a perception perceives something transcendent and that it posits its object existentially in its certainty of belief and posits it with a transcendent sense of such and such a structure. This is a type of truths which, understood in phenomenological purity, includes not the least opinion concerning the unqualifiedly transcendent world, the existent world.

In this regard it should also be noted that every process of making determinations on the basis of natural experience, e.g., of explanation based on objective considerations, but also conceptual grasping, describing, theorizing, as every other performance of consciousness which is carried out in the natural attitude, can afterwards undergo that reductive methodic transformation into the purely subjective, into the phenomenological. Instead of placing myself further upon the ground of the world and universally ⟨192⟩ upon the ground of objects and worlds of objects which I have naïvely acquired, grasped, and accepted, or instead of *remaining* on this ground I can subsequently set out of play the execution of the experiential certainty *in* which and *by* which I have this ground. Therefore I subsequently alter my thematic interest and now look at this entire subjective process. I make this *exclusively* my theme: only the reflective experience which has it as existing is to be accepted. Only this pure reflection is to give me the ground upon which I stand sure and think, the ground of pure subjectivity. Here I find the stream of pure lived experiences with their real and ideal contents. Now I consider more closely what they produce in themselves by way of experiencing, thinking, or any other way, how they construct their meanings, how they actualize them, how they anticipate new meaning.

38. THE ACCESS TO PURE SUBJECTIVITY FROM EXTERNAL PERCEPTION.

You recognize now that all our pure descriptions of the last series of lectures were carried out in the phenomenological reduction – except that we did not make that scientifically clear. For we spoke always about the subjective and about how the subjective makes something objective present to consciousness in forms of intentionality; previously we excluded nature in the strict sense, but also in the broader sense of the objective world and the pertinent sciences of the world; having turned purely within, therefore purely reflectively, we wanted first to establish nothing else but what we could see in perception itself, really and intentionally. But only the conscious execution of the reduction and clarity concerning its sense makes science possible here. Only in that way do we protect ourselves from the natural relapse into the natural attitude and the confounding of the correlative directions of judgment.

All that we have thus far learned about pure subjectivity we have learned ⟨*⟩ as pertaining to external perception, and thus also the conscious exercise of

the phenomenological reduction which alone makes science possible here.
‹193› External perception was, as it were, a first and immediately graspable peak
of pure subjectivity, and beginning with it we were to work on to all of
subjectivity, to its in fact infinite multiplicity of single types and of structural connections. How much there was to see and to describe phenomenologically already on this one peak, this one type of purely subjective givens,
how one must first learn to see here, how completely foreign this world of
pure internalities is to us who are always naturally oriented – that you will
have felt keenly. Surely you have also felt the extraordinary difficulty of
even following phenomenological descriptions and of finding one's way in
the fullness of accumulating distinctions.

You could not be spared the efforts, and no one can. Whoever wants pure
psychology as a science of the disclosure of pure internality must first learn
that in the attitude of externality the internalities are hidden and that it
requires a fully new attitude, a totally altered species of perception and
thought in order by infinite efforts to disclose for the seeing eye of the mind,
the "mothers" of all knowledge, the "mothers" of all appearing objectivity.
For the seeing eye: because we are not here to set up speculations concerning the "inner essence of the psyche" and to think up "metaphysical"
substructions, but to bring about a psychology as experiential science. But
also necessarily a psychology as eidetic science based on intuitive sources.

But experience traces back ultimately to perception, to a seeing and
grasping of something itself; and all other intuition, as it grounds the
original procuring of eidetic insights, is a merely modal variation of perception. Psychology is the mind's self-knowledge first in the form of phenomenologically purified originary self-seeing of its own hidden self-being
and self-living and then in the form of the rigorous science grounded upon
this experience. All difficulties in coming to a true psychology, to such
genuine and pure self-knowledge, rest upon the proper essence of the mind:
to bring about objectivating producings in its subjective life, in its
‹194› subjective passive courses of mental occurrences and its active doings, and
at first to experience itself for itself only naïvely as objectified mind in an
objective world; a world which pure mind as objectifying has created in
itself cognitively as idea and as life-theme. But only the phenomenological
reduction and the pure psychology made possible by it discloses purely
objectifying subjectivity. Of course it was infinitely toilsome historically
to work through from the first presentiments of this hidden subjectivity,
constituting all objectivity for itself consciously, to a method which
could be consistently pursued, in which this subjectivity could come to
disclosure. For it is everywhere thus, that in subjective producing only the
objective product, in subjective doing as internal activity only the objective
process of activity is visible; and it requires first an artificial method of

pure reflection even to see the pure internalities. And when one finally sees them, they are something completely foreign. For the eye is trained only for what is objective. Only what is objective in its empirical types and the typology of its structure of objective properties is well known from the training of our entire perceptual life. A similar training for the internality disclosed by the phenomenological reduction must first be acquired; a familiar internality, so to speak, an empirically typified internal world must first be created by this training. Now that you have become acquainted with the species of internal givens and their analysis, the species of real analysis and of intentional explication and unfolding of sense in our portion of the analysis of perception (despite strong inner resistances), you must not think that this portion is a finished one even for the sphere of perception alone, or that the distinctions which appeared to you often as excessively fine were actually particularly fine at all, actually penetrating into the profoundest depths. – What we were able to deal with concerned first and in truth still quite rough exhibitions and merely one-sided moments out of an exceedingly fine total texture, difficult to apprehend. As little as we are able even to think of actually carrying through the supplementary analyses, even for external perception alone, nevertheless the beginning and the preliminary exercise suffices to place in your sphere of vision the opposite sides and the corresponding tasks. Going on in this way I plan to lead you so far ‹195› that you can see the all-inclusive nexus of pure subjectivity as a realm of its own, as a self-contained world, and as the field of tasks for a pure psychology.

Let us therefore stick with external perception and pay attention to this, that we keep our regard turned exclusively toward the series of appearances processing in perception and the intermingling of appearances and what appears and of the objective meaning included in them. We had not heeded and therefore had not drawn more closely into our discussion those possible alterations of style which such processes of appearances can assume, whenever perception ceases to be perception in the strict sense, continuing harmoniously in the mode of progressing existential certainty, nor those modalisations of certainty itself into doubt, negation – thus of perceptual existence into doubtful being, presumptive being, not being, etc. Here the hybrid overlappings and reciprocal transformations of appearances in the conflict of different apprehensions, and similar occurrences, come into question. Also the forms of determining more closely a feature already actualized within the scope of a harmonious perception and the constantly open possibility for such closer determinations and eventually different determinations, must be described precisely; e.g., the seen coloring of this thing is determined ever more precisely in drawing closer, the uniform coloring is not actually uniform, it need not be, it can turn out to be a spotted coloring, the spots can gain ever new shapes in coming closer, etc. In short, in contrast to the external horizons of perception every such feature already given as fulfilling has its internal horizons.

But still much more is lacking. We immersed ourselves in the single perceptions and their perceived object and also in the external horizon which the perceived object has as a surrounding circle of the unknown perceptual properties, but not in the further external horizon in the sense of the surrounding world of things. Thus we did not investigate and did not even become attentive to the causal relations and to what, in the multiplicity ‹196› of perceptions entering into synthetic connection with one another, grounds the distinction between merely sensuous phantoms and spatial objects experienced as realities, therefore, what bestows upon the object-pole its sense-determination as real substrate of causal properties. We had hit upon that as well as upon much else in the universal preliminary considerations concerning nature and natural science, therefore for quite other purposes. But now it must become a theme of "constitutive" analyses in the purely subjective attitude; it must be made intelligible what levels of the intentionality of the appearances of a real thing in its relation to the appearances of other things co-comprehended by way of horizon, as possible environment, are responsible for the sense-bestowal of reality and causality.

39. ANALYSIS OF PERCEPTION WITH REGARD TO THE PERCEIVER HIMSELF.

But now it is necessary to bring to light a colossal and, I might also say, monstrous, *one-sidedness* of all these considerations. What we studied were perceptions in a determined precise sense, namely as the processes of the appearances of what is objective and, eventually in supplementary remarks, in its relation to other objective elements. To have perceptions means then: to have appearances and what appears by them and what is perceptively meant. But we have perceptions not as if they had fallen down from heaven; we have them by perceiving; and this perceiving, whether it is in the form of a doing, set into work voluntarily by the I, or whether it happens involuntarily, has its own properties which admit of being studied in their function which is necessary for the having of appearances of a thing. There is no empty having of appearances. Here what matters is to perceive the appearing of the thing *visually* in seeing, *tactually* in touching, etc., and only thus do we have these or those appearances. Here, in the exemplary fact, we hit upon necessities which immediately refer us to essential necessities.

‹197›   Therefore, our body as unity of perceptual organs now enters the

thematic consideration, for the intentional internal analysis of our perception. The study of the intentionality in which things come to perceptual
givenness is not to be carried through without a study of the corresponding
intentionality of one's own body in its perceiving function. But my body
is given to me as a thing – are we not then moving in a circle? But we know
already from our pre-psychological reflections that the body is at once
a thing, and at the same time a function and a specific body – now we are
concerned with a responsible scientific development of the intentionalities
mutually related to one another. Thus, there would be needed a novel intentional analysis, namely the sort in which the kinesthetic systems of hand
movements, head movements, movements of walking, etc., are constituted
intentionally and are joined together in the unity of one total system. Of
course, the exact clarification of the peculiarity of kinesthetic processes as
the subjective "I move" belongs here, the clarification of the two-sidedness
of every bodily organ with regard to its movement as objective spatial
movement and as kinesthetic, and finally, of course, the universal intentional clarification of the total uniqueness of the body, which is simultaneously a spatial externality and a subjective internality, simultaneosly a
spatial thing, a bodily mass, and at the same time an internal body, an
organ, a habitual system of subjective functions, always ready to pass over
into actual subjective functioning. In this way, a vast dimension of analyses
is drawn into the thematic area of subjective research, one which becomes
intertwined with the intentional analysis of the sphere of external perception in the previous sense, and which enriches its results with essentially
new results, which are quite indispensable for a phenomenology of the
givenness of the spatial world.

With the *body*, experienced as belonging to the objective world, a new
species of objective causality also enters the phenomenologically constitutive investigation. Beyond the fact that the body is experienced as exercising perceptual functions in all external experience, it is also experienced as
pushing and shoving, etc., in the spatial world, as interfering in the course
of nature by objectively altering it. It is practically an organ in a particular sense and also the organ of the I as ruler of the body, as one who acts ⟨198⟩
voluntarily as well as thinks voluntarily, etc.: but the *I-aspect* which we hit
upon again and again can at first remain in the background. –

It should be noted that even after the introduction of this great theme,
the body (and body in relation to itself, in relation to the thing-world, in
relation to its perceptual there and its existing in somatic causality), the
entire investigation takes place in the method of phenomenological reduction as an investigation of pure subjectivity. The reduction is formed quite
analogously with the way in which it is in the investigation of external
perceptions in the strict sense of perceptions of spatial things purely as

such. The body is that too, but still more. If the body becomes a theme of physiology, then it is taken simply as an existentially posited natural object. The physiologist stands upon the ground of the experience of nature. In phenomenology the perceiving, the experiencing of the body is the theme, and the body itself purely as experienced therein, as perceptive meaning.

What is new here is that this perception, although it also has the form of a perception of a spatial-thing, offers something completely novel and thereby a novel type of perception, as correlatively the transcendently meant and posited object which is called body, is something novel in its fundamental essence. How does that intentionality appear phenomenologically as to the aspects of specific perceptions of body, the intentionality in which "the body" as perceived comes to harmonious self-givenness; and how do the subjective modes of the perceived body as such appear, purely in reflective perception, thus in the field of the purely subjective? In no moment is the body as objective actuality claimed or theroretically treated as existing. Thus throughout.

In this expanded sphere of research, the distinctions of normalcy and abnormality pertaining to the essence of the experienceable body as such become very significant. Already in the doctrine of the peculiarity of kinesthesia the distinction between *unrestrained* and, in this sense, free, and *restrained process* of kinesthesia confronts us. Already restraint acquires significance as something like abnormality. Added to these, we have the ⟨199⟩ experiences of those well-known yet very marvelous alterations of the entire perceptual world which we call maladies, abnormal alterations of the perceptual organs; the manner in which all visual appearances can be altered for me if my eyes are altered, etc. There one soon becomes aware of this: that what we normally experience simply as the world signifies a world-sense which depends upon the presupposition of a normal body in its normal functioning. This presupposition is not formulated; but, as little as we, directed in perception toward things, think about our perceptual organs which are necessarily co-functioning in it, just as little do we remember that they sometimes become abnormal – although we do know of this from experience. But once such experiences have been made, the world-sense constituted in the normal functioning of the body, which until then was simply "existing world," receives a new layer of sense; now, the world is no longer the normally experienced world, but the normally experienced world in its relation to the normal body lines up with multiple abnormally appearing worlds, related to the bodily modifications of normalcy. But all these worlds, as different as they might appear, are from now on each a "different appearance" of *the same* world appearing differently precisely " in each case according to the disposition of the body." This is clearly the way to physical nature in its ultimate form of sense, as the natural scientist attempts to determine it in thought, that nature which is not itself sensuous, therefore free of all sensuous features, but which has its "modes of appearance"in the sensuous features and in the full sense-worlds of normal intuitions. In that way, a new concept of appearance springs up, as well as a new concept of objectivity.

By the phenomenology of the body in its interwining with the phenomenology of physical things, including here the phenomenology of organisms considered biophysically, fundamental segments of a phenomenology of nature are produced, that is, of the phenomenological clarification of subjectivity as constituting nature in itself experientially, namely as experiential sense and experiential tenet, or as a system of free accessibility – but only fundamental segments.

40. THE PROBLEM OF TEMPORALITY: PRESENTING – RETENTION AND   ‹ 200 ›
PROTENTION (POSITIONAL AND QUASI-POSITIONAL MODIFICATIONS OF
PERCEPTION AND THEIR SIGNIFICANCE FOR PRACTICAL LIFE).

Many large themes open up, as soon as one fixes in view even perception alone as directed merely toward spatial objects. To study external perception phenomenologically in its real and ideal components means to be led immediately beyond mere external perception. That happens to one – and happened to us ourselves – as soon as one reverts to reflection. We immediately come upon a new type of perception, the reflective immanently directed perception in its double character of phenomenologically reduced reflection and natural reflection. Perception of the body was a new type of perception, and even that did not close the series. In this way a universal theme, perception as such, is distinguished from the particular types of perception as particular themes. Also, one sees at once that perception as such (whatever particular species of perception or perception of whatever species of object) has its modifications in other species of experience, first in memory as retention and as recollection and on the other hand also in varying forms of expectation.

But one encounters this, not only by surveying the regions of perceptions, but also by the plainly very necessary study of the immanent structure of each concrete perception itself. The concrete unity of a perception as a continually streaming lived experience, existing only in the form of streaming, is a synthetic structure; or, it can be regarded as such in an ideal analytic consideration. The streaming is a process which has an immanent stretch of time as its form, a stretch which we can think of as structured in partial stretches and in time-phases, time-points as it were (in which case we must not think of mathematical ideal points). Here, we soon confront the difficult problems of the original consciousness of time. If, in the reflective attitude, we pay attention to a streaming perception, then we can perhaps fix our attention upon a momentary phase which is set off by its contents, ‹201› perhaps upon a phase of the sound of a violin which is set off by the beginning of a scratching noise – in this way we can make marvelous observations. If we retain this phase, then we are not really retaining it as perception. For, at once it has already passed away – a new sound phase is there in its stead, characterized as a living perceptual phase, as a new sound-now. But how is the phase which has passed away present to consciousness? And likewise the phases which are still further back? They must be also present to consciousness in every momentary now, throughout a stretch of time. For, otherwise, how would we have more given than the respective momentary sound-now? How could we have the consciousness of an enduring sound continuing through a stretch of time? The momentary now is not a stretch: plainly, together with the momentary consciousness of the sound-phase emerging *originaliter*, we have a consciousness of the one that has just passed, as of its "sinking" into the past.

Together with every sound-phase newly emerging in the form "now" the phase which has just been given as now is given in a new mode, in that of the past, "retentionally;" not only is it present to consciousness retentionally instead of being perceived, it is present to consciousness in an ever new mode, as ever more and more past in the continuation of the a priori never stationary process, of the emerging of an ever new now. Each past is changed into a more-past; this once again, etc. The intentional clarification of this process, or the clarification of the manner in which a stretch of time is present to consciousness as a streaming process, is one of the most important themes in the doctrine of pure subjectivity. For, it is always and everywhere only in the form of a streaming life.

In this connection we encounter the multiplicity of the modes of givenness of the temporal as temporal, the modes of givenness of the now, the past, the past of the past, etc., also of the *future* in its own modalities.

And we encounter also the description of temporal orientation and the temporal perspectives, thus universally, the peculiarity of temporal appearances as appearances of: the special species and layers of intentionality by which the temporal appears for us as such in immanence.

‹202› In this way, it becomes evident that concrete perception as original consciousness (original givenness) of a temporally extended object is structured internally as itself a streaming system of momentary perceptions (so-called originary impressions). But each such momentary perception is the nuclear phase of a continuity, a continuity of momentary gradated retentions on the one side, and a horizon of what is coming on the other side: a horizon of "protention," which is disclosed to be characterized as a constantly gradated coming. This momentary continuity of retention and protention belonging to every originary impression undergoes a modification difficult to describe, in the flowing off of the originary impression; in any case the multiplicity of appearances of the linear stretch of time is multi-dimensional.

If we then look around further, then we have to attest that each concrete perception, for instance that of a sound continuing on, often has or in any case can have the form of a perception which comes to an end; and after its end it is not nothing. It has changed into a concrete retention, into the lived experience of the concrete sound which has just faded away. But this can be re-awakened, retention can pass over into an intuitive recollection: this is indeed not an actually repeated perception, but still a peculiar consciousness in which it is as if the sound were again constituted for our hearing as continuing on and on. "The" sound: it is not a sound of mere fancy, but a sound is given in believing certainty as reproduced, as reawakened, as having been for us, as having been perceived. The intentional analysis of recollection is again a large new problem. The traditional psychology and theory of knowledge has had no inkling of its hidden depths, and only phenomenology has made us capable of seeing them.

Recollection is re-presenting. In contrast to it, perception is presenting, and indeed original presenting, insofar namely as it makes a present as originally occurring be existentially present to consciousness. In this respect, if we take presenting concretely, the present is also a concrete and *originaliter* given present, that is, e.g., the enduring sound which is ‹203› *originaliter* given in the streaming duration precisely as this presently enduring sound. And so every other object given *originaliter* as enduring. On the other hand, a re-presenting also makes a present an object of consiousness and brings it intuitively to givenness as what it re-presents, e.g., as the recollection of an enduring sound.

At the end of the last lecture, I spoke of the various kinds of modifications ‹*› of the type of lived experience, perception as such, of retention as still having consciousness of what has gone by as perceptual present, of having consciousness in the mode "just-having been," of protention as the original foreseeing of what announces itself as "just-coming." Further, of recollection as perceiving again, as it were, re-presenting the past again intuitively. All such forms, of themselves refer back to a corresponding perception and are therefore called its modifications, modalities of perception. Apparently reproductive fancy and perceptive pictorial consciousness belong in this same series. As, e.g., if we fancy ourselves into a land of fairy tales, or if something of the sort is placed before our eyes perceptively by a painter, in a perceptible picture. But a closer analysis shows that fancy, taken as *pure fancy*, draws us into a new realm of modifications. The perceived, the remembered, the expected is characterized as existent:

presently existent, past existent, etc. This existent can be changed modally; instead of certainly existing, also possibly, probably, dubiously, emptily. But it always remains existent; it is always actually believed by the subject, in whatever modalities of belief. But one modification stands opposed to all that: instead of an actual believing, a fancying of belief according to which what is perceptively or reproductively represented is merely in one's mind as if it were, as if it were perceived or as if it were given as existing, as if it were past or coming. The belief is not an actual one, but a quasi-belief. Since every lived experience in pure subjectivity is only as present to consciousness perceptually, even if not noticed, therefore *idealiter* for every
‹ 204 › one there is a possible corresponding fancy of the same content. Also, every fancy can itself be again modified to a fancy in fancy and so on *in infinitum.* We have perceptively the intention "unqualified image," "image of an image," and so on *in infinitum.*

These two series of modifications which branch out from perception are called the positional modifications, with actual belief and modalities of belief and the *quasi-positional* modifications, having the marvelous character of *belief as if.* Together they have all-inclusive significance in pure subjectivity. They all play a continuous role already in experiencing life. For, we have a continuous experiential world not merely by streaming perception. Apart from the fact that this itself in its concretion is a mixture of abstract moments of perception, retention and protention, it should be pointed out that a concrete retention and a concrete protention, which allows us to expect something concretely new, are attached to each perception which has streamed away. Further: what has already sunk into the depths of the unliving past, thus is no longer in our grasp by living retention, emerges again, becomes again intuitive as recollection. A past which can be pursued in various directions is constituted by syntheses of recollection, a past which, thanks to its synthesis which can always be established with perception and with the protentions directed toward the future, constitutes the unity of filled time.

Therefore, a world is there for us as a possession of knowledge to be acquired by perception and one which remains once acquired, only by recollection and anticipation, as a unified multiplicity of objects to which one can return again, to which one constantly has or can gain access, which one can re-present to oneself as they were and as they continue to be for possible future perceptions, which one can count on and with which one can deal.

While the positional modifications of perception in their synthetic connections bring it about that we can become conscious of actualities which remain, in pure subjectivity, and can have them as demonstrable unities of
‹ 205 › experience, the fancies furnish us with possibilities, in connection with the actualities of the positional sphere, ways of imagining something as being

different, as when we fictitiously change in thought a gray object into a red one. But this is the presupposition for a praxis which transforms objects. I prefer the red which I have thought of to the gray, and now perhaps I find practical ways of realizing the imagined possibility.

(This implies that the imagined possibility is recognizable as a practical possibility, as being in the domain of the practical "I can" –but that already belongs in another line.)

If within the framework of the phenomenological reduction, one passes in this way from the various types of perception to their positional and quasi-positional modifications, then in the investigation one expands his sphere of vision in a purely subjective context, in which each new form has the fundamental characteristic of everything merely subjective, that of intentionality. Whereas we first had the externally perceived as such, thus purely as appearing in the course of perception and motivated by our own bodily kinesthesis, and various directions for purely subjective analyses were predelineated from that starting point, now we find something quite analogous in the case of the modifications, only in more complicated fashion. Recollection shows us everything that perception shows us, but modified as recollected – but not merely the same thing in a new color, so to speak. For, new marvelous properties come with it, as e.g., this, that starting with the recollected object two reflections are possible, one upon the recollection, the other into it; *one* reflection leads to the present lived experience of recollection, the other to the past perceiving of the object, so that thus recollecting contains a having perceived. As the I of the present belongs to the present recollection, so to the past perceiving belongs the I of that time.

If instead of recollection we take fancy as a modification of perception, then we find again this double reflection. It leads not only to the present fancying I, but to the I in the fancy as an also-fancied I and indeed one which is imagined along as quasi-perceiving, as quasi-living such and such ⟨206⟩ courses of appearances, etc. Therefore, imagined appearances, imagined syntheses, imagined acts of belief are included in it.

41. REFLECTION UPON THE OBJECT-POLE IN THE NOEMATIC ATTITUDE
AND REFLECTION UPON THE I-POLE AS UNDERLYING IT. ALL-INCLUSIVE
SYNTHESIS OF THE I-POLE. THE I AS POLE OF ACTIVITIES AND
HABITUALITIES.

Thus, by the phenomenological reduction, together with the actual pure subjectivity, i.e., together with its reduced objectivities, their appearances, their modalities of belief, the I related to them and its I-acts, we also arrive at imagined pure subjectivities with corresponding imagined nexus.

But all these imagined components and the imagined subjectivity are nevertheless imagined in the actual pure subjectivity. We pursue these in direct exhibition of lived experiences and syntheses of lived experiences without ever positing the experiential world of the natural attitude directly. We are constantly dealing with consciousness as consciousness *of* that of which it is conscious as such, with perceptual appearances *of* what appears in them, and described as what is appearing and just as it is appearing in them, with memorial appearances *of* what is remembered in them, etc. Everything objective, which is purely and simply there in the natural attitude, is here put in quotation marks and is *only* posited as the meant of meanings, as the experienced of experiences, the fantasized of fantasies, etc. These can be considered singly or in synthetic connections. And *if* natural experience in its experiential belief anticipates implied infinities of possible experience, then it is the phenomenological consideration which, without placing itself naïvely on the ground of experience, discloses precisely these infinities as purely subjective and thereby discloses to us what naïve experiencing includes intentionally as "simply existing world."

In our descriptions offered as suggestions we had preferred a direction of description which in phenomenology is called the *noematic.* That is, we had directed our regard at the start toward what is objective, as it is given sub‹ 207 › jectively as to its objective sense, as to modalities of being and as to the subjective modes in which it is given. From there we went back to appearances which lie deeper and which are appearances in a new sense, the sense in which this object appears in its subjective *how,* e.g., the perspectival aspects or the corresponding temporal perspectives in which the temporal as such is constituted. But we hit upon the I itself again and again.

But furthermore reflection, it should be noted, instead of passing from the object first to its appearances can also pass immediately to the I as the I which performs acts and has objects, has them by appearances.

In the noematic attitude (and combined with it, in the direction of regard toward the multiplicities in which the objects are constituted in their subjective *what* and *how*) under the title of existing objects taken purely as objects of experience, the first result of the synthetic unity of progressing perceptions and other modes of experience is a polarizing of the subjective occurrences. The one experiential world runs through pure subjectivity, through the flow of the variety of synthetically united lived experiences as a connected multiplicity of poles of unity. Indeed if we go back to the stream of immanent lived experiences itself, then it is also a pole-system in relation to the phenomena of the original constitution of temporal objects, and finally the entire immanent life is constituted for itself as a pole-system.

But this polarization has its marvelous counterpart in the I-polarization. From everything which is given directly as an object, reflection leads not only to constituting lived experiences in which the object is constituted as a pole, but at any time a reflection directed toward the identical I is possible: and this I is the subject of all lived experiences and the subject for all its objects as a pole of unity of its intentionalities; but it is not itself a lived experience. Previously we saw that the object as appearing in the multiplicity of the lived experiences and meant as existing is irreal vis-a-vis these lived experiences; it is not a real moment of them, for it is an identical object in lived experiences separated by immanent time. On the other side also, ‹208› the I is not to be found in the real stream of lived experiences, neither as a lived experience nor a part, a real moment of the lived experiences. I who now perceive and perform this perception am identically the same one who find myself in recollection as the I who has perceived the past. I recognize the absolute identity in reflection. All my lived experiences are related to me, as the same I, but also by my lived experiences all objects which are constituted in them as object-poles are related to me. Of course every reflection which I relate to myself and every synthesis of reflections in which I find myself as identical is itself a lived experience and makes me objective — objective for me.[1]

But this unique distinctive character is clear, consisting in this, that an all-inclusive synthesis pervades the streaming of lived experiences and all existence synthetically constituted in them as persisting, an all-inclusive synthesis by means of which even unreflectedly I am constantly a pole of identity in relation to which everything else is "objective."[2] When I reflect upon myself, then I am as subject of the reflecting a functioning I, on the other side as object of the reflection an object, which I designate as *me*. Above everything else that can be an object is the functioning I as ideally identical pole for all objects.

But here one must note that this I is not the human being even though I am accustomed to say, in the natural attitude and in spatial apperception, "I, this human being." As every spatial object, so is the body which I claim as mine a unity of my appearances; I am the pure I of these lived experiences as mine and the I for which their experiential unity, the body, is constituted.

But this pure I – which plainly Kant had in mind, as he spoke of the I of transcendental apperception – is not a dead pole of identity.

It is the I of affections and actions, the I which has its life in the stream of lived experiences only because it on the one hand exercises intentions in them as intentional lived experiences, toward and busied with their intentional objects, and because on the other hand it is stimulated by these ob- ‹209› jects, in feeling is touched by them, is attracted to them, is motivated by them to actions. Insofar as it is that, it is "awake" and thereby particularly

---

[1] Kant's transcendental I.
[2] Synthesis of transcendental apperception.

"awake" for these or those objects and in various ways. But it can also be a dull, sleeping I. That is, nothing stands out either immanently or transcendently, everything has flown together indistinguishably. Then neither is the I itself in its way a prominent subject-pole, for it is then not a functioning pole in changing I-formations, touched by particular affections, awaiting them, drawn toward them, then, following their tug, reacting in actual turnings toward them and in I-activities. The sleeping I in its peculiarity is of course revealed only from the perspective of the awake I by a reflection of a peculiar sort which reaches back and seizes it. More closely considered, sleep has sense only in relation to waking and implies a potentiality for awakening.

Let us consider the acts of the I. The I as awake exercises acts in the specific sense. For example: I perceive attentively, I "consider" something, I am directed in memory toward the past, I grasp it, I exercise a contemplating re-presentation, I explicate the object, I determine it as substrate of the properties belonging to it, I relate it to other objects, compare and distinguish them, I evaluate it as beautiful and ugly, I imagine it different and more beautiful, I wish that it were different. "I can" shape it differently, will it changed and actualize the difference. The I is constantly there in such occurrences which can be exhibited purely internally – not as an empty word, but as a directly exhibitable center, as a pole.

Every *actus* has the character of something arising from the I-pole, not passively flowing forth from it, but going out from it in the unique active way. But every such *ego cogito* is restricted to the presupposition that previously the I was affected, that means, that previously a passive intentionality in which the I does not yet hold sway has already constituted in itself an object by which the I-pole has been affected and determined to the *actus*. On the other hand, every *actus* just as it has been put into play by the I as produced *from* it is at once itself a lived experience inserted into the same stream of lived experiences to which the passive lived experiences belong.

⟨210⟩   But that leads to an enrichment of the world of objects which, once constituted, can again and again affect and motivate new activities of the I, whereby ever new specifically I-produced objects are constituted and inserted into the surrounding world of the I. For the I does not simply turn toward what is already passively given; and it is not merely an I of perceptivity. Rather, by comparing, e.g., it constitutes likeness; by connecting in the way of relational determining, it constitutes relations of objects, states of affairs, property relations, relational complexes; likewise then relations of value, practical relations, activities, means for goals, etc. Even such objectivities have their original mode of givenness, are perceived in a broader and the broadest sense of the word. But their originality is originality as a result of an active doing of the I on the basis of something or other given passively beforehand. And only as issuing and having issued from the activity of the I is it there for the I. And once there, it is henceforth its enduring acquisition, something to which the I can at any time return in a ray of vision, something to which it can subsequently look back receptively, which it can again re-present, identify objectively, take as reference point for new relating actions and treat in other ways.[1]

Now that we have gained a notion of the I as point of origin of all producings, all logical, axiological and practical producings and products, of the mental formations produced by the I, not only is this higher level of the surrounding world of objects, which has come into being through these mental formations produced by the I, of interest to us, but of no less interest is correlatively the distinctive change which thereby takes place with the I itself. The pure I-pole is numerically and identically the same, it is the unique center of the entire pure subjectivity with which we become progressively acquainted from our point of departure, each beginning with his external perceptions and experiences. But just as an object-pole in the ‹211› progress from its appearances to ever new appearances which are connected in harmonious synthesis is the same in numerical identity, but nevertheless as being determined ever anew by ever new objective constituents, from then on includes sediments of these determinations, so similarly with the I. But of course the I is not a mere object in the manner of a thing which is constituted as a unity of appearances and constituted as a substrate of determinations of material features. The I performs activities. But it is not an empty ideal polar point, merely determined as the point of intersection of the activities which flow forth from it and are then given as already there; rather, precisely thereby it is also a pole of corresponding habitualities. But they are not in it as perceptually given and exhibitable material properties in a material object; rather, they are dispositions which accrue to it by a genesis, by the fact that it has carried out the respective *actus*, and which belong to it historically only in recourse to them. With the original decision the I becomes originally the one who has thus decided. It can then immediately see itself as that and later see itself as the same, as the same one still thus decided. The I has its history and on the basis of its history it creates an I which persists for it habitually as the same I.

E.g., if I become acquainted with a spatial object by considering it singly and gain for the first time a "unitary representation," a "concept" of it,

---

[1] The state of affairs, that the table here is brown, is as state of affairs a form produced by the I, and only as such does it enter the realm of objectivities which henceforth exist for the I. Then they exist even when they do not exist perceptually, that is, exist in their original producing and being produced. They are, for instance, background objects by means of retention or objects which are present in the realm of those things of which one is not actually conscious, but can be brought to recollection and re-actualized by awakening.

if I acquire it as substrate of traits acknowledged as distinctive of it, then that is an active producing beyond passivity and yields just this "concept."

If I subsequently see this object again, then it is no longer a new object for me, but it is *eo ipso* the comprehended object. If we go back to the I of the original act and of the later recognizing act, then the following is clear. In the original act I acquire a cognition, but not the momentary cognition of the act, rather cognition as a conviction which persists for me. The subsequent execution is indeed the execution of a like act insofar as the content may be alike, but this act is altered not only in this, that it awakens the ⟨212⟩ previous act and takes on the character of familiarity with regard to the objective content, and not only in that I, re-establishing the recollection, can now say to myself: I now believe the same and see the same that I have previously found; rather, I must say: I have had knowledge of this previously, and this knowledge has persisted with me as a conviction. This is my conviction, and the renewed seeing confirms this conviction which meanwhile was mine all along.

Take a proof that I have carried out for the first time in its implicit activities. If later I come back to it in my thoughts, then that is not only a memory of having previously proved it and a newly occurring co-belief from the present in what was previously proved; but my conviction, I say, has not altered, I still have it as at that time instituted in the proving. And I say, I am still the same one – I, who have framed this conviction, am the same one – insofar as I still have this conviction. The fact that I have exercised an activity and have gained a certain conviction, a certain result of positional producing, has a prospect toward the future for the I. With the institution of this conviction, a being-thus has accrued to me myself as something remaining, not an empirical expectation as to how I will behave later.

42. THE I OF PRIMAL INSTITUTIONS AND OF INSTITUTIONS WHICH FOLLOW OTHERS. IDENTITY OF THE I IN MAINTAINING ITS CONVICTIONS. THE INDIVIDUALITY OF THE I MAKES ITSELF KNOWN IN ITS DECISIONS WHICH ARE BASED UPON CONVICTIONS.

The I has no material properties; it has determinate being exclusively as a subject of self-instituted convictions.

But the I which executes primal institutings and by so doing institutes itself in a correlative sense as an I of self-instituted, original convictions, also becomes, in a community, an I which understands and follows other I's in their self-instituting and originally instituting activity and, within the unity of its own life, executes co-belief, co-valuing, etc., in an institution which follows by its "assent," i.e., by accomodating itself fittingly to the other's motivation and the other's conviction. The convictions which are instituted in the I in this way are not born forth from the I itself; it does

not form them itself nor institute them itself in the originality of its I. It ‹213›
follows after another, is guided by another, by his convictions and his motivations. It thinks, values, acts, not as itself and on its own, but it follows
the suggestion of the other; it lives in him, putting itself in the other's place
and living with him, and consents, goes along, expresses its opinion as
agreeing with the other's opinion. On both sides we have two ways of expressing an opinion:

1) Opinion, decision, or conviction based purely on rational motives,
in which something is "seen," intuited, attained by seeing.

2) On the basis of "blind" motives, which can of course be understood
by being disclosed and which with their intelligibility also have an indirect
rationality but not a seeing rationality, not a rationality which includes
necessity. Its rationality would still have to be delimited. This is a field
of associative-apperceptive transfer from the sphere of seeing to what is
anticipated without being seen, made on the basis of the analogy with what
was *previously* seen, but not supported by any seeing verification.

But a distinction can also be made between rational motivation and that
motivation (that psychic causality, passive causality and causality of the I)
which motivates me to adopt teachings of reason at all, which puts me in
such a position that I can see and must see by following passive affects.
When I follow the other, it is possible that I can reproduce his insight and
that I do so. In this way I follow him rationally and decide according to his
reason and simultaneously according to my own, since his becomes my own
when I follow his example.

My decision is a decision fashioned after another's and yet I have decided
by free exercise of reason. I can justify it to myself. On the other hand it
remains true that it does not stem purely from me, I am not the author;
I follow another's authority but on the basis of my own reason simultaneously. Possibly, I have insight and follow my insight but the other has
no insight at all; therefore, I do not follow his insight by fashioning mine
after it.

But we must first also distinguish between going along "passively" and
deciding on free deliberation in favor of the other's decision, with this
difference: on the basis of reason (possibly purely on the basis of reason) ‹214›
or on the basis of unjustified motives. Thus I have:

1) Convictions arrived at by suggestion and only that;
2) freely following the other, convictions arrived at by active assent;
3) convictions of assent arising from one's own reason (possibly following
   his way toward insight and his insight itself).

I am as originarily instituting myself on my own; I am the subject of
convictions instituted after others' example, freely motivated by others.

‹ * ›   Every change of conviction is a change of the I; I do not have convictions
as I have fleeting lived experiences, but I have them as properties of the I,
which I have as the result of my own originally instituting activities or as the
result of my own decisions which freely follow other I's and their decisions,
but which I may lose by other activities and by being necessarily motivated
by them. As long as I do not give up the conviction, it is accepted by me.
I, as who and what I *now* am, am the one thus and thus convinced as a result
of a decision originally my own. The I has no other properties at all. Much
is connected with this basic peculiarity of the I. Thus, for example, what we
call self-preservation, and that with reference purely to the I. Ultimately,
the life of an I is pervaded by an aspiration to come to a unity and to unanimity in the multiplicity of its convictions such that the I wants to become
an I that remains true to itself or can remain true to itself insofar as it is
no longer inclined to abandon its convictions and, essentially connected
with that, to become unhappy. This is of course an idea, but it designates
the sense of the striving for self-preservation in its ideal meaning.

The concepts of personality, character and individuality in that emphatic
sense of language referring purely to the I also refer to this field of convictions to be formed by the I and defining it as an I.

The I has its mode of continuing through time as an enduring I amid the
fluctuation of its acts, and thus of its convictions, its decisions. But it does
‹ 215 › not merely endure on in the manner as it were of an empty stage for such
fluctuation, or better, in the manner of a mere substrate of this fluctuation.
Rather, what we call "I" in the proper sense (abstracting from the communicative relation to a you or we) means a personal individuality. This
concept implies an identically persisting unity constituted amid the fluctuation of decisions. It is a bit analogous to the unity of a real thing vis-a-vis
the fluctuation of the thing's conditions. In the way in which the I lets itself
be motivated to its fluctuating decisions with reference to the surrounding
world of which it is conscious, and thus in the particular character of its
decisions themselves and of their connections, the I preserves an individual
style which can be recognized. The I-pole has not only its fluctuating sediments but a unity constituted in this style throughout their fluctuation. The
I has its individuality, its individual total character which identically permeates all its decisions and determinations; as an individual character it has
peculiarities, special properties which are called properties of character.

In the decisions, as they emerge in the comprehended connection of
already known decisions of this I, such and such properties of character,
and thus its individuality as such, become manifest to apperception and
knowledge.

---

* Concluding lecture. July 30, 1925.

But we should add here: in associatively inductive experience expectations are formed as to how the respective persons (or my I for myself – in which case the experience is my own experience of myself) will behave, in accordance with their behavior thus far.

But the empirically inductive unity which is formed, the substrate of the directions of expectation, is here an index of an internal unity which can be understood by following, one which can be disclosed intelligibly. The decisions of an I themselves imply a predelineated consequence for further decisions, and this is a sphere of intelligibility, but of course in many respects one which still requires clarification.

43. THE UNITY OF THE SUBJECT AS MONAD – STATIC AND GENETIC   ⟨216⟩
INVESTIGATION OF THE MONAD. TRANSITION FROM THE ISOLATED
MONAD TO THE TOTALITY OF MONADS.

What we have set forth suffices to give you an idea of pure subjectivity, self-contained and everywhere inseparably connected. Taken in its concretely complete nexus this subjectivity comprises what we call the concrete pure subjectivity or the monad; thus in this context, "monad" is not a metaphysical concept but the unity of the subjective within the phenomenological reduction, to be explored in direct intuition by painstaking analysis.

The analytic investigation is static here, dissecting whatever relatively self-contained connections are to be made prominent at any particular time, and pursuing everything immanently real and ideal in all essential correlations. But then genetic investigation is also necessary, the exploration of the geneses, passive as well as active, in which the monad develops and evolves, in which, within the monad, the monadic I acquires its personal unity and becomes a subject of a surrounding world, which is partly given to it passively in advance, partly actively shaped by itself, and then at the highest level becomes the subject of a history.

One more big step should be mentioned, though here unfortunately it can only be introduced with a few words: within the phenomenological reduction the investigation is first naturally carried out just as we have done, that is, as an investigation of that pure subjectivity which the investigator finds before him in first originality, namely, as the pure subjectivity of his I, of his life, of his appearing surrounding world, most simply taken abstractively as *solus ipse*; but I have found that the phenomenological reduction can be extended beyond this realm of the *solus ipse* or extended into the other subjects appearing in external experience to me, the exploring I (and in the natural attitude appearing, so to speak, as "children of the world"). The result is a pure phenomenology of intersubjectivity which extends to

‹217› the universality of monads which become manifest by empathy in my monad, and are given me in pure self-experience.

If phenomenology is executed also as a purely eidetic science, then the result is a science of the essential properties and essential connections which belong not only to a monad as such but to a communicative totality of monads.

44. PHENOMENOLOGICAL PSYCHOLOGY FOUNDATIONAL BOTH FOR THE NATURAL AND FOR THE PERSONAL EXPLORATION OF THE PSYCHE AND FOR THE CORRESPONDING SCIENCES.

Let us now pass on to a concluding consideration. Pure phenomenology, as a science referring to pure subjectivity, can of course also be called psychology, pure psychology in a quite determinate sense. But there are various sciences with the name "psychology," all very closely connected, all essentially related back to our pure psychology.

Let us put ourselves once more on the ground of the natural world which the natural performance of experience gives us. There resulted – since the founding of modern natural science – on the basis of the abstractive exposure of the theme of a merely physical nature, a definite preferred direction of ascent for scientists in exploring the world: from physical nature to psychophysical nature, thus to the exploration of the psyche as spatialized and objectively temporalized in physical nature as a causal annex of the physical body. In other words, there resulted an exploration of animal and human spatio-temporal reality which is essentially oriented toward the properties to be explored inductively, those of the physical organic body, the specifically somatological properties and the psychic properties connected with them. Here already it became evident as our look penetrated more deeply from inductive externality to psychic internality, that soon an existence of the psyche having its own proper determination was exposed, an existence which is *presupposed* by all psychological induction, and therefore is not to be understood merely inductively.

But if one seriously wants to become acquainted with the psyche's own
‹218› essence, and especially to become acquainted with it in pure self-experience, as it is and can be seen in abstraction from all physis – then one must of course carry this abstraction out in the right way and in strict consistency. In other words: if inductive external psychology, psychophysical and experimental, instead of operating with the rough notions of prescientific life concerning psychic internality and basing experimental inductions upon them, is to gain scientific concepts of this internality, then it must adopt the method of phenomenological reduction. Therefore it requires a proper science of pure subjectivity, as we have constructed it. This then soon turns

out to be the properly central science yielding all properly psychological knowledge, and even the most extensive psychological science.[1] Of course the inductive is not to be despised; it gives cognitions by which we acquire from without rules for the practical judgment of psychic connections indicated by the body. But it also makes us acquainted with the rules of the empirical coordination of the psychic with what pertains to the physical body.

A different direction of research, as it were the reverse of that which begins with physical nature and natural science, would have required a particular exposition; it was intimated in the way our lectures proceeded, but unfortunately could not be given further exposition, in order not to curtail the central psychology of pure internality. The direction of progress from physical nature on led to an extension of the idea of natural science. But the socio-cultural sciences are the opposite of all natural scientific disciplines in the narrower and in the broader sense. They are the sciences of personalities and their personal formations.

What we have said in the last two lectures within the phenomenological reduction with reference to I, personality and personal formations as products of specific acts of the I, makes it easy to understand that a purely ‹219› personal research is possible even on the ground of natural experience. And thus it is also easy to come to understand what gives the socio-cultural sciences of modernity their peculiar character vis-a-vis the natural sciences.

Now let us consider again the thematic directions. Let us assume that the direction of interest toward mere nature has been adopted. In one-sided unbroken consistency the interest is directed toward what gives extensive realities purely on their own a proper existence, and toward a truth which disregards all relativity of restriction to single persons, groups of persons, the factually experiencing and thinking communities or civilizations of any contingent particularity. Everything "merely subjective" in its various senses is thus excluded as disturbing the consistency of the theme. This is then the path of natural science. If the mental then becomes itself a theme, with physical nature being maintained as the founding theme, then there arises a natural science in the broadened sense directed toward animality and humanity.

But one could take the thematic direction toward the mental quite differently. And one has done that also, though while following inconsistent thematic directions of pre-theoretical life. Just as pretheoretically an inter-

---

[1] Mistakes in the attempts of psychologists to form descriptive concepts of the psychic itself rest on the fact that they are incapable of seeing intentionality in its specific character and of treating it accordingly. The nexus of consciousness is an intentional nexus; unity of consciousness is the presupposition for all inductive apperceptions in logical inductions and must be studied before that in its unity and the internal regularity which creates unity.

est, e.g., that of curiosity, can be directed toward merely physical things and their properties, so also and even much more frequently, toward the personal.[1] And the personal can also become a consistent theoretical interest. Of course: we live in the all-inclusiveness of experience which flows on, and whatever appears in its harmonious progress in the mode of actuality remains of course as it stands there; it remains in acceptance even though it may momentarily not be in execution. A phenomenological reduction does not take place. The personal interest can also be consistent in that way and in its consistency can urge me on so that I never encounter anything but ⟨220⟩ what is personal. I direct my interest purely toward the personal, that means, purely toward how persons behave as persons and behave toward one another, how they define themselves and others, how they form friendships, marriages, unions, etc., how, busied with the things which surround them, they form them into works, and how they form mental meaning in a useful way, the sense of signs, of signals, of terms expressed, of trophies, treatises or of works of art, of religious symbols, of office buildings, of useful organizations, etc. If I do this, nature as nature is never my theme in all that, neither the physical nor the psychophysical. Of course things continue to be there, the physical world, animals and human beings with their physical bodies and as somatological unities. But in the personal direction of interest precisely the person or the multiplicity of associated persons is the theme, and the spatial things are included in the theme only as belonging to the personal surrounding world. "Surrounding world" is a term with personal signification. But "nature" is a word which has excluded all personal significations – both concepts are concepts with a thematic content which the theoretical attitude has circumscribed. In the personal direction of regard toward myself I am the I that has experiences, thus such and such courses of appearances in which spatial things and also my entire world of things appear, just as they appear for me and are accepted by me.

If I reflect upon myself, for instance, for purposes of a deliberation concerning a way of life which I should adopt, or if I even execute an ethical deliberation, then nature in the sense of the natural scientist is only there for me insofar as I could institute a direction of regard which would investigate nature beginning with my correlative appearances: but that would not even occur to me in this attitude. Likewise if I am directed toward other persons as such or toward personal communities. Then my interest pertains to their surrounding world, purely as it appears and is accepted, to physical or personal factors which determine them in pleasure or pain.

---

[1] That a consistently personal interest can actually remain forever within a purely personal nexus in experience and theory, thus that this nexus is itself included in the all-inclusive experiential world, is a structural fact parallel to that of nature.

Insofar as I relate personally to them, I also judge their surrounding world and do so on the basis of the acceptance which I myself execute: but I do not at all judge in natural scientific fashion. As a consequence, a ‹221› consistently personal science is directed purely toward persons and their surrounding worlds and toward the personal surrounding world common to all who belong to the community circle in which the personal scientist includes himself.[1]

Since in fact the mind, namely the entire realm of personal subjectivity and its formed products, is the exclusive theme in all socio-cultural sciences, they all belong under the broader title *psychology*–as long as we take this title so broadly that all thematic research directed toward subjectivity in every sense is included within it. In the whole of modernity psychology has been aspired to as the parallel to theoretically explanatory natural science.

In order to appropriate to psychology a particular task in this regard, all that remains is to distinguish the universal investigations directed toward the essence of personality and of its formed products as such from investigations concerning particular and individual (and typically universal) personalities and correspondingly particular formed products.

Thus an eidetic essential science of the psychic opens up, in contrast to the descriptive concrete socio-cultural sciences and those which possibly press further toward explanation: quite *similarly* to the way a universal, be it empirical or eidetic, doctrine of the essence of nature (physics, chemistry, biology) is contrasted with the concrete sciences of nature. Therefore this psychology would be the fundamental socio-cultural science, that is, the one which establishes in a generic way all explanatory principles and theories for the explanations to be accomplished beyond mere description in the special socio-cultural sciences. But this psychology was never developed, simply because naturalistic psychology was predominantly substituted for it in modern times, psychology as a natural science, and because this itself never went on to develop a pure internal psychology which it itself needed. One can indeed say that Locke's psychology was an advance toward such an internal psychology, but an unsuccessful one, because he ‹222› was not able to draw the essential distinctions and besides did not see the essence and the problems of intentionality at all. But that is precisely a further main point. Whoever does not see what is essential to intentionality and the particular methodology pertaining to it, does not see what is essential to personality and personal productions either.

---

[1] This problem is not touched: how is it to be understood that the "mind," a mental "world," can become a self-contained region of all-inclusive science, corresponding to the parallel problem: how is it understood that nature becomes such a theme? Self-containment of the experience of nature, as well as of the experience of the mind.

Thus we recognize that phenomenological psychology is the unitarily explanatory foundation both for the natural exploration of the mind and for its personal exploration in the socio-cultural sciences. But consequently also for further possible disciplines which arise from the alternation of the personal with the natural attitude; I mean those disciplines which can be concerned with the psychophysics of social mind so to speak, e.g., as ethnology, as the exploration of the empirical parallels between physical and mental national character and the like.

All psychology in the historical sense and in the reformed sense which can naturally join it refers to the already given world and belongs to the sciences of the world. One step further in the all-inclusive consideration of the world by carrying out the transcendental-phenomenological reduction, and we make the world as such our theme together with every natural consideration of the world, from an ultimate standpoint which leads us into transcendental mentality. The fundamental science then becomes transcendental phenomenology, a *psychology* of the highest sense, a new sense which includes all critique of reason and all genuine philosophical problems.

45. RETROSPECTIVE SENSE-INVESTIGATION.

‹*› The lectures treated the development of the natural concept of the world and the tasks of the possible experiential sciences (they aimed in particular at psychology and the socio-cultural sciences) and the possible eidetic sciences of the world, of any possible world at all.

It is presupposed implicitly in this sense-investigation [*Besinnung*] that a ‹223› world is already given to me and to us by experience[1] and that we can perform universal descriptions by considering in what characteristics it is given universally to all of us, that we can, therefore, gain fitting universal concepts and universal judgments in what is given universally, that we can see their truth and thus universally perform sense-investigations as scientific thinking. In these sense-investigations we produce a science of the universal structures of the experienced world as experienced.

We presuppose then further, as something to be taken for granted, that experiential sciences of this world can be produced on the basis of the thus universally experienced world and in reference to the structures known scientifically in their universality, therefore in reference to the structure of the experiential world as such. To speak more clearly: from the world actually experienced at any time in any experience, we pass over to an all-

---

* Penultimate lecture. July 26, 1925.
[1] Orientation toward the *one* experiential world, which includes all orientations – that of the natural sciences and that of the socio-cultural sciences.

inclusive survey of the experiential world as such, which means: we "disclose" the experiential world by expanding actual experience and entering into recollection, expectation and possible experience and investigating the sense of what we can assert about the world on the basis of expanded and ever further expanded experience, experience which is actual now, previous experience, and anticipatable experience, but also of possible experience. If we now imagine ourselves theoretically interested in the actual world, then there arise for us the tasks of theoretically exploring this experienced world.

The universal sense-investigation concerning what universally typical object-types and forms of combinations all-inclusive experience offers us is then the foundation for the universal determination of possible themes of the sciences of the world as to possible all-inclusive regions and as to possible researches directed toward the world-contexts. It is clear then that the universal doctrine of the structures of the experiential world as such, itself provides a segment of the science of the world, though one which still needs to be deliberated.

Now one will say: if I follow the experiential world and determine its universal characteristics on the basis of experience and even do so conceptually and scientifically, what is left for a further science and consequently an eidetic science to produce here?

First: to experience, to take cognizance experientially is not to determine in thought. The experienced is a theme for experience *in infinitum*. But the ⟨224⟩ experienced can also be a goal for theoretically determining knowledge. If science knows the objects of experience theoretically, and universally any objects at all in their regions, it intends thereby to create a stable possession of knowledge, of such a character that it permits the possible confirmation of the course of actual and possible experience, or the determinations of the objects of such experience, on the basis of incomplete actually accomplished experiences, but without in each case continuing in experience *in infinitum*.

This presupposes that: 1) Experience is incomplete and a first stroke for experiential knowledge to be acquired by progressing *in infinitum*. 2) A describing, a conceptual understanding, which merely follows experience and is adapted to it, is unsatisfactory insofar as more is possible, namely, an experiential knowledge a priori to the actual continuation of experience. This "a priori" is a universal presumption of being able to know "in advance." 3) This may not succeed at once and completely; but it is possible to progress in steps and in approximations. In such a way that progressively again and again closed, limited constituents of actual experience, by the ascertainment of what is experienced in them, can provide the substrata for theories which make it possible to construe infinities of possible experience – though not of all. These theoretically construed infinities have only a relative justification insofar as they are only approximations, laden with imperfections, the improvement of which is a consequence of progress on the path of further experience and further theory (and possibly in quite different though connected directions of experience and theorizing). But, in any case, there can be here a *consistent progress* and an approximative mastery of the experienceable *by an a priori which*, even in this approximative relativity, can gradually and relatively satisfy theoretical and practical interests and on the other hand includes the satisfaction of being on the way to the idea of a conclusive truth. *All-inclusive experience* ‹225› *in its unexplicated infinity includes an "a priori" and an infinite gradation of approximative a priori regularities.*

This is a *presupposition*, an intending ahead, a further development of the conviction already included in natural life, that one can reasonably know beyond actual experience and that such reasonable knowledge allows one to construe "in advance" the course of future and possible experience and its givens. There is a "knowing" to be acquired and comprehended in statements on the basis of experience, a "knowing" which transcends it as actual experience. All experiential knowledge of life is restricted by the particular respective life-practice, which predelineates how far the determinacies are to be determined in advance; theoretical interest and science are "practically uninterested," and thereby unlimitedly all-inclusive in their focus.

Science necessarily presupposes that its universal theme, its region of the world, is already given to it as a theme, just as a most universal science of the world presupposes the prior givenness of the world. Fundamental sense-investigation concerning the universal structures of the experience of the world gives the universe of regions as possible themes, as possible theoretical goals.

How knowledge makes theory, what theory is in more detail, how it is formed justifiably in subjective work, will not be mentioned in more detail. We are not doing theory of science.

But we reflect on its sense: how does the all-inclusive experiential world look if we pursue it experientially and disclose it in harmonious experience – in this sense: what remains its universally contained content, meant as experience and accordingly given as existing with a stable sense, however the particular, concrete content may be shaped; thus, what is invariant in the world, however it may be in factual particularity? This leads to the eidetic study of the world of natural experience, to its eidetic a priori.

Let the procedure be naïve just insofar as we presuppose no logic as universal doctrine of science. We proceed "scientifically," but we wish to know nothing of "scientificality." We follow the "evidence," that is: we say what we "see," and what we ourselves grasp in fact, of universalities,

of whose veritable existence we are directly convinced, and for instance ‹226›
produce convictions (as acquisitions in universal statements) of whose
truth as verifiable correctness we can at any time convince ourselves, as
long as, persisting in freedom, we are not hindered from advancing in
thought. But we take this as something practically intelligible; we take it
as we know it from life itself. And in any event we confirm it in universalities
of sense-investigation which we again justify the same way. If we speak
further with regard to the world regions to be demarcated and the nexus of
sciences which have their thematic goal in them, the title "science" is itself
to be taken naïvely. This region should then be thought of just as a goal of
cognitive interest directed purely toward it, and indeed of a "thinking"
knowledge, subordinated to ideas of conclusiveness, a knowledge which
goes beyond experience. All our sciences are fundamentally naïve although
they create ingenious methods and constantly reflect about methods in
order to be able to create and improve them (since method is always already
presupposed in order to be able to form a method).[1]

They follow the evident method in the formation of knowledge and are
not yet aware that there is something further to ask concerning the evidence
of the production of knowledge itself. Therefore, we can also have before
our eyes the working method and typical performance of science in general,
the type of its setting goals and realizing them in typically established ways,
without entering into more detailed considerations.

In an evident investigation of sense, we can aim purely at the invariance
of the world as experienced and possibly to be experienced, determine it
for ourselves in evidence and only then ask: how far can knowledge still
intend something particular for the experiential world and its determination, what can be the aim here, and what measures would for instance have
to be taken? We describe the experienced world universally, and the invariant is something shown descriptively.

It is shown descriptively that the subjective and in contrast to it the non-
subjective are intertwined in the experiential world, and if we say that ‹227›
"nature" in the sense of natural science executes such and such exclusions
of the subjective, then we point out in truth descriptively the abstractively
established unity of a merely physical nature. Likewise, nature in the extended sense. The psyche as psyche of the body, the inductive peculiarity
of a human being or an animal, and the necessity of the question concerning
the unique essential nexus in the psyche itself: which leads to a new method
of disclosure, the *phenomenological reduction.*

What is lacking in the lectures: I show descriptively that this entire

---

[1] Method means: goal-directed activity in an intelligible, insightful manner, which is
fit to lead to the goal. Still better, we should say: goal-directed doing which, with its stage-
points, these products, presents the way which the doer goes, goes by doing and seeing.

species of consideration of the world ascending from nature – which naturally considers human beings as animated bodies, as inductive unities (whereby, however, the inductive in the psychic refers back to its own essential ground of unity) – leaves open a second possible consideration, the personal. While nature is always "there," while subjectivity is always there as I-centered psychic life, as an animating psyche, the positing of this nature (the physical and psychophysical) need not be accomplished – that is, as a theme, as a consistent goal for experience and goal for theoretical knowledge.

For, one can instead be thematically (in this sense) oriented toward *human persons* in their personal nexus or toward their *personal surrounding world*. There is a difference between speaking simply of things (simply of the spatial world, of spatial events, causal events, etc., directed thematically toward them as what they are themselves and "conclusively") –therefore, as objective nature, and on the other hand being thematically directed toward things as things of a personal surrounding world, as things of which persons are conscious, as things experienced by them, thought of by them, etc. Then they are intentional correlates in personal life or of persons; they are then not objects simply but "posited in relation to these determinate persons" – but this is still a very unclear expression. For, they are not thus first posited (and thematized) as objects, as nature, and then posited as such in reference to the persons; rather they are not at all themes in the manner of objects of nature and as such; instead, the themes are persons ‹228› and everything personal, as such inseparable from them; and inseparable from a person is his surrounding world, even if it may contain specters, fetishes, etc.

A double thematic direction results here, from the start: 1) the description of the personal surrounding world, namely of the persons or personal communities in question, purely as it is theirs intentionally, according to their belief; 2) on the other hand, the attitude taken by the one who is exploring this personality, his attitude toward the true existence of all these objects of the surrounding world; for he is himself a person and knows himself to be in a certain personal connection with them – he is necessarily a member with them of a personal total mankind; but this happens in the same way as when persons within a community agree or disagree concerning a determination, argue with one another, and convince themselves of truth and untruth. Possibly, they find the others as subjects of supposed objects which belong to their surrounding world, which in "truth do not exist at all," but are illusionary, etc.

But in all this the persons themselves and their personal living, working, creating in relation to their personal surrounding world are the subject matter. And even if natural scientists are the themes, as persons who, interested in nature, explore it, then nature indeed belongs to their surrounding world, as the goal of their work, as their theme; but they themselves are the primary objects. A person does stand there bodily; and I myself, when I take myself as a person – as whenever I simply say "I" and call the other "you" – have my body and bodily existence for myself. But within the scope of the personal attitude I am not posited for myself as an object of nature, just as the others are not; not as a physical thing of nature and not as a psychophysical reality existing in space – but my body is now given for me in the surrounding world as the center of the rest of the surrounding world, as a spatial thing of the surrounding world with somatic properties, in which I hold sway, and even as that by which I exercise an influence upon the rest of the surrounding world, etc. And likewise the other. The personal attitude takes the I itself as its theme, as an I which has its possessions, as an I which is active and which above all has its surrounding world as an already given possession at any time – one which is ever again new in content, yet as a whole continually identified for him as the ⟨229⟩ same surrounding spatial world, of which such and such things, etc., confront him subjectively, appearing to him subjectively in such and such sides, in such and such an orientation; these are the personal subjective modes, which have also their forms of variation, including clear and unclear appearing, the noematic modes of attentiveness, and the perspectives as well, insofar as by them the existential objects have their *how* in the personal sphere, pertaining to the surrounding world of persons, a *how* which occasionally comes into question for them. Thus, something's appearing large at a distance but small up close, as well as a thing's "growing hazy" in the dark but becoming distinct and clear in the light of day. A person is a working and living I which has his psychic basis, his body with a body-psyche, in which he holds sway, and his extra-corporeal surrounding world as the world of his working and suffering.

Generally speaking, the personal attitude is practical in the broadest sense, [oriented toward] what is experienced, what is thought, what is evaluated, etc., as the thus varying prior givens which belong to the substrate of personal actions or affections and which motivate it in the activity of thinking and in activity which is practical in the narrower sense.

If I am in the personal rather than the natural attitude, then of course the other stands before my eyes bodily as a spatial object, and makes himself known in the body seen by me, by empathy and expression. But I do not take his psyche in the natural way of considering and thematizing, as really united with this bodily organism, even though this unity may be "constituted" for me; rather, his body is a bodily organism for me just as bodily organism in this subjective mode, and he himself a bodily member of my surrounding world; and he is simultaneously posited by me as himself having his body as the center of his surrounding world and as experiencing just this material surrounding world, and having such and such thoughts, valuations, aspirations, etc., in relation to this surrounding world and to a broader one which is not properly experienced. This is my practical interest and possibly my theoretical interest – theoretical, if I am a socio-cultural scientist. And then all the cultural objects belong in my realm of research. Culture is not a layer of properties pertaining to natural objects as psyches, rather, it is a psyche in objects of the surrounding world, objects which admittedly are natural objects whenever they are investigated from the point of view of natural truth, but which as such have only natural properties.

⟨230⟩

The natural attitude, considered from the part of the socio-cultural scientist, is something personal; the natural scientist is a special personal type who is interested not in what is personal but in nature, i.e., who pursues "objectivity" by laying aside everything merely subjective (personal).

The world, considered personally, is the nature of the natural scientist, for all personalities interested in nature; from the orientation of the socio-cultural sciences, nature, and correlatively the natural scientist, is a personal theme. History is an all-inclusive personal science, a science of the personal and of its facticity taken all-inclusively. Eidetics is the all-inclusive science of ideally possible forms of personality in the unity of a personally regarded and thereby historical world. But this eidetics itself is of course for its own part only possible personally as a fact in a historical world; and all possibilities here, no matter how much they can become related again to possibilities, trace back to the all-inclusive fact of history.

But is there not *one* experiential world, and how are the two worlds mutually compatible: nature and the world of mind (personal world, human-historical and animal world)? Certainly there is one unique experiential world. But what does that mean? The first thing is this: I, the one experiencing, and we, the ones experiencing, live and are forever experiencing in the unity of a personal life (whether we reflect upon it or not). But in our experiencing we can be focused upon nature, which means: the experience of nature is a milieu for a thematic intentionality to be carried out practically – it is a set of themes. But the direction of regard toward personality and the personal can also be taken; personal experience can provide the milieu, instead of the experience of spatial things. Various species of experience are able to be effected together, precisely because they all – even if they can not be effected – belong to concrete life.

But the purely phenomenological attitude, as "purely" personal, "purely" historical, provides the ultimate clarification.

A difficulty will be found here, to be sure. As socio-cultural scientist,

I am oriented toward the "purely" personal. Thus if I were oriented toward ‹231›
nature, I would lose my theme which is a self-contained theme. (That would
still have to be explained). What is therefore left for the phenomenological
reduction to do?

The historian extends his thematic interest to a unitary horizon of
experience which unites in the unity of one humanity all personalities and
communities which are of interest to him, a unity to which he himself also
belongs. And this humanity is a humanity in the spatial world and the
spatio-temporal world itself, which of course comes into question for
him only as a personal surrounding world. The socio-cultural scientist
as such, even if he is for instance not an explorer of human personalities
and their personal products, but an investigator of "animal life," of animals as personal subjects in their animal surrounding world, is related to
the surrounding world common to him and all of us and so to the animals
also. Every investigator knows that he belongs to a scientific community of
investigators, as a historical community propagating itself through the
ages; and together with this special community he knows that he is inserted
in the community of scientists as such and of "earthly" humanity as such
in the unity of its history. Therefore, the spatial world common to all, in
which everything personal is included, lies in his horizon. It is spatial and
spatio-temporal by the individual personal bodies, to which the persons
belong; and these bodies have their all-inclusive horizon of spatial things
in the world of spatial things as such. This world contains a natural truth
to be explored interpersonally in natural investigation as its "objective"
element – to be explored precisely in the natural attitude of the natural
investigator. Of course, it also contains somatological truth and inductive psychological truth, i.e., everything knowable by maintaining the
natural attitude and by continuing the interest to everything mental which
can be known inductively – thus, the natural characteristics of psyches and
of races, etc. – proceeding as an inductive parallel research, possibly
intertwined with personal facts and cognitions, insofar as it seeks their
physical parallels. All that lies in the horizon of the socio-cultural scientist, although of this world-horizon only the personal is his theme; and
accordingly the all-inclusive world itself only as surrounding world, as ‹232›
presupposedly (by virtue of continuing harmonious experience which gives
it as already there) harmonious actual world, in relation to which all
surrounding worlds which are of thematic interest to the socio-cultural
scientist are, as already said, its personal aspects. But precisely its truth
is not in question for him as his theoretical theme.

Natural science shows that all of nature admits of being isolated and
pursued purely for itself as a theoretical theme, and phenomenology shows
the same with regard to its possibility. But personal investigation is also

able to be executed as purely personal investigation, as is shown in the genuine socio-cultural sciences and as again can be made evident by the epoché of all natural theory. But, precisely considered, nature as such is not in parentheses; as experienced and existing for experience and showing itself pre-theoretically in its being experienced, it is continually presupposed. It is just not a consistent theme for experience, namely, in that consistency which wants to end in an experiential theory. Belief in the world is included in every personal relation to the surrounding world, and thus a positing of the existence of physical nature; – investigating consistently in this direction in experience and theory, each person, or someone taking his place in a community, would investigate toward the "true nature." But the interest of the socio-cultural scientist for the personal, for personal living, working, creating, and for the cultural world which arises thereby, excludes this direction of investigation, except as a particular theme, in the investigation of scientific personalities and of the sciences as personally formed products.

Therefore the state of affairs is such that the unitary experiential world is and remains always in acceptance precisely on the basis of experience, and accordingly it is the all-inclusive world for natural sciences and socio-cultural sciences. The natural scientist does not perform a "reduction" either, with regard to mind, although he excludes the mental from his theme. Its being constantly there for him continues on, if he understands himself properly. Likewise, the socio-cultural scientist does not perform a phenomenological reduction with regard to nature, i.e., the thematic exclusion does not signify setting experienced nature out of acceptance in the sense of the phenomenological epoché.

‹233›   The one experiential world, ever constituted, already given in the constant all-inclusive acceptance of natural experience, is the basis, the ground, for all sciences. Notwithstanding, every science has its thematic restriction and in our case only this is of particular significance, that the investigation of nature and the investigation of mind can be separated, as "pure" in each case. On the other hand of course, as I must state explicitly, they can also be combined, insofar as a combined inductive consideration is possible, which investigates personal contents and bodily-organic constitution in their parallel inductive relationship.

Things are things of nature, persons are again persons "in" nature, insofar as they "have" bodies, actual natural bodies, which are nature, and insofar as they themselves [persons] have parallel properties of nature. Or, things, natural objects, psyches and persons considered naturally – persons considered purely personally and the world of mind considered in pure self-containment – everything is included in the one experiential world. And the phenomenological epoché "switches" this off in its entirety –

therefore also personal mentality in its existence in the natural world. It reduces all that to its phenomenality and takes its own position not in the world, but in the subjectivity for which the world is experienced, etc.; not in the personal subjectivity which is experienced as existing in the world, and also at the same time as having the world as its surrounding world, but rather in that subjectivity which is constantly there experiencing personality and in that life which is not an objectively personal life but which rather encompasses this personal life subjectively and presents it subjectively in itself. The disclosure of pure subjectivity: the actual execution of the indications begun in the lecture would include the entire doctrine of constitution, but resting on that and gradually becoming detached from it, a universal doctrine of the structures of individual subjectivity and intersubjectivity.

That would be a great work. Therefore, I could only project its plan, and that would already be much. This was thought of as a species of näive research which at first asks about nothing but what is showable directly, by disconnecting the objective world experienced and posited by "me." But in the background a purpose can serve a motivating function: ⟨234⟩

1) I am an inductive psychologist, but would like to know how the psyche looks "internally." I intend of course "parallel" and altogether inductive research. Naturally I hit upon this, that here a great science of psyches arises which is not inductively related to externality but is immanent, a science to which induction itself belongs as internal.

2) Likewise, I can be a personal researcher and be interested in personal internality. Here I would have to consider specifically in what ways personality and personal doing, the creating of personal products, enters the naturally experiencing regard. In any case, the personal I has an "internal" life to be disclosed, and a personal self-development. And there I come again upon the demand for a deeper exploration of pure subjectivity, and this leads to the same result as above. Therefore, I could give merely the outline, the presentation of a pure internal psychology as fundamental science for the socio-cultural sciences – but also for a natural psychological research; also the purely subjective consideration of inter-subjectivity (lecture of July[1] 10); then from the psychological reduction to the transcendental-phenomenological.

[1] Correction, reading VII for II. *Tr.*

SELECTED BIBLIOGRAPHY
(Works explicitly referred to by Husserl)

DILTHEY, WILHELM. *Aufbau der geschichtlichen Welt in den Geisteswissenschaften. Gesammelte Schriften* VII. Stuttgart: Teubner, 1958.
——. *Einleitung in die Geisteswissenschaften. Gesammelte Schriften* I. Stuttgart: Teubner, 1959.
——. *Ideen über eine beschreibende und zergliedernde Psychologie. Gesammelte Schriften* V. Stuttgart: Teubner, 1957.
HUSSERL, EDMUND. *Ideen zu einer reinen Phänomenologie und phänomenologischen Philosophie. Husserliana* III. The Hague: Nijhoff, 1950. English: *Ideas: General Introduction to Pure Phenomenology*, tr. W. R. Boyce Gibson. New York: Macmillan, 1931.
——. *Logische Untersuchungen.* 3 vols. Halle: Niemeyer, 1913–21. English: *Logical Investigations*, tr. J. N. Findlay. 2 vols. New York: Humanities Press, 1970.
KANT, IMMANUEL. *Kritik der reinen Vernunft.* Hamburg: Meiner, 1956. English: *Critique of Pure Reason*, tr. Norman Kemp Smith. New York: St. Martin's Press, 1961.
LOCKE, JOHN. *Essay Concerning Human Understanding*, ed. A. C. Fraser. Oxford: 1894.

INDEX